Warrior
PRINCESS

Warrior PRINCESS

My quest to become the
first female Maasai warrior

MINDY BUDGOR

ALLEN&UNWIN

First published in the United States in 2013 by skirt!®, an imprint
of Globe Pequot Press.

First published in Great Britain in 2013 by Allen & Unwin

Allen & Unwin
c/o Atlantic Books
Ormond House
26–27 Boswell Street
London WC1N 3JZ
Phone: 020 7269 1610
Fax: 020 7430 0916
Email: UK@allenandunwin.com
Web: www.atlantic-books.co.uk

A CIP catalogue record for this book is available from the British Library.

ISBN 978 1 74331 447 0

All photos by Mindy Budgor unless noted otherwise.

Text design by Sue Murray

Printed in Italy by 🐾 Grafica Veneta S.p.A.

10 9 8 7 6 5 4 3 2 1

To Faith, Kinyi, Lanet, and Nic

Dear Reader,

The following is a true story about my quest to become the first female Maasai warrior. This is my personal perspective of what happened. Why a nice Jewish girl gets this thought in her head, and has a diehard desire to do this is your story to read. Ultimately, I believe this story belongs to all of us who have angst about finding the inner self. Names and dates have been altered to protect privacy, and to make the telling of the story comprehensive.

Best always,
Mindy Budgor

Contents

Prologue: *Dinosaur!*

Deep in Kenya's Forest of the Lost Child, 9,799.9 miles from home and at least 50 miles from a toilet or electrical jack, I stared, my eyes bugged and unblinking, as trees toppled to the ground. Trunks fractured in half, leaving spiky shards of wood in their place.

A massive white tusk shot into the sky.

I screamed.

"Dinosaur!"

A gray, wrinkled butt appeared through the trees about twenty feet in the air. A tail whipped around angrily. Power-less, I watched the monster take a step backward, closer to camp. Closer to us. This journey—and life itself—was about to come to a thunderous end.

Lanet, the leader of my tribe, grabbed hold of our beaded belts and yanked Becca, my partner in warrior training, and me backward. Jolting us from our paralysis, he tossed over our spears, pushed us out of camp, and ran off to join the other warriors. One of our tribe mates—a buns-of-steel body with a sparkling smile and extra-long earlobes that wrapped around the top of each ear in Princess Leia–style buns—waved for us to follow. The deep, heavy voices of the Maasai echoed through the forest, "oooooooOOOOOO!!! oooooOOOO!! ooooooooOOOOO! OOO! OOO! OOOO! OOOOOOOOOO!! Sorr, HORR OLAG OLAG!!! SORR!!!!"

With our thighs pumping and our beaded necklaces jin-gling, we ran after him, the tops of our spears guiding and protecting us from branches. We hopped over fallen trunks and shrubs and wove in and out like skiers gliding through trees. Ensuring that we were okay, the perfectly molded war-rior turned his head every few seconds, giving us a bright, encouraging smile. Seconds later, he stopped in front of a mammoth tree. He smiled, nodded his head, and pointed his spear up the trunk.

I turned to Becca, panting like a golden retriever. "He . . . he . . . wants us to climb the tree."

"Go! Go! Go! I am not going to die on day damn one! This is NOT my time to go!" she screamed, as she slapped my butt to get moving. Needing no more encouragement, I hustled up the tree as if my ass was on fire.

BECCA AND I had been escorted to our bush home only that morning. We were quickly assigned our first task: Chop branches until you can't chop anymore. And then chop some more. Given that this was Day One, Task One, and I was surrounded by a tribe of men with spears and swords, I decided for the first time in my life to follow directions now, ask questions later.

After three hours of nonstop chopping, I sat on the cold dirt for a much-needed rest. I surveyed the scene. Rays of light seeped through breaks in the dense canopy of leaves, babbling calls of colobus monkeys echoed in the trees, and Becca's curly bob bounced as her sword hacked at the joint of a branch.

I glanced at the palms of my burning hands. Blisters the size of half-dollars—the result of a two-foot metal sword with a wooden handle furiously chafing my once-flawless skin—had already sprouted. My Red Dragon nail polish, however, was intact. When selecting the luxury items I would tow into the forest with me, the precious bottle of polish was nonnegotiable. The shiny red lacquer combined with fresh blisters gave my paw the ferocity of a lion's. And if I didn't yet *feel* like the badass warrior princess I planned to become, the one who would show the Maasai tribesmen that women have a voice and power to match (nobody's ever accused me of aiming low!), at least I looked like her.

Fake it 'till you make it.

Becca sidled up to me, her arms piled with branches. "Of course you're inspecting your nail polish. What are you going to do when an ape eats one of those treasured thumbs?"

When Becca and I finally returned to camp (a generous term for the small patch of land that made up our communal living quarters), we were greeted by a three-foot fence surrounding it, made of a thousand crisscrossed branches.

"I guess this is supposed to protect us from animals," Becca said.

"Good luck to us," I said. "An elephant could tear down this piece-of-shit fence with a pinky toe."

As Becca studied our new security system, I glimpsed a patch of leaves wiggling softly about a yard in front of us. Becca shook the fence lightly, causing the entire thing to wobble. "Yeah. This is a piece of shit. But when it's your time to go, it's your time to go."

I didn't subscribe to Becca's hippy-dippy *c'est la vie* attitude. My own worldview was much more aggressive. "When death comes knocking, open the door, kick it in the nuts, and run for your life."

And that's when I saw it. Another movement in the trees. This time the leaves didn't just jiggle. An entire cluster of trees swayed like windshield wipers, right to left.

Only one day in the bush, and we were face-to-face with the enemy.

Now, FROM OUR perch in the tree, we could see three elephants chilling just outside the piece-of-shit fence.

Becca punched me in the arm. "Dude, you thought the elephant was a dinosaur!"

"Look at the size of them," I said. "They're five times bigger than any elephant I've ever seen. The tusks are the size of airplanes!"

She huffed, "Yeah, it's like a trippy version of *Jurassic Park*. But the good news is that the piece-of-shit fence is holding up quite well."

I laughed, "Doesn't it look like they're waiting to be invited inside or something? It's like the elephants have etiquette! The top of the fence doesn't even reach their ankles, but it's working!"

We watched Lanet and the rest of our new family scurry to build a fire. Within minutes, a low flame was burning. Three men ignited two sticks each and hid behind big, thick trees, taking turns making the deep, throaty *oooOOOooo* calls intended to scare off our guests. One by one, the warriors threw their torches at the elephants. The monsters didn't budge.

From the relative safety of my branch, I tried to remember why I'd decided to become a warrior. There was a purpose outside of myself, which was to help give Maasai women a much-deserved voice in their tribe, but the purpose within me was to develop and listen to my own voice. Before I took this major leap of faith into the forest, I had come to the realization that the life I was "living" was not mine. I was existing in other people's shadows. I knew what was important to me, but I wasn't staying true to myself. I felt that by being stripped of basic needs such as a roof, toilet, and electricity and left alone with my thoughts and nature, I would be forced to stop hiding in anyone's shadow. Becoming a warrior was important culturally, but I went on this journey because I needed to learn that casting my own shadow mattered, not standing in the ones cast by my parents, my peers, or their expectations of me. But death by elephant on day damn one was not part of the plan.

Suddenly, I flashed back three months in time to my home in Chicago, where all this bush business began.

1

The Itch

CHICAGO SHIFTED TO winter as I passed my days poring over
business school applications. What I thought was going to be
a relatively simple process—due to work experience that I
was proud of and thought to be impressive—turned out to be
tedious, frustrating, and upsetting. I was forced to face my past
academic errors; the few Cs that I got in college that were now
rearing their ugly heads blocking me from the schools where I
felt I belonged. Even more painful, they came from trying to
be something that I'm not. I began my undergraduate degree
intending to become a doctor because that's what my parents
wanted me to be.

In a dark auditorium that smelled of antique wood and dis-
infectant, classmates in my college anatomy class would elbow
my ribcage when my deep breathing turned into a rattling snore.
I found my professors uninspiring and the content mind numb-
ing, but the root of the issue was that I cannot handle being
caged, and the hours spent memorizing made me feel suffo-
cated. I remember talking with my guidance counselor during
my freshman year about the fact that everyone has a passion for
something and I wasn't feeling the love.

"If you explore enough avenues, then you will find your passion and hopefully you will have the courage to follow the signs
to get you to your goal," she said.

I responded by telling her that the signs leading me to becoming a doctor were big black Xs, Do Not Enter signs, and U-turn arrows that flashed brighter than all of the lights combined on the Las Vegas strip.

With a heavy sigh, she said, "I can guide you, but you are the CEO of your own life, and ultimately you have to choose what is right for you." The title CEO resonated in my head like a Mozart sonata, but okay, I got the message.

Taking her words to heart, during my next semester I explored art history, literature, business, and economics. Finally, in my first entrepreneurship class, I found my calling. Moving from the back of the class to the front, I found challenge, danger, love, and freedom in the process of starting with a vision and blending determination, timing, and luck to make that idea a reality. I started my own business while still an undergraduate, a journey that allowed me to live on the edge of success and failure, an intersection that made use of all my passions. But now, seven years later, as each business school admission's counselor reviewed my past academic history with tsk-tsks or a telltale shake of the head, I realized the conversation had ended before it began. The Cs on my records blinded them from seeing what I could do, but I knew that with determination, timing, and luck, I would be admitted to a school I wanted to attend. When my way is blocked, I simply look for a detour.

I come from a family of hard-core straight shooters, and while logically I prefer to be told the truth, I frequently find myself longing for a pair of earmuffs to block a family member's version of how my life will play out—always in a neat, conforming box.

My father was born in a displacement camp, and both of his parents were Holocaust survivors. His worldview is comprised of hard work, no cutting corners, following the chain of command, and the drive to survive. The actions associated with that line of thought work for him personally and professionally. My mother, on the other hand, was raised by a financially privileged family in a life of garden parties, symphonies, and world travel. It was apparent early on that my brother, who decided that he would be an investment banker while still in the womb, would become a clone of my father. But I wasn't the obvious offshoot of anyone. I was just different.

When my parents enrolled me in ballet class at age five, I couldn't understand why the teacher was so damn serious. Where was her smile? What was up with the fussy glare? I decided to add a little fun in her life, so while all of the other pink tutus pirouetted around the stage, I busted out a cartwheel, bulldozing the tutus over one by one. My father began to look at me sideways from that moment on. So my first day of ballet was also my last, but the cartwheels continued.

In my teens, I set my sights on becoming a figure skater. Although I loved skating instantly, the short neon skirts and twists and turns in the air proved to be operationally unfeasible. One day during training, my coach pulled me aside and basically told me that my butt and thighs were too large to be a good skater and that I needed to shed some pounds and practice being more graceful. Out of the corner of my eye I could see an ice-hockey team on the next rink, smashing each other into the boards. I looked at my coach and said, "I think I should play ice hockey." Her response was perhaps typical for 1990:

"That sport is for boys! Just go home and talk with your parents about what I said, and I'm sure we can change you so that you have a chance to be a good figure skater."

At least that's how I heard it. I ditched the toe picks before I left the rink, my sights set on ice hockey. I went home and explained the situation to my parents.

"My coach told me that I'm too fat to be a figure skater."

My mother responded, "Well, that wasn't very nice, but you could stand to lose some weight."

My father piped in, "You can't be a quitter. Eat less and try harder."

Their advice fell on deaf ears.

"I've decided to play ice hockey," I insisted.

My mother gasped, "Ice hockey! Mindy, *no*! You're a girl!"

My dad weighed in, "You're going to become a lesbian if you play ice hockey!"

"I feel like a wild beast figure skating," I protested. "I'm never going to be great or even good at it, and I'm just not having fun."

When my parents continued to try and convince me otherwise, I found another solution: Call the grandparents. My dad's mother respected my chutzpah and within a couple of weeks, I had ice-hockey gear and a coach. The sport's blend of precision and ferociousness fed my soul, so I joined the only girls' team in my area. We ended up becoming pretty good, traveling all over the East Coast to play, but that wasn't enough for me. All of the local high schools but mine had an ice-hockey team. Unacceptable. I met with the principal of my school, and he told me that we couldn't start a team because there wasn't enough interest.

"I don't believe you're correct, Principal Marco."

He looked at me blankly, shrugged his shoulders, and waved me out of his office. My parents, by now convinced of my dedication, helped me craft a strategy to gather signatures, find a coach, and raise the money to start the team. Principal Marco was unable to say no to all of that ammunition. The plan worked, and I spent three years as the only girl on the team.

As a 21-year-old college sophomore, rather than applying for an internship with an eye toward a steady, full-time job, I decided to start a company: a concierge laundry and storage service for students. The only small problem was that it required I drop out of my senior year. Predictably, my parents had a fit. For two months my mother called at least twelve times a day with dire warnings of failure while I completed the business plan.

Even though the added work of starting an actual, real-world business meant I officially graduated a semester late, I did negotiate my way into walking across the stage with my class. After I got my diploma, my mother changed her tune and became the biggest cheerleader of my company. She would fly to Chicago for a week at a time, helping me with everything from responding to client e-mails to making sure that I had a comfy pillow in my office for the frequent times I slept under my desk. Four years later I sold the business for enough money to buy a condo, with savings left over for a few rainy days.

I was quite proud of this accomplishment, but when the sale was complete, I didn't have another project to sink my teeth into. In what seemed like thirty seconds after I sold my company, the parental phone calls started to come in. Under pressure to find a job, I tried the corporate route for a few years. Sadly for me, the environment was lackluster, and the entrepreneurial fire in my belly quickly faded. I found myself consistently questioning my purpose in life and feeling overwhelmed with anxiety because the future looked bleak. How was it possible that at age twenty-six I was still being influenced to do something that I knew wasn't best for me? Did I feel a need to fit in and please my family so badly that I was willing to compromise my happiness?

After a significant amount of time thinking about this, I got a grip on my identity again, handed in my resignation, and started applying to business schools. Back when I was growing my business, I often found myself questioning my decisions and seeking outside advice on day-to-day operational decisions, increasingly worried that I didn't know enough to see if someone accidentally did a calculation wrong or was stealing from the company.

I reasoned that perhaps the theoretical knowledge of business school, combined with my practical "street" experience, would enable me to build something significant not only in my eyes, but my family's as well. But for some reason, my father felt that an MBA was not going to net out in the black for me.

"Mindy, we dealt with you starting your own business, and you ended up being lucky on that one. But now you've quit a good job and are taking on a huge amount of debt to go to business school. What is your end goal?" He continued, "Stay focused and stay in one spot."

I didn't have anything to say, but the very thought of doing something I wasn't passionate about made me want to do the opposite. As usual, I forged ahead with my plan in spite of, or perhaps because of, the doubts of my family.

ON ONE particularly freezing afternoon, with the city submerged in white and the wind chill factor a cozy twenty below, I watched my breath form frosty clouds while I walked to get a coffee. Chicago was gorgeous, but the winters were dark and depressing. That's when I had an *aha!* moment. If I could fill out applications anywhere, what was I doing here getting frostbite under four layers of clothing? As a hansom cab driver clanged his horse's bell down Michigan Avenue, I had a vision. I could ditch the doom and gloom of Chicago and jet out to sunny California, where I could take up temporary residence in my parents' empty beachside condo, only a mile from their home in Santa Barbara. I'd complete my admissions essays and increase my majorly deficient vitamin D level at the same time.

By the time I got home from my coffee run, I'd mentally packed my bags. Santa Barbara was just what I needed. A city that's Zen to the millionth power. Where feng shui holds sway even in the bathrooms. It was the ultimate refuge, except for one tiny problem: my parents. They couldn't stop me from quitting a job in Chicago, but they wouldn't be too keen on supporting what they'd consider a pretty lax lifestyle. In my family, you either work or go to school, which will lead you to more work. My father's ironclad code of ethics is simple: "Work until you die." If there was a corollary, it is this: "Better yet—die at work!" Going home could end up becoming pretty toxic, so I created a list of pros and cons to prepare me for what I was in for:

Pros	Cons
Sun	*Daily family shit storm*
Beach	*Daily family shit storm*
Hiking	*Daily family shit storm*
Surfers	*Daily family shit storm*

After I completed my list, I compared the thirty-day weather forecasts for Chicago and Santa Barbara. In Chicago, fourteen degrees was the high, while Santa Barbara was a steady seventy-eight degrees. That overrode all the cons, and my decision was made.

I called my parents to pitch the plan. My mother, clearly regretting her words even as she spoke, gave me the okay.

"But for one month *only,* Mindy, and I will be the one to tell your father!"

Done and done. I was beach-bound.

In short order, I put my Chicago pad up for rent and was lounging on the Santa Barbara beach in a Polo T and sunglass-print capris, laptop in hand. All would have been well in California, except that submitting applications and interviewing stretched on for an additional two months past my mom's time limit.

"Mindy, I knew this would happen," my mother squawked as she combed through the new OPI nail polish colors at our local salon. "You need to figure out what you're doing next. What is your *plan*?"

"I've told you this already, Mom. I didn't think about how much free time I was going to have between submitting applications and hearing back from schools."

My mother slammed the bottle of Miami Beet back on the display.

"But it just doesn't make sense. What did you expect to do with three months of time off?" she asked.

"Mom! I just told you that I didn't think about it, and then you ask me what I planned."

Pissed off and more than a little hurt, I continued, "Fine! I've just made up my mind. I'm going to do something until I hear back from a school—I don't know what—but it will definitely *not* be in California."

"I've been telling you to go to New York," she said. "Everyone is thin and there are tons of smart, single Jewish men."

My mother, if you can believe it, wants the best for me—it's just that a twenty-seven-inch waistline and a Jewish husband define "the best."

"Yeah, yeah. I need to marry a doctor or lawyer before I get too old and bitter," I said.

She glared at me over her glasses. "Tick-tock!"

The next morning I considered my situation. I had twelve weeks until I heard from business schools—even longer if I was put on the wait-list—and I had to find a way to fill that time. I couldn't afford to come up empty after the scene with my mother, so I sent out a mass e-mail to solicit ideas. A college friend responded, raving about a trip she took to Kenya to help build a clinic in the Maasai Mara, a large game reserve in southwestern Kenya named after the Maasai people, a seminomadic tribe that had been the first inhabitants of the area thousands of years ago. The Mara is famous for its lions, leopards, elephants, buffalo, and the annual migration of zebra, Thomson's gazelle, and wildebeest.

The stars were aligning.

I called my friend immediately. "When's the next trip?" I asked.

"In March. You should go!"

Timing and luck were on my side, and just that quickly I made my decision.

That night, driving to my parents' house for dinner, I was actually excited to share the news of my plan. My mom, for all her judgmental ways, was a bit of a hippie once. In her early twenties she fled to Israel to live on a kibbutz for three years and then in Jerusalem for another three. I knew the free spirit was still in there. Somewhere.

When I arrived, my family was seated at the mahogany dining table. Across from my empty chair was my grandmother, Lee, who we dubbed the royal nickname of Queen Lee when a friend gifted her with a tiara—the perfect accessory for a woman who walks around town as if it's her kingdom.

Holding her signature gin and tonic in her manicured hand, Queen Lee was dressed in a chocolate-brown cashmere sweater with dark sepia leather piping, a cream-colored silk turtleneck, and skinny, stovepipe, no-hip/no-butt camel tweed trousers.

Over the years I'd developed a theory that there was a direct correlation between Queen Lee's accessory count and her level of concern for me. It started when I was sixteen and she caught me with three pairs of Manolo Blahniks I absolutely couldn't afford. When she called me to her house for a lecture on finances, she was wearing rings on both hands and a tightly tied scarf around her neck. The more worked up she got, the more embellishments were added.

Tonight my grandmother wore two scarves twisted together, and peeping out between the scarves was a gold snakeskin necklace. Chunky gold and aquamarine art deco earrings glimmered under her platinum blowout. She looked at me with penetrating green eyes that felt as if they could pierce my gut as her stiff fingers wrapped around the bamboo handle of her fork. And then I saw it: two rings on her right hand and another on her left hand. I hadn't seen three rings since the shoe debacle. This was serious.

Queen Lee's lips tightened, and I could tell she was about to erupt. I'd hoped to speak up before she had a chance to let me have it, but I was too late. She dropped her fork and took a large sip of the gin and tonic, only the sound of ice cubes clinking against her glass broke the silence in the room.

"Mindy, I saw you at Jeanine's yesterday at 11 a.m. with a croissant in your hand. This is ridiculous. You must get a job. Take anything! Start at minimum wage. Go work at Vons. The service in the deli is pitiful!" She scanned the table for a nod of support from my parents.

My mother looked horrified, most likely at the thought of my eating a croissant rather than the idea of the deli job.

My father was irate. "Don't tell her to work in a grocery store and take a job away from a hard-working person who needs to feed a family. She can find something else that uses her skills." Dad took a few bites of salad. "But Mindy, I do have to say you are on a dangerous path of running through all the money you made from selling your business and ending up destitute. In this economy you need to hunt and beg for a job, and I can tell you right now that you aren't moving back in with us."

His words stung. I looked around the room. My mother was poking at her plate in silence. She just wanted to see me happy, thin, and successful. And while I yearned to be a Dolce & Gabbana size six, these conversations made me want to dive headfirst into three pounds of chocolate cake. My grandmother wanted me out of her town because my lack of employment embarrassed her. And my dad, a physicist who's happiest holed up in his office with his nose in a textbook, just wanted the conversation to stop so he could go back to studying how South African succulents could be used to solve world hunger.

I clinked my water glass with my knife.

"I'm going on a trip," I announced. "I have plenty of money saved to pay for my travels, and I'll be back after I have an answer from business schools. And if I don't get in school this time, I'll get a job and apply again."

I knew I wouldn't be able to leave it at that, but I tried.

"Where are you going?" my mom asked, already breathing heavily.

"I'll be volunteering in Kenya."

Queen Lee smiled and banged her G&T on the table. "Phenomenal!"

I was both shocked and grateful for her unexpected enthusiasm.

"Hold on a second," my mother said. "Why are you going so far away? Can't you get an internship or volunteer in your own country for a few months?"

Did she forget that she once took a similar trip? That I came by my craving for adventure naturally?

"No, Mom. I'm going to Kenya because I have a friend who went on the same trip, and it sounds fantastic. I'll be building a clinic in a tiny village in Kenya."

My mother was starting to shake.

"You will get diseases! Aaron?!" she pleaded with my father. "Please talk some sense into her. This is craziness. She can't do this."

"Calm down," my dad said. "This might be good for her, and I just might give her some of my miles." His positive response shocked me. I'd figured he'd tell me to set up a tent in the backyard, buy a cardboard giraffe and elephant, and pretend that I was in Kenya.

My mother's face turned from Casper-white to Elmo-red. She pounded on the table.

"Aaron! You're going to help her get cholera and malaria and dysentery? Or killed by a raging elephant? Or kidnapped?"

Ignoring her rant, he turned to me. "When you're in Kenya, you need to go on a safari. And don't leave without seeing the Maasai tribe. There's a book in my study that you should take home with you tonight."

"That's the tribe that drinks blood and carries spears, right? We're actually building the clinic in the middle of the Maasai Mara, so maybe I can stop by for a shot of the hard stuff," I said.

Queen Lee laughed as she lifted her drink, "Don't forget about their houses. They are made of cow poop. You can smell them from a mile away."

My father said, "The Maasai have been around since the fourteenth century, so there's a bit more to the tribe than drinking blood and carrying spears, but, yes, that's who I'm talking about."

After dinner, Queen Lee pulled me aside. "I think your plan is great and, I must say, very mature. Your mother will be okay. Go home and pack. Come over to my house tomorrow, and we'll discuss the details of your trip." She gave me a peck on my forehead.

Before I left, I tried to give my mom a reassuring hug, but she was too consumed with flailing her arms and yelling at my dad.

2

Habari!

Six weeks later, as I finally walked through the musty Kenya airport hallway, I couldn't figure why I'd accepted my father's gift of miles. It would have been wiser to drain my life savings to avoid the travel hell that resulted from the itinerary he'd planned.

I was surprised anyone could stand to be near me as we waited in the customs line. I reeked of sweat and grime, which baked into my skin in the hundred-degree heat of the airport. Huffing in exasperation, I slid my passport across the countertop to a Kenyan man in a peach button-down shirt and a skinny navy tie.

"*Habari*. That is how are you in Swahili," the agent said in a British-Kenyan accent. "Miss Mindy Anne Budgor? Twenty-seven years old? California?" He flipped through my passport, the pages packed with stamps, evidence of yearly family vacations all over the world. "Israel, Poland, Morocco, Spain, Italy, Ireland, Belize. You have traveled to many countries, but Miss Mindy, I must tell you, Kenya will be by far the best."

One flash of his smile released all of my pent-up frustration, and I had a feeling that he might be right. I claimed my shiny black duffle, tossed it over my shoulder, and felt the first real inkling of excitement since I'd stepped on the flight. An employee of the volunteer center picked me up, and we rode the forty minutes outside of Nairobi to meet the rest of the group

13

at a miniscule airport, where only planes the size of extra-long kosher hot dogs could pass through.

My group was made up of twenty-five volunteers—twenty-two of whom were members of the same Illinois family, the Bergmans. This particular family went on a trip like this every year to support a foundation created in honor of a family member who had passed away as a young adult. The foundation adopted a village in Kenya, and over the years the family came back to build classrooms and kitchens. Their latest project was the development of a clinic. When I heard about this family, I was immediately drawn to them. Any group of people who could be so committed to improving desolate villages in a faraway land were people I wanted to get to know.

The pilot hurried us to the planes. The tires teetered on the runway as we struggled to get airborne. I pressed my head into the glass of the window to survey the land below. The passport agent was right. Kenya was gorgeous. Thin, twisting valleys etched through parched, dusty-brown land dotted with fluffy green treetops. The pilot pointed out the volunteer center, a pinprick of a settlement in the middle of the savanna.

Our plane descended, curving and diving, skimming the treetops and landing on a thin, fifteen-foot-wide grass runway. The only indication that this was a landing strip came in the form of twelve silver rocks with white markers painted on them. Our group deplaned, two of the passengers with extra luggage in hand: used barf bags.

I scanned the land around me. To the north the trees were so thick that my eyes got caught in the leaves; to the west was the volunteer center; to the east were flat, uninhabited lands spotted with acacia trees and bushes; and about one hundred yards to the south was the beginning of a steep mountain where I could see two rail-thin, black-skinned individuals in bright red short dresses with spears in hand walking peacefully into what looked like uncharted land.

Julie, a Canadian volunteer in her mid-thirties, greeted our group. She pointed to the men I'd seen and explained that they were Maasai warriors and that we'd meet them after dinner. They would be our guides and protectors against animals or any other danger for the duration of the trip. All of my expectations were based on my dad's picture book on the tribe. In truth, I knew virtually nothing about the Maasai except that they were known for killing lions and drinking blood.

As we made our way along the grassy landing strip toward the volunteer center, Julie gave us our housing assignments. I was to room with Becca Bergman, one of the Illinois family members who hadn't yet arrived.

Walking down a perfectly manicured stone path, I passed mini-mansion after mini-mansion. This volunteer center was first-class. My new living quarters had cathedral ceilings with exposed wooden beams, two olive-green down-filled sofas, a coffee table, and a fireplace. In the bedroom, oversize mattresses with crisp white Egyptian cotton sheets and burnt-orange comforters were tucked into handcrafted wooden canopy beds. The bathrooms, one adjoining each bedroom, were made entirely of stone. These facilities were Queen Lee–ready!

I took off my hiking boots and was almost knocked out from the stink. Eyeing the shower, I stripped down as quickly as I could. The steady flow of warm water tickled the small of my back, and I spun around like a little princess. This was the life.

Thoroughly rinsed, I settled my avocado-oiled self into bed and began to doze off. Within moments, an insistent banging woke me. I slowly tightened the towel around my chest and sauntered to the door, where my new roommate was still banging her fist.

There we were, Rebecca Bergman and I, separated by a pane of glass. I looked her up and down. She was dressed in vintage blue-linen overalls, a canvas newsboy cap tipped to the side atop her Shirley Temple curls, circa 1983 cherry-red Ray Bans covering her eyes.

"Well, do you plan on unlocking the door?" She asked in a slightly annoyed tone. I turned the lock, opened the door, and immediately felt the gust of her free spirit breeze past me. Becca stepped one saddle shoe and then the other into the center of the foyer, where she dropped her bags, giving every indication that she planned on leaving them there until she went back to Illinois. It appeared she was marking her territory, and I was quickly getting nervous that our orderly home was about to become a pigsty.

"Don't you want to unpack?" I asked.

She waved off the luggage and stepped over it. As she darted in and out of each room, I was able to piece together that she was almost twenty-one and a self-published graphic novelist who quoted Hemingway as easily as she did Prince. Becca was the polar opposite of my MBA-bound entrepreneur self. I quoted only Warren Buffett.

Becca whipped out *Middlesex* from her hunter-green rucksack and flopped on the sofa. My cue that the get-to-know-you session was over for now.

Later, while getting ready for our first group dinner, I leaned into the mirror to pluck a few stray hairs from my brows. I could see Becca watching—and judging—in horror. "Maybe I could work on you next," I offered.

"Not gonna happen," Becca said as she surveyed her reflection.

"All I'm saying is that even tree huggers need a monthly brow wax," I said.

Becca shook her curls out of her face, took a step closer to me, and put up her fists like Oscar De La Hoya. "We can discuss after a few beers."

As we walked along the pebbly path to the gazebo where we would eat all of our meals, I heard a slithering on my right. I gasped.

"That was definitely a snake," I said, my voice shaking.

"Welcome to Africa," Becca said and continued on, completely unflustered.

The gazebo was a spacious pavilion with four Mission-style wood tables, benches, and heaters lining the periphery of the room. There was a cozy fireplace where I knew I'd be curling up at the end of the night. The spread of food was impressive: a buffet of lasagna, steak, mashed potatoes, salad, asparagus, bread bowls, cheese platters, and bottles of red and white wine. Very Western. I stood there, deciding what to eat first.

"I'm told we're in Kenya, but this feels more like a bar mitzvah at the Four Seasons," I told Becca.

"Then you must feel right at home," she said, half joking. "Right now, I don't really care where we are. I'm hungry!"

Just as we were finishing our feast, Julie, the volunteer coordinator, clinked her water glass to get the group's attention. "Now we'll meet the Maasai warriors who will be your guides for the remainder of your visit."

From the darkness, a gentle jingling grew louder. A procession of six magnificent men with taut ebony bodies adorned with colorful beaded necklaces, bracelets, and anklets walked up the steps into the gazebo. The artificial lighting from the high wooden beams made their skin look iridescent and the kitchen-knife-length scars on their bodies stand out like molded clay. The way they carried themselves and their unflappable facial expressions commanded immediate respect. These were men who had been through battle. And they were here to protect us.

I turned to Becca with a look of both satisfaction and anxiety. She mirrored my reaction. We turned back to the sight in front of us: fierce young men in red, blue, green, and white tartan tunics. Two draped cloths were together in a knot on top of each of their well-defined shoulders. The result was an unobstructed view of their muscular legs. Each clutched a spear in his right hand, and swords sheathed in burgundy leather hung from their beaded belts. Screw my dad's coffee table book—nothing could compare to the reality of these perfectly chiseled beings. But another look at their spears and swords quickly reminded me that these primal men were not actors. They were real-deal bushmen, not to be messed with. I was intimidated by them and turned on by them at the same time.

The warriors took their seats in director's chairs arranged in a semicircle near the fireplace. I tried to see if they were wearing anything under their "dresses." Unfortunately, the Maasai had taken a lesson from Emily Post, and they knew to close their legs when sitting.

The man sitting at the center, or twelve o'clock, on this half-clock dais took the lead. In a tempered voice, he introduced himself.

"Hello everyone. My name is Winston, and I am your lead guide. This is . . ."

He pointed to ten o'clock. "I am Peter," the warrior said.

Eleven o'clock: "I am Felix."

Twelve o'clock: "You already know me! I am Winston!"

One o'clock: "I am Jackson."

Two o'clock: "I am Gideon."

Three o'clock: "I am Peter, too."

Winston gave the audience a toothy grin. "You can call them Peter One and Peter Two."

"I would like to start by giving you a general overview of our culture," Winston said. "When I am done, we will take any questions on your mind.

"The Maasai are one of forty-two Kenyan tribes that have upheld our ancient cultural ways. We speak Maa, which means 'my people.' We used to be a tribe of over one and a half million, but after decades of natural disasters and diseases such as small-pox, our tribe shrunk to under half a million living in Kenya and Tanzania. Maasai are considered fierce warriors. We believe that Ngai, our rain god, gave us all of the cattle in the world, so if anyone other than a Maasai is seen with a cow, then that person must have stolen it from the Maasai. This belief led to many fatalities with our neighboring tribes, and it was only after hundreds of years did we develop peace over this issue, but you must know that the cows are the Maasai's. Our goal is to live in harmony with the land and animals, but we also protect ourselves just as a baby gazelle must protect itself from a preying lion."

In a profound way, these men were probably the most powerful beings I had ever encountered.

"We believe that our people originated in the fourteenth century. Since that time, our life hadn't changed much until recently. Our culture is now at a crossroads, and there is a widespread fear that the Maasai culture will no longer exist in fifty years. I will tell you about that later, but first I want to lay the foundation."

When he leaned back in his chair, I noticed Winston had made an unfortunate concession to modern civilization—he was indeed wearing shorts under his tunic.

"We are seminomadic, which means that it is rare for us to stay in one place for very long." His voice was commanding, but playful. "Our men are known for going on walkabouts that can last for months at a time. We leave our wives and children in order to take our cattle and goats to graze in new areas. In our culture, cattle, goats, and children signify wealth. If a man has cattle, but no children, then he is considered a poor man. One must always be in balance in all areas of life.

"Our tribe has twelve geographic sectors, and each sector has its own leadership. We have the Keekonyokie, Damat, Purko, Loitai, Siria, and more names that you will not remember. Only a few sectors remain that follow all of the traditional customs and remain basically untouched by people who are not Maasai."

With my elbows digging into my knees, I hung onto Winston's every word.

"Our homes are designed and built by the Maasai women. They cut the trees and branches with axes, haul up to one hundred pounds of timber at one time on their foreheads, and put the home together from the start to the finish. It is their pride and joy. They plant the sticks in the ground in a circle or star shape and then create a plaster out of mud, sticks, grass, cow dung, human urine, and ash."

I wanted to be open to new ideas, but the idea of living in a home constructed of poop and pee made me nauseous.

"The result is a three-by-five-by-one-and-a-half-meter palace. Families of seven or more live under one roof. We cook, eat, sleep, socialize, and live together with small livestock. Sometimes it can become very crowded and uncomfortable when the goats lick your face in the morning." Again, that smile. "The next topic is our diet."

This is what I'd been waiting for. How these men could be so fat-free without an exercise machine in sight? I was sure my mother would be interested in any tips I gleaned that might help me control my own weight.

"I am sure that many of you have heard that we only drink blood and milk and only eat meat," Winston said. "We wish that were still true, but now because of drought and disease, the number of cattle and goats that remain is not sufficient to feed us properly, so we have been forced to cultivate our land and produce kale, potatoes, and maize. Many traditional Maasai look down on their neighbors who cultivate land. Eating meat and drinking blood is now only a luxury. Many people ask me why we drink blood. I turn the question and ask you, 'Why *don't* you drink blood?' Blood is very rich in protein and builds a strong immune system. A *mzungu*—that is the Swahili word for white folk—recently told me that a study was done on a group of warriors and they found that their diet and fitness level put them at an Olympic standard. This was not a surprise to me, as our health is ideal, but it will be a good standard for you to compare."

While the thought of drinking blood terrified me, I couldn't help but feel a desire to be like these warriors.

"The other thing that many white people are amazed by is that we do not celebrate birthdays."

There were murmurs in the audience.

"That doesn't sound like a good setup." I whispered to Becca. "No birthday cake? That sucks."

"We do not record a date of birth," Winston continued. "Instead, our society is broken into age groups that have different responsibilities. Every fifteen years or so, a new and individually named age group is created. The first is childhood, and this is when boys herd cattle and goats, but it is mainly playtime. Girls at the same age do the cooking and milking. After childhood, when the boys are around twelve to fifteen, they graduate to the next stage of life, which is when they become warriors, and they stay warriors until they are twenty-two to twenty-eight years old. This is when boys become men. Then the warriors move to the next group—junior elders—and after junior elders, a Maasai man becomes an elder."

"Everyone in front of you is a warrior," Winston said with pride. "This stage is crucial to our society. Warriors protect our community in times of war like your military protects you. A warrior must be able to go face to face with a lion if it tries to kill our cows. A warrior must fight when forty elephants rampage into our community, threatening the lives of our family, livestock, and crops. A warrior must be fearless while also able to entertain and dance at celebrations. A warrior is coveted and loved by the community."

I too was in love! Winston's passion for his heritage was apparent with every word. I'd been searching for something to feel that strongly about, and Winston found it right here on the very ground where he was raised. I was envious. I wanted what he had—a deep, almost spiritual sense of purpose and confidence.

Scanning the crowd, Winston decided it was time to wrap up the first lesson on the Maasai people. "There are many things to discuss, like the fact that we have multiple wives, but I want to end with the fact that our culture is in danger. The government has taken our land for resorts, wildlife reserves, and ranches. Children in school are taught that some of our traditions—the very things that make us Maasai—are bad. The drought is killing our cattle, which is killing us. I ask you to think about how to help preserve the Maasai, as there are many things to learn from our natural way of life. Does anyone have questions? Is anyone awake?"

Awake? I was riveted!

The rest of the group seemed overloaded with information, but I raised my hand. "Why do you put big holes in your ears?"

"We stretch our earlobes as a sign of beauty," Winston said. "We use many things to keep them stretched. I have part of an elephant tusk in mine, but Peter Number One found empty film cartridges from the last group of tourists, so he put them in his earlobes."

Winston clapped loudly. "Now we have a treat," he said. "We will dance and sing for you."

Everyone on the wooden benches sat a bit straighter as the six warriors lined up near the railing of the gazebo. Winston was third in line and began to belt out *EEEEEEEEEEY-AAAAAAA*—a chant so loud that I felt the vibration down my spinal cord. The five warriors called in response. Winston sang a verse in Maa, the Maasai language, while the other warriors accompanied him with throaty grunts: exhaling, their necks thrust forward, and inhaling, their necks recoiled. Their breathing was in rhythm with their pelvises, lunging forward and backward, over and over again. The gazebo pulsated with their hypnotic song and dance. I didn't take my eyes off the men for one nanosecond.

These guys are in heat, I thought. *This must be their mating call.*

While the group continued, Felix stepped forward and propelled his sinewy, six-foot-five body four feet into the air, landing gracefully like a gymnast on the balls of his feet. Peter Number One stepped forward and jumped even higher. Winston stepped in and bounded even higher than Peter. Determined to beat him in this jumping contest, Felix jumped again and seemed to shoot at least five feet off the ground. The warriors responded with a high-pitched call and a high-five for his winning leap.

BACK AT THE MINI-MANSION, I lay in bed, eyes fixed on the blades of the ceiling fan cutting the air. The first image I had fresh from the plane of the Maasai walking peacefully through the virgin land was all I saw in my mind's eye. The purity of the Maasai's way of life made me think about how so many things in my own life were manufactured or determined by everyone else but me—from the car I drove to the food I ate to whom I dated and where I worked. I wasn't the creator of my daily life, and that fact had seeped into my subconscious and bankrupted my confidence.

I remembered the times I knew I was being true to myself, like playing ice hockey and starting and running a business. Those endeavors had come from the deepest part of my heart, but that honest, driving force within me was inconsistent, flickering on and off like rolling electricity outages.

Hypnotized by the fan, I questioned my integrity. Integrity meant to be whole and undivided, and that was my problem: I felt divided. Sometimes I saw myself as a puppet being yanked, pulled, and pushed by my parents and society's expectations. What would I do differently if I were the only person pulling my strings?

As the fan's blades continued to chop, the messages lodged in my brain began to battle. A clear and confident voice that I knew was fully mine said, "You have all that you need within you to be successful." But then another voice that I also accepted as my own countered with, "But you really should be smarter, thinner, richer, and, of course, married with children." My heart raced when I thought of what would happen if I did end up without a job, a place to live, something to be wholehearted about. Did I have the skills to survive? My mind turned back to the Maasai. They seemed to live fearlessly and confidently, dealing with life as it came moment by moment. There was no past, no future . . . only now. Closing my eyes, I saw myself walking among the Maasai, not just *with* them, but also as one with them.

3

Sealing the Deal

THE NEXT MORNING'S breakfast buffet was a carbo-heaven of fluffy golden pancakes, cinnamon buns the size of my head, and two-inch-thick waffles loaded with powdered sugar. Before I could pile my plate with goodness, I heard Queen Lee in my ear: "A second on the lips is a lifetime on the hips!" Almost ten thousand miles away and her presence was still powerful enough to shock my system. Of course, I ate the pancakes anyway.

After breakfast, the group gathered for our first day of work. If our skin color didn't give away that we were tourists, our accessories certainly did—a combo platter of fanny packs, SPF 99 sunscreen, and rainbow-colored visors. Felix, the warrior who'd won the jumping contest the night before, was leaning against the driver-side wheel of a double-decker bus/Mack truck hybrid. They called the green, canvas-roofed mammoth a lorry in the British style, and Felix motioned for us to climb the ladder attached to its side. Although we each had to jump to reach the ladder, one by one we hoisted ourselves on board, settled into taupe canvas seats, and waited for the day's journey to begin.

Winston leaped onto the lorry. He was dressed in a similar tunic, or *olkarasha,* as the night before, but this one was bright red, white, and blue.

"I love America!" he yelled, laughing. Winston was an unexpected—but pleasantly surprising—combination. His confidence said, "I can kill a lion with my teeth," while his childlike spirit teased, "Let's play Twister." My Western marketing mind could immediately envision him on a global speaking tour, training corporate executives on "How to Find Your Inner Warrior."

"Your trip will be a lot of hard work," Winston said. As his eyes darted to his feet, mine followed. He was wearing flip-flops, but these were no lightweight Havaianas. This Chief's footwear was made from tires; the treads had been shaped into soles, while cut-up pieces of rubber crisscrossed the tops of his feet. Brilliant! Those shoes could probably last for seventy-five thousand miles.

He continued. "It will be hard, but it will be truly amazing because I am your guide. Last night I was on good behavior, but you must know that I am actually . . . fantastic!"

The truck roared with laughter. "The ride to the construction site will take about forty minutes. Oh, and to answer the question I know everyone is wondering: I am the premiere warrior in all of Maasailand. I have killed seven lions, and no one will ever top me."

His charisma was irresistible. We hadn't even left, and he already had us eating out of his hand. The lorry's engine ignited and the combustion vibrated the seats, leaving our butts numb and shaking our kidneys like maracas. We rocked slowly from side to side like a ship moving through rippled water. The truck climbed over boulders, up and then down again. Our teeth chattered and our knuckles turned white from gripping the seats. Conversation was minimal as each passenger focused on holding down his or her breakfast. We rolled along as if going from the crest of one wave to another until someone shouted, "Look out the window!"

Every head turned to see Kenyan children in school uniforms. The girls wore chunky blue wool sweaters paired with matching linen skirts that fell just below the knee, revealing thin, almost skeletal calves. The boys wore blue polo shirts and khakis. Their sandaled feet carried them as they ran alongside the lorry, waving and screaming, "Habari!" Everyone waved back, thrilled to greet the locals.

When we arrived at the construction site, we gingerly descended the lorry's ladder, dropping off the bottom onto uneven land. Once on solid ground, visors were straightened and shirts were re-tucked into chinos.

My eyes skimmed the site. I could see the outline of the future clinic, each room marked by a rock border. Winston introduced us to Amani, the construction manager and also a local Kipsigi tribesman. He was dressed in a taupe mesh T-shirt, khakis, and a puffy down turquoise vest.

I couldn't hold back. "Aren't you hot?" I asked. "It's like a hundred degrees out here and you're wearing a vest."

"What's a vest?" he asked.

"*This* is a vest." I grabbed a handful of his Patagonia.

"Oh. No, I am not hot. It is winter now." He assessed my skimpy T-shirt and black capris. "You don't feel cold?"

"Do I look cold? I'm sweating like a pig, and I haven't even started to work yet."

"Right, get to work!" He pointed me toward a pile of stones.

Amani didn't assign us specific tasks; he simply told us to hop to it. I wanted to try out all the different jobs until I found my niche. I started by making mortar. The directions were simple: Take a wheelbarrow of water, a forty-pound bag of cement, and mix them together with a shovel until someone tells you stop. It was fun—for a bit.

Next, I tried out the wheelbarrow task. I was instructed to push it up a hill, load it with boulders, and bring the full load back down to the construction site. After seven round-trips, I decided to have a chat with Amani.

"Can I see the plans for the clinic?" I asked.

"Why?" He looked at me with a wide smile.

"Well, this process seems inefficient. If we change the location of the clinic to the top of the hill, we won't have to bring the rocks from top to bottom. Or, better yet, have the boulder delivery truck drop the load at the bottom of the hill."

The business side of my brain was working in overdrive, but my suggestion was met with radio silence.

"I really think that if I could just look at the plans and maybe change them a bit, we would save a lot of unnecessary labor."

"Please go and enjoy your work," he said, giving me a pat on the back. I walked away, deciding to leave the wheelbarrow brigade until the operational process was improved.

While trying to scope out my next self-appointed construction project, I noticed a Kenyan man wearing a denim painter's uniform with frayed sleeves working on the periphery of the site. I hiked over and sat down beside him and pointed to myself. "Habari. I am Mindy."

He pointed to himself with his cement-covered, calloused finger. "Amos."

Amos handed me a stone and a miniature ax to carve my rock. He showed me how to chisel. I found a groove, determined to become the best mason the native crew had ever seen. Whenever my energy waned, I'd look up to see a taut warrior body whip out his machete to cut a bag of cement and was immediately reinspired.

Suddenly the sun that had been beating down on my back turned to shade as the shadow of a huge body fell over me. I looked up and locked eyes with Chief Winston.

"Mindy, you are a woman. Women cannot do this sort of work," he said, inspecting my stone. "You should settle down under a nice tree for a rest or sip some water. You are not suited for the job of a strong craftsman."

Suddenly, I didn't care if this guy was a Maasai chief or not. His blunt dismissal of my efforts pissed me off. I gently placed my chisel on my thigh, and gave him my best glare.

"Excuse me?" I smacked the silvery dust from my stone off my capris.

Winston smiled. "Mason work is for skilled men."

Snapping back, I said, "And for some reason women can't carve a rock?"

"You have fight. I know of women like you. You would be a very good Maasai wife," he laughed.

"Well, you'd be a great American husband," I said, "since I see that all you've done today is stroll around demanding that everyone else do the work."

He smiled, put his hand on my shoulder, and plunked down next to me. As he bent his knees, the two plaid sheets that made up his tunic parted like a theater curtain, creating a perfect slit to display his imposing thighs. I tried not to stare, but that was just not possible. He soon followed my gaze and closed the curtains. Show over.

Under the scorching sun, Winston and I talked and carved stones. For now, it seemed, he would allow me to do this "man's work." I learned that he was university-educated and had a master's degree in biology.

Surprised at his level of education, I asked, "Do many Maasai get master's degrees?"

"No. I am the only one of thirteen children who went to school. I was lucky to be the favorite of my father. None of my brothers and sisters even made it through primary school."

As we talked, I realized that he knew everything about every tree, plant, and animal in the bush, and his favorite book was also a favorite of mine.

"How many times have you read *To Kill a Mockingbird*?" he asked.

"Once. And you?"

"Three times. That Boo Radley character meets me in my dreams."

The more I chiseled and chatted with the Chief, the more I wanted to learn about the nature of his tribe.

"Last night you said that the Maasai are at a crossroads," I said. "What does that mean?"

"Well, there are many issues, but one problem is that in areas where religious schools are being built, children are abandoning their culture," Winston said. "Many school administrators tell Maasai children that their practices are wrong. Like Felix. His schoolteacher told him that notching his ears was bad, so when he told his mama that he would not take part in that cultural rite, their relationship was harmed forever. A few places in Kenya remain untouched by Western culture. It is rare to find a Maasai who still practices our culture in its purest form, but if you do see the authentic ones, you will see perfection."

I told Winston I wanted to see perfection.

"Absolutely not," he said. "These locations are not well-known to white people. They are far removed, with much danger from animals, and the depth of the way we do things will be too much for you to handle." He gave his chisel back to Amos and got to his feet. "Now we need to talk about something serious." He bent down, bringing his face so close to mine that I swear I could smell animal blood on his breath. "Tell me about your long shoes."

"Long shoes?" I was confused. The Chief rose, positioned himself a few feet in front of Amos and me, stood on his toes, and strutted down an imaginary catwalk.

He turned back, "You know, the ones that Beyoncé wears!"

"High heels?" I couldn't believe that *this* was the very serious discussion. When Winston wasn't making me mad because of some insult about women, he was cracking me up. "Yes, I have lots of very pretty long shoes," I said.

Winston wanted me to describe some of my long shoes. I told him about my red patent-leather pumps, my silver-studded stilettos, my four-and-a-half-inch black patent-leather Mary Janes, and my royal purple, open-toed platforms with flirty silk flowers. The Chief was hypnotized.

"But these are my new favorites," I said, pointing to my hiking boots that, after almost a full day's work, blended in with the Kenyan landscape: muddy with red dust and strands of golden grass lodged in the seams.

BEFORE THE DAY was over, I changed jobs once more, this time to haul bricks from one side of the clinic to the other. I walked back and forth with two thirty-pound loads clenched under each armpit and two mini bricks dangling from each hand.

In the middle of a haul, I looked up to see Amos and the Chief pointing and laughing at me. I dropped my rocks.

"What?" I asked. Amos said something to Winston in Swahili, and they both burst out laughing. I nudged the Chief on the shoulder. "Amos has a Swahili name for you," he said. "He is calling you *Tausi Punda*."

"What is that?"

"Well, the exact translation . . . well, it means . . ."

I was anxious to know my new nickname. "Just spit it out!"

"Peacock donkey!"

I didn't know what it meant, but it didn't sound like a compliment. And the crazy thing about the nickname was that my brother had been calling me donkey basically ever since he was able to speak.

"You've got to be kidding me. That's not nice."

"No, no! You are taking this the wrong way. He has this name for you because you are beautiful like a peacock and work hard like a donkey. This is a very nice name." Winston's eyes suggested sincerity and, frankly, I was excited to have a Swahili nickname—it felt like I was becoming part of their inner circle.

Soon, every warrior and Kipsigi tribe member on the construction site was calling me Tausi Punda, and our days on the worksite continued.

AT 3 A.M. ON our ninth morning, I awoke to the sound of my BlackBerry alarm. It was March 25, and I had a reminder: "Business School."

I'd already gotten two rejections, and today was the day I'd find out the status of my final application—my last chance.

"What was that?!" Becca howled from her room.

"Sorry. It's my BlackBerry reminder. I have to see if I got into business school."

"Only you would have an alarm for something like that," she said. "You are in Kenya. Screw school. Go to bed!"

I logged into my school account, only to realize that, due to the ten-hour time difference, I wouldn't hear until later in the day.

I followed Becca's advice and crawled back into bed.

After breakfast, I opted out of going with the group on the scheduled visit to a village market. I needed to do something physical to release my anxiety, so I went to work at the construction site. I knew that if I didn't get into school, I could apply again next year, but I was still nervous. While I firmly believe in the notion that failing is a great learning opportunity, I didn't want to fail at this. Part of it had to do with not wanting to go home and see disappointment in my parents' eyes. Even though I was charting my own path, I still wanted them to be proud of me.

Sweat dripped down my forehead as I carried brick after brick from one side of the clinic to the other. I thought about a Plan B—maybe I could stay in Kenya and work at a microfinance institution if I didn't get into school this year. I also began to wonder if I continually went against the popular vote because of some screwed-up self-fulfilling prophecy, unconsciously meeting my family's negative expectations. The issue was unresolved even after a few hours of labor. Exhausted, I returned to carving stones with Amos.

"Tausi," he said and smiled.

Today I was just peacock without the donkey. How did this man who didn't speak my language know what to say? I smiled back and settled on the dusty ground shoulder to shoulder with Amos. Turning my face to look at his eyes, I could feel his heart open up and invite me in. Even though we didn't speak the same language, there was a body language that crossed all borders. Amos felt my anxiety without me needing to say a word, and he responded by making me feel comforted from the inside out. No words were necessary.

When the workday ended, it was time to check my application status. I turned on my BlackBerry and . . . ping!

"Your application status has changed. To view your status, please click this link . . ."

Word had traveled through the warrior grapevine, and Winston, Felix, and Peter Number One stood by as I waited for my answer. There we were, a five-foot-five-inch mzungu and three nearly seven-foot men, all of us staring into the peephole of a BlackBerry. Given that the nearest cell tower was about as close as the nearest Starbucks, it took a few minutes for the Web page to load. But apparently my phone battery didn't have a few minutes, and it died before I got my answer.

I looked up at the cobalt blue Kenyan sky. *Whoever's up there has quite a sense of humor,* I thought.

I turned to the warriors, who actually looked quite worried. Before I could say anything, the Chief piped up. "Tausi Punda, if you have any problem, I will call the admissions staff. I will tell them that I have killed seven lions and that I am the leading warrior in all of Kenya. I will tell them that my aim is so precise that I can throw my spear from the Mara to that business school and hit the student who was admitted instead of you directly in the eye on the first day of class, so unless they want to start school with a funeral, they must admit you now!"

I smiled and declined his offer, tempting as it was.

Back in my room, I charged my phone and logged in, finally ready to hear from my last-chance school.

"Wait-listed."

Ugh. Wait-listed meant I might not get accepted *anywhere*. But then, wait-listed also meant I *wasn't* rejected—at least I was still in the running!

So, now what? Business schools take students off wait-lists up until a week before classes start. I could be looking at another five months before I had an answer. I couldn't hang out in California. Queen Lee and my parents would have a fit. I could see my grandmother now, calling the deli to see if they had openings. My father would be waiting at the airport, his welcome home gift an application from the temp office. And my mother would go into therapy, wondering where she went wrong.

I looked out the window of my mini-mansion and saw three warriors with swords tucked into their beaded belts, spears in hand. I went outside and joined them. Instead of needing to explain who I was and why I wanted to join their little circle, the men simply made physical and mental room for me. That was all I needed to feel welcome just as I was. At that moment, I didn't need to be enrolled in graduate school or be ten pounds thinner or be better at whatever I was supposed to be better at to be accepted. We gazed at the magenta and amethyst sky. Clouds were outlined in gold, and rays of light created a shimmering canvas as far up as the eye could see. The confidence and calm of the warriors helped me decide then and there that I would not repeat past mistakes. I was not going to conform this time. I always found success when I followed my heart and passion, and I vowed that was exactly what I would do.

My FINAL MORNING in Kenya arrived. I hadn't yet seen a sunrise, so I rose at 5:45 to a dark lavender sky and went on a trek with the Chief. The morning dew left a soft wet film on my skin as I trailed Winston through the dry plains of Northern Maasailand, one strenuous step after another. One of his gargantuan strides was equivalent to ten of mine. Only a few steps into the hike and already my heart was throbbing from the brisk pace and high altitude. Beads of sweat bubbled across my forehead and between my breasts. Barely able to catch my breath, I asked the Chief the question that had been gnawing at me since I met him: "What does it take to become a warrior?"

"You need to be a strong, brave man who is willing to do anything to protect your community," he told me.

"You say 'a strong, brave *man*.' How many female warriors are there?" I asked.

"None," Winston said. "Women aren't strong or brave enough to do the work we do."

Flashbacks of people telling me I wasn't capable played in my head. My chest tightened and my blood boiled. I slowed my pace to catch my breath for what I knew was about to be a battle.

"Okay, hold on a minute," I said, my hands on my thighs as I tried to catch my breath. "How about you explain what's actually involved in becoming a warrior?"

"You need to be a man," he said. "You need to go through rites of passage that only a man can do. You need to live where you can only eat meat and drink blood and herb soup that makes you lose your mind. You need to get circumcised like a man and not wince from the pain. You need to be fearless. You need to protect and entertain your community and be able to face any animal head-on. You need to be able to throw a spear and use a sword with total accuracy. And you need to be a man."

"Yeah, I heard the man part, but don't Maasai women want to be warriors?" I asked.

"Of course they do. Who wouldn't want to be like us?"

"And they've never been given a chance?"

"No."

"But everything you just said is something a woman can do—something I can do—except for the penis part," I said.

The Chief wasn't entertained. "Women aren't built emotionally or physically for the work that warriors do." He shrugged his sculpted shoulders and turned back to the mountain.

Winston's words and that shrug made me furious! I can take no for an answer if there's a good reason, but the idea that women couldn't be warriors just because they weren't men wasn't sitting well with me.

Suddenly my mission became clear. The move to Santa Barbara, my family's constant questions, the trip to Kenya, the rejections, the wait-list—it had all been leading to this moment.

"Chief, how about we make a deal," I said. "If I come back here someday, will you take me through the rites of passage to become a warrior?"

The Chief stopped and turned to me. A patch of sunlight lit up his face. "You must be crazy."

I shrugged and smiled a big Peacock Donkey smile. "Maybe."

The Chief scanned the twisting valleys of green below us. "Sure. I guess if you come back and can live without trail mix, long shoes, and daily updates about Hollywood, then I will take you through the rites of passage to become a warrior." He laughed. "This will be an easy promise for me. You will be back in sunny California faster than a hippo can swallow you whole."

All I needed to hear out of the Chief's mouth was "sure."

Ready to seal the deal, I presented my hand and we shook on it.

I SPENT THE REST of the day informing everyone that I was going to become a warrior and prove the Chief wrong. Winston listened and shook his head in disbelief. Most of the extended Bergman clan laughed in disbelief, but some pulled me aside to ask if I was serious.

"I am totally doing this," I responded.

One woman had a minor panic attack, "Have you spoken with your parents? They are not going to let you do this. This is not something that a nice Jewish girl would do." She paced back and forth and with right hand over her heart. "I think I will call your mother. Together we will make sure you don't do this. If you were married you wouldn't have such thoughts." Accustomed to the overbearing Jewish mother thing, I paid her no heed.

As I walked down the stone path to dinner that evening, another woman, who appeared to work at the volunteer center, stopped me. Someone I hadn't met before.

"You are Mindy?"

"I am."

"My name is Faith. I am Maasai."

I smiled, "Good to meet you."

"I have heard that you want to become a warrior."

"I do," I said with a slight chuckle.

Her eyes focused in on mine, "Why do you laugh? For many years women in my tribe have been trying to become warriors. If you have the chance to show girls, boys, women, and men that a woman can be a warrior, then you must do this. You must take it very seriously."

It felt like the air had been knocked out of me. All I could do was nod my head as Faith walked away. Suddenly, my little spur-of-the-moment adventure took on a meaning outside of me. In a flash, my smile evaporated, and any hint of playfulness was replaced with a determination to achieve the goal.

4

Two for the Road

ON THE INTERMINABLE plane ride back to Santa Barbara, I couldn't get Faith off my mind. What had started as something of a self-serving, self-aggrandizing plan had taken on a much deeper and broader importance. This was now a mission that I *needed* to complete. I'm not a religious person, but I do believe a higher power exists that creates openings for people to use their talents, leaving it up to the individual to accept or reject those crossroad moments. Becoming a warrior was not going to be an opportunity that I rejected. Why a plump, white, Gucci-wearing Jewish girl from California was given this chance seemed ludicrous on the surface, but I wasn't going to waste energy figuring out the *why*. Now was the time to figure out *how* to make this warrior thing happen.

I closed my eyes, wondering what the training and rites of passage would be. The Chief mentioned living in a cave for at least a month or two with other warriors. I could do that. The diet would be limited to meat, questionable herbs—and blood. The thought of drinking blood made my stomach roll, but I could do it. But what would happen if a lion or a hyena attacked me? Would the other warriors protect me, or would I be on my own from the start? Would I learn how to defend myself gradually before moving into dangerous territory? Also, I had heard that there was a circumcision rite of passage. While I didn't have a penis, I clearly had a vagina, and I knew that in some cultures circumcising the vagina (clitorectemy) was not off-limits. Was I willing to undergo that procedure? Was Faith expecting me to get circumcised, to give up a good sixty years of varying levels of pleasurable sex (maybe fifty-nine given my recent dry patch)? There must be a way around this issue. My mind darted to the people I'd be living with in the cave. What if they didn't accept or grow to respect me? The Maasai I had been exposed to were peaceful and welcoming, but were they only that way because they were at work? This train of thought was leading me nowhere good. I wiggled in my seat and gave my mind a mental shake. If I continued to think like this, I would never go back to Kenya.

I decided then and there that I was not going to overanalyze the opportunity. I was not going to scour the Internet for the average number of lion-mauling deaths per year or the potential diseases one could get from drinking blood. I told myself that Winston was going to keep me as safe as possible until I learned how to do the job myself. He would be by my side every step of the way. Relieving myself of the pessimistic thoughts allowed me to focus on the benefits. I would be exposed to a culture so drastically different from my own that it would cause me to question accepted beliefs about humanity and the world. I would be relying only on myself and my tribe without the luxuries I took for granted as necessities. I would be doing my best to show women that they didn't have to accept the status quo. Most important, I would follow my heart. I vowed I would not let fear or self-doubt keep me from taking advantage of this once-in-a-lifetime chance.

WHEN I ARRIVED HOME, my parents picked me up from the airport. My mother, carrying Pink Panther–colored roses, embraced me with a tight, but short-lived, hug. She crinkled her nose and said, "Sweetie, you really need to take a shower, but you look thin!"

My dad took a whiff, "Sweet Jesus. You smell like you've been grazing in the savanna!"

Exhausted after the long and restless journey, I tried to get a little shut-eye on the twenty-minute ride back to my temporary housing at the beach condo.

Fat chance.

Just as my eyelids drooped, my father spoke up.

"So, Mindy, since you haven't told us about business school, I'm assuming you didn't get in?"

"I was put on the wait-list."

My mother gasped, "Oh, that's terrific! Congratulations!"

My father turned and gave my mother a confused look, "Why are you congratulating her? She didn't get in."

"Yes, but she still has a chance, and it's at a school she loves." She continued, "Mindy, you need to do everything possible to impress that admissions committee. Put that creative mind to work!"

While my father agreed, he also needed to sprinkle in a little pessimism. "Remember that you didn't get in, and in this economy I highly doubt anyone will be accepted off the wait-list. I just read an article about how business schools are overloaded with very qualified applicants because of the layoffs."

I rolled my eyes, "Yeah, and don't forget . . . I am at risk of being destitute."

"Now you get it," my dad said.

My mother snapped back, "They wouldn't have put her on the wait-list if she didn't have a chance!"

I was way too tired to speak up, so I let yin and yang battle it out.

Raising his voice to just the right level to startle me, my father said, "So what is your plan? Did you follow my advice and reach out to companies while you were in Kenya so that you could get to work right when you got back here? Opportunities aren't going to knock on your door."

I wanted to blurt out that I was already employed by Maasai, Incorporated and that my new title was Warrior Candidate, but being flip with him would lead nowhere. Instead of responding like a child, as I often did, I needed to impress upon him my determination to follow my heart.

"Have the two of you ever thought that I actually care about my future? You make it sound like I laze around tanning, shopping, and sipping martinis all day. And while that life sounds fantastic after a trip filled with hard work, sweat, dirt, poverty, and no shopping, one thing you need not worry about is my interest in living a happy, successful, and independent life."

We were parked in front of the condo, so my father turned around to face me.

"I am incredibly concerned about you. You don't properly filter risk. Your mom and I thought that it was just a phase you would grow out of, but the belief that you are invincible is still a driving force in you. If you found a steady job with a solid company, we wouldn't worry."

I stared at him, wondering if I should be offended or relieved. I finally understood where he was coming from.

"Thank you for explaining your thought process to me, but I'm an adult. Don't worry about me falling. I can promise you that I'm going to stumble and even take major spills, but it is my job to lift myself back up again. And if I don't fall, then I won't grow."

I looked at my knees—both spotted with scars—and said, "I remember what happened when I got each one of these scars." I pointed to my right knee, "This one was from skateboarding." I pointed a scar on my left knee, "This one was from rope swinging and crashing into a tree." And then I opened my left hand

42

to reveal the two-inch scar on the palm. "And this one is from slicing a head of lettuce helping to make dinner." I continued, "Both of you know that I have more scars, but none of them are from repeating the same accident."

I grabbed my bag, opened the car door, and said, "This is my attempt to manage your expectations—I'm going to continue to make mistakes, but not because I'm trying to intentionally hurt either one of you. I will continue to scar because I'm living my life."

THE NEXT MORNING, I watched the sunrise from my bedroom window, already yearning to return to Africa. Flipping to my stomach and snuggling deep into my bed, I allowed my mind to drift to Maasailand. I grabbed a handful of pillow and dreamed of digging my fingers into the Kenyan ground, taking hold of a handful of moist morning dirt. I imagined meeting Faith after successfully completing the rites of passage. I would tell her that it was possible: A woman could be accepted as a warrior in her tribe.

My conversation with my parents the previous afternoon had felt like a big step in cutting the cord, but my speech didn't stick. Over dinner that night, my father returned to the theme of finding a job. Sadness swept over me. I felt that he had no confidence that I was going to be able to survive on my own, but I remained firm in my resolve to get back to Kenya as soon as possible to start training as a warrior.

I stepped onto my balcony and scanned the beach, which was dotted with surfers zipping up their wet suits and happy couples in linen tops and khaki pants unleashing freshly groomed dogs to run free. Everyone was so fit and happy in Santa Barbara. Evaluating my shape in the mirror, I figured that it would take at least a month to get strong enough to undertake rigorous training. I needed to hit the gym—big time. Now I had an immediate goal that took me one step closer to becoming a warrior.

I opened my laptop and started searching for a top-notch personal training program nearby. After scrolling through page after page and clicking on site after site of lame-looking, same-looking trainers, I finally landed on the Peak Performance Project (P3), run by Dr. Marcus Elliott, a Harvard physician. P3 was a training program for Olympic-level athletes, not open to commoners like me, and from what it looked like, not interested in taking on any new clients. Obviously, P3 was where I needed to be.

The gym was only a mile away, so I hopped into my flip-flops and drove over to a shiny gray warehouse located, ironically enough, next door to an Oscar Mayer weiner factory. I paused, staring at the Wienermobile—the bright-yellow bun on wheels holding a twenty-seven-foot red-hot fiberglass sausage on top. The thought of a juicy dog in a warm, baked bun topped with ketchup and spicy mustard put me on the verge of dropping my workout-for-warrior plan, but I restrained myself and entered the P3 office. My eyes feasted instead on the adult jungle gym fully equipped with massive television screens, big beastly equipment, and steamy men lying sweaty and exhausted on the black rubber flooring. I wiped the drool from my mouth, a visceral reaction that was of greater quantity and quality than my earlier hot-dog reaction. This was a completely superior type of wiener factory.

I explained to the first person who would listen that I needed to get in shape to become a warrior in Africa, surely a goal that they heard every day. Cody, the gym's manager, quickly evaluated my ability to ever become an Olympic athlete and looked me square in the eye,

"I don't think Dr. Elliott is taking on any new clients—and are you aware that this gym is strictly for professional athletes? Do you need directions to the YMCA?"

Being rejected was not an option. I needed to get in tip-top shape, and this was obviously the place to do it. This place was serious. I grabbed a business card that said President and CEO, walked outside, and sent an e-mail straight to Dr. Elliott. I explained that I was off to Kenya to face almost certain death as a lion's lunch and, if he had any interest in saving a fellow mortal's life, he would tell me what time to arrive the next day to begin training.

Apparently the note had an impact. A few hours later, Dr. Elliott accepted me on the condition that I come in four times a week and not disrupt his program by bothering the serious athletes.

The next morning, my training at P3 began. In one corner, three men in their twenties were sprinting along the indoor track. In the center of the room, a thirty-something gym god decked out in Under Armour gear rotated between sets of pull-ups and one-arm push-ups. I could have, and cheerfully would have, bounced a quarter off his butt. The slight bend of his upper body toward the machine revealed the top of his underwear, which hugged his muscled waist and created a perfect view of the dip of his spine down to the top of his buttocks. My estrogen shot through the tin roof. How the hell was I, a normal sexual woman, going to last in this meat market without "disrupting the athletes"?

But then the workout with Mike, my personal trainer, began—what felt like two hundred push-ups and enough sets of planks and weighted lunges to make my quads and abs go numb. The first few sessions were so intense that even the motion of squatting to sit on the toilet brought forth a groan that would have sent the hairiest, scariest lion back to his den trembling in fright. But after the first two weeks, my muscle memory woke up and I began to feel like an athlete again.

Assuming that the Maasai walk about fifteen to twenty-five miles a day, Dr. Elliott prescribed three-hour hikes five times a week—an essential component of training, as my entire life would be spent on foot in the wild. Mike also encouraged me to start figuring out how to hoist myself up a tree, so I incorporated this task into my hikes. Little did I know how important a survival skill this would prove to be.

ABOUT THREE WEEKS into my training, I was feeling a bit cocky and decided on my next hike to put myself in the path of a mountain lion that had been sighted in the area. I felt strong enough to kick butt with a wild cat, but after three hours with no sign of the lion, I veered off the trail and continued to climb. Gingerly, I took step after step, my arrogance swiftly fading as I realized that if something bad happened, no one would be able to find me. I was able to forge ahead by telling myself that this is what I was going to have to do in Kenya, and in a much more dangerous environment. Until I heard a rattle.

Holy shit. Holy shit. Holy shit. My worst nightmare was now a reality. I'd thoughtlessly put myself in harm's way, and a snake was going to bite me. I was going to die. What the hell was I thinking, trying to find a mountain lion? My father was right! I don't know how to judge risk.

I heard the rattle again and saw the snake out of the corner of my eye. I stood completely still as it moved toward me.

I stopped breathing.

The snake slithered over the top of one of my hiking boots. Shit. Shit. Shit. My heart banged against my chest cavity. I prayed—opening up my pleas to every god from every religion in hopes that one of them would hear and help me. As the snake shimmied on its way down the side of the mountain, I ran so fast back to the main trail that when I stopped I got whiplash. I had never felt this type of paralyzing fear. And just as easily as the switch turned *on* in my brain to go on the trip, the switch turned *off*. I called Mike.

He picked up, "Shouldn't you be on a hike right now?"

"Mike, I'm not going to Kenya."

"What?"

"Mike, I can't do it. I almost just died."

A typical human would have been a bit more emotional, but Mike was in the Marine Corps and a MMA fighter, so he responded nonchalantly, "But you clearly didn't."

"Listen, Mike, I'm completely freaked out about a snake crawling over my shoe. What the hell am I going to do when I'm face to face with a buffalo? I'm not the right girl for this. This is not going to work."

Mike told me to meet him in thirty minutes at our usual running spot on the beach. I got there first, so I took my boots off and let the sand gently massage the arches of my feet. My heart slowed to a normal pace by the time Mike arrived.

He plopped next to me and said, "I've only known you for a month, but from the first time we met, I could tell that there was something very different about you. Yes, you're right that you're not in the perfect physical shape to go on this journey. And your outdoors experience leaves much to be desired."

I nodded, "Yeah, the closest I've been to the outdoors up to now is a cruise to Alaska."

Mike continued, "But what will carry you through this journey is your heart and your complete audacity. The things you don't know now, you will either learn or not. It doesn't really matter. All that matters at this point is that you believe you will make it through. You're capable. Stop your bellyaching and accept it. The only person getting in your way right now is yourself."

I thought about this and nodded slowly.

"I get it. I guess it's time I started acting as if I were already a warrior."

Mike punched me lightly on the arm and said, "You already do, and you already are."

A FEW DAYS LATER, I was back in my groove. Mike gifted me with a wooden stick that was supposed to resemble a spear. He made me run the track with that dorky stick over and over to get me used to what I would encounter with the Maasai. I also worked on strengthening my wrists and forearms by gripping a thirty-pound plate in my hands and steering it from side to side like I was driving a bus. When I had walked into the gym the first day, I could barely do three push-ups in a row. By the time I left, I was able to do sets of twenty-five back to back.

The added strength helped get my head in the right place. I realized that believing in myself was going to have to be a conscious daily effort. Some days it would come naturally, some days I would need to fight for it, and some days I wouldn't have the will. I didn't have the innate belief that I was going to be able to accomplish this mission, so I needed to train my brain just like I trained my body.

Walking out of the gym after a particularly ass-kicking but exhilarating workout, I patted my new and improved abs. Four weeks had come and gone. I was as physically ready as I could be to return to Kenya. I jumped into my car, grabbed a pad and pen, and began to develop a list of things I needed to do before I got on a plane to Nairobi:

1. Buy socks and underwear (love Under Armour, so go online to buy).

2. Research water purification situation—go to camping store.

3. Buy Chanel Red Dragon nail polish.

4. Don't forget tweezers, nail clippers, and tampons.

I tapped my pen on my steering wheel, wondering what I was missing and idly noticed a plane flying by.

"Good morning, Mindy!" I said to myself. "I need to buy a plane ticket!"

I checked the calendar in my BlackBerry to see when my schedule was open: Day after day was blank. I could leave right now if I wanted to. I was completely free. I felt the familiar throat-tightening anxiety. I suddenly wanted company on this death march of a journey. My first call was to Mike. Would he go if I paid for his plane ticket?

His response was a resounding "Hell no! This is only for a crazy Jewish girl who has something to prove."

Scrolling through my address book, I realized that the people I knew were more used to the Ritz Carlton than roughing it with a rucksack. Then I flashed back to the handshake with the Chief and remembered my free-spirited roommate, Becca.

Two rings and she picked up.

"Hello," Becca said in her bouncy voice.

"Becca, this is Mindy."

"Mindy?"

"Mindy—Mindy your roommate from Kenya."

"OH! Hey! What's up?"

"So, you want to go back to Kenya with me to become a warrior?" A few seconds passed with no answer.

"Becca, are you there? Did you hear me?"

"Oh yeah. I totally heard you, but this song that I love just came on the radio—can I call you back?"

Having already accepted Becca as Becca, I said, "Yeah. Sure. Call me back right away because I'm ready to buy plane tickets!"

Six minutes and a few hundred antsy taps of my right foot on the car mat, my phone rang. I told Becca about my plan to return to Kenya. She didn't even need time to think about it—she was in as long as her expenses were paid. Paying for two people would be expensive, but I could swing it.

The only other unsolved issue was what I was going to tell my parents. I'd stayed clear of them this month by doing temp work in-between workouts, but leaving the country was another matter. They couldn't stop me from going back to Kenya (unless, of course, my mother had me committed and put in a straitjacket), but they could make me feel awful enough that my trip would be tainted. Guilt trips galore would ensue. My mother would cry, my father would question how this could lead to a steady job, my brother would fly in from New York and tell me that I was breaking up the family, and my grandmothers would claim that they were too fragile at their late ages to deal with the stress that this trip would produce.

As the light turned green on Gutierrez Street, I plucked at the sweat-soaked Under Armour T-shirt clinging to my skin and remembered reading an article about how Under Armour's sales of women's products paled in comparison to the men's side of the business. I looked down at the shining white logo of interlocking shields and *bingo!*—I had the idea that would make this whole thing come together. I would tell my parents that I was working on a marketing plan for Under Armour to increase sales of their women's apparel. In my parents' eyes, adding this to my résumé could help me get into business school, which was even better than working another temporary job while I languished on the wait-list. It wasn't a complete fabrication. After all, I had loved Under Armour ever since I saw it hug the gym god's goodies, and there was something about the brand that made me feel powerful when I wore it. Like a Westernized version of a warrior uniform.

Back home, I hopped in the shower and practiced the pitch to my parents as I shampooed my hair. I only had one chance to convince them that my plan was sound. Otherwise, I ran the risk of leaving my family with bad blood between us, and that was not something I wanted to do, especially considering the danger associated with the journey. I turned on my business brain and thought about it as if I were making a presentation in class. As far as they knew, I would be developing a free marketing plan for Under Armour, providing hard-core gear testing in the field, and offering the company an opportunity for social responsibility with a tribe of incredibly fit people. How could they possibly object? Machiavelli Mindy was driving this car.

Feeling optimistic, I bought the plane tickets to Nairobi and texted Becca:

We are leaving in exactly one week. Flight details were sent to you via e-mail. Can't wait!

WITH TICKETS PURCHASED, I decided that I might as well call the CEO of Under Armour, Mr. Kevin Plank, and tell him what I was up to. After all, I had nothing to lose, and he would probably be bowled over by the brilliance of my idea. I actually managed to reach his assistant (aka gatekeeper) and launched right into my spiel.

"Hi, my name is Mindy Budgor, and I'm about to become the world's first female Maasai warrior. Does Mr. Plank have time to speak with me?"

Deep-space silence.

"Hello?"

"Yes. Hello. Can you please repeat what you just said?" she asked.

"Of course. I'm leaving in seven days on a trip to Kenya to become the first female Maasai warrior, and I'm wondering if Mr. Plank is available for five minutes to discuss my upcoming adventure and a possible connection to Under Armour."

More silence. Then came her polite voice. "Thank you for your call, Ms. Budgor. Mr. Plank is not available, but I will certainly give him your message."

I had made enough cold calls in my life to know that I would not be hearing from Mr. Plank. Sure, they were missing out on an amazing opportunity, but all I really needed was a story to quiet the potential family drama that my announcement would create. And I had that completely mapped out. My parents would never know this marketing plan only existed in my imagination. By the time I returned as a Maasai warrior, they would be so proud of me that they would have forgotten the whole Under Armour ploy. I hoped.

Getting them on my side was next on my to-do list, so I invited my parents and Queen Lee to dinner.

At precisely 6 p.m. came an authoritative knock. Queen Lee, always punctual, was dressed in green from head to toe: lime-green slacks, a honeydew silk blouse, and a green-apple bag that matched her pear-shaped emerald ring. I brought the Queen into the living room and instantly handed her a G&T with four squeezed limes.

She gave me an approving nod and scanned the room. She looked curiously at the dinner table, which had four small vases with a single hydrangea in each, and said, "You've gone to a lot of trouble. I assume you have something big to spring on us tonight."

I smiled. She knew me well.

My parents arrived a few minutes later. I dimmed the lighting just a bit and doubled the alcohol in the drinks. I was going to control the flow of this event as much as possible. My mom sat down and took a decent-size sip of what looked like a glass of Perrier. Almost spitting the vodka and soda across the table, she called out, "Mindy!! Are you trying to get me drunk?!"

My dad and I chuckled and I said, "Oh, I just thought you'd want to relax a bit."

"Mindy, please. I can't drink this."

I brought my mother a glass of Perrier and placed the mild version of fajitas I'd made in front of my grandmother and me and the spicy version in front of my mom and dad. My mom eyed the tortillas warily and said, "You know, fajitas still taste excellent without the tortillas." She looked down at her plate and continued, "That's the way I'm going to eat mine."

I rolled my eyes. Even when I was in shape, she remained worried about my weight. As soon as everyone started eating, I shared my news: "I'm going back to Kenya!"

My mom was trying to chew quickly in order to respond and nip that plan in the bud, but she wasn't fast enough. I kept talking.

"And I'm going with a nice Jewish girl from Illinois who I met while volunteering. We have a truly incredible opportunity."

My mom looked at me, desperately wanting to speak, but her mouth was on fire. That's what happens when you add something like twenty jalapeños and a heap of Aleppo pepper flakes to a single serving.

I continued, "We'll be working on a marketing plan for a major company while living with the Maasai."

My dad looked up from his plate, "This food is perfectly spiced, and the Maasai are great. Did you see my book?"

My mom drank her entire glass of water. "Mindy, I *don't* understand why you have to go back to Africa! Really, this is just ridiculous! You were lucky that you didn't get a disease last time, but you won't be so lucky again."

My father gave me an all-too-familiar look of suspicion. "So what company is it, and what exactly are you going to be doing for them?"

"The company is Under Armour—an athletic apparel company—and I'm going to be part of an initiative to increase sales of women's apparel."

"And explain why the Maasai are involved," my dad prodded.

"Because we're working on a female empowerment initiative with the tribe that we believe will have broad-range appeal to women."

Just as he was about to ask another question, Queen Lee lifted her G&T and said, "Well, I think it's terrific. I don't want to think about the drek you will live in, but it's your life."

My mother continued to plead, hoping that I would change my mind, but I knew I'd won. In my family, the Queen had the final word.

THE NEXT WEEK seemed to fly by. Seven days and no return calls from Mr. Plank. I had my last workout at the P3 wiener factory. I almost got a little teary when I said good-bye to Mike. He'd become so much more than a physical trainer to me.

"Don't get all emotional on me. I will see you right back here when you are officially the first female Maasai warrior." He grabbed my shoulders, looked deep into my eyes, and said, "You got this," and slapped my butt as I walked out the door.

By the time I boarded the plane, not only had my mom come to terms with my journey, but she even had an errand for me to run in Africa.

"Where are you staying your first night in Nairobi?" she asked.

That was the only thing I did know, "The Holiday Inn."

She handed me a manila envelope and said, "A man named Nic from a nonprofit is going to pick this up from you when you arrive. My friend Teri asked me to have you deliver it to him. It's a tape of *The Lion King* and some documents." With that she handed me a package that would set our course in ways neither she nor I could ever have imagined.

I didn't ask any questions. Instead, I stuffed the package in my carry-on, gave my mom a big hug, and disappeared in the security line.

5

New York to Nairobi

EXITING THE TERMINAL at JFK airport, I was blasted with the muggy summer heat of New York City, my first pit stop en route to Kenya. I would stay in town for a couple of days until Becca arrived, and then she and I would have one night together at my brother's place before boarding a plane to Nairobi. I hadn't given my brother the details of my upcoming trip, and the only thing my parents told him was something along the lines of, "Your sister is off to Kenya to do something that is supposedly going to help her get into business school."

My brother, a Columbia Business School graduate, didn't have any issues getting into school. He had been laser-focused on working in real-estate investment banking since he took his first breath in this world. Any admission advisor looking at his application got a clear and confident picture of his professional trajectory. There was no risk in accepting my brother into school—he was the type who would have a job lined up within twenty-four hours of admittance. My path, on the other hand, appeared random and jarring in a business school context, and my brother knew it. He had been trying to coach me but finally gave up a year earlier after setting me up with an interview at a bank where he had a good relationship.

The memory was indelibly imprinted on my brain. My high heels clacked as I walked through the colossal lobby. I entered an extravagant, but admittedly tasteful, conference room, and within minutes of two BSDs (big swinging dicks) coming into the room, I would have had preferred fifteen root canals with no laughing gas. They grilled me, and I lost it when they asked me this key question:

"What happened between July 12 and July 22 in 2005?" (which was four years earlier).

I was stumped. "Excuse me?"

"There is a gap in your resume from July 12 to July 22 in 2005, and I am asking you why that is the case."

I had known I had no chance of employment at this bank after question one, and I replied politely for as long as I could because of my brother's relationship. But this question was the tipping point. Polite Mindy switched off and bitchy Mindy turned on. I was not going to let this guy stomp all over me. I leaned over the desk and looked him straight in the eyes and said, "Do you remember what you did from July 12 to July 22 four years ago?"

He looked like he was going to reach across the table and strangle me. The other dick looked at the angry dick and said, "Well, thank you for coming in. I don't think this is the right place for you. I wish you the best in your future endeavors."

Although my brother was furious after I told him the story, the experience allowed us to build a relationship based on who we were, not what we are "supposed" to be. We've gotten along better ever since.

WITH A BACKPACK slung over my shoulder and purse dangling from my hand, I rang my brother's doorbell. He opened the door, gave me a big hug, and started scanning my possessions.

"I don't think you'll need your Louis Vuitton bag on this trip. Speaking of which, what exactly are you doing?"

Stretching out on his camel-colored leather sofa, I gave him what was now a canned speech.

"I'm working on a marketing plan for Under Armour that will help them increase sales of women's apparel and help me get into business school."

Silence.

"You are so full of shit! Is that the story you told Mom and Dad?"

I smiled, "Indeed."

He went to the kitchen, poured scotch into two glasses, and said, "I'm assuming the real story requires a bit of liquor."

The scotch burned my throat as it went down, but in short order, I was loose as a goose and telling my brother how I felt deeply connected to the Maasai and needed to at least try to become a warrior. He listened intently and then tried to reason with me.

"I know how you get when you have an idea, but I just want to make sure that you have thought through everything."

I held my hand up to stop him, slurring my words. "I purposefully did not think through everything. Close analysis of this journey would have stopped me from going."

He gave me a worried look, "That alone should tell you something. Mindy, this could be very dangerous. Do you actually believe that you know the Chief?"

I let him talk.

"I'm sure he was nice when he was working, but you don't know what he's like when he's off duty. And that doesn't even factor in the other people in the tribe. Just one pissed-off tribesman could be the end of you. You know that some of them are going to fight against you. It's not like they're going to welcome you and say, 'Yes, please change our culture. The very culture that we have been happy with for thousands of years.' You could get seriously hurt. I mean, you could get raped or killed."

I nodded as he spoke. His concerns were valid and had crossed my mind, but no one was going to talk me out of the trip at this point. Today was not one of those days when I needed to convince myself I had the power to survive.

My brother continued, "And what about the way they live? You've never even backpacked and now you're just going to roam free in the wild? Mindy, you are not going to the Brooklyn Zoo. There won't be any gates protecting you from the lions. And what if a lion mauls you? Is there even a hospital where you are going?"

I shrugged my shoulders and said, "The Maasai have been living in the wild for thousands of years. If something happens to me, then I figure no one will be in a better position to take care of me than the Maasai."

He finished his scotch and said, "I know you're going to do this, but I wasn't going to let you go without giving you a piece of my mind." He continued, "So is the whole Under Armour thing made up?"

"Absolutely not!" I shrieked, swinging my drink and spilling it on his couch. In my drunken haze, I mopped up the spill with the bottoms of my pant legs and said, "Well, sort of, but I did call the CEO. He just hasn't had time to get back to me yet."

My brother laughed, "How is it possible that you are drunk already, and did you actually just use your pants to clean up your mess? And furthermore, explain to me how you are going to write a marketing plan when you are in a cave."

I thought about the logistics. "Well, I might not be able to get the marketing plan done from the cave, but I am going to stay in contact with Mr. Plank to at least begin a conversation." I continued as seriously as my drunken state made possible. "They really do have an opportunity for growth, and I know I can help them."

My brother took the now-empty glass of scotch out of my hand and put it in the sink.

"The stuff your brain comes up with never ceases to shock me. Just try to call or e-mail every now and then, and don't do anything stupid to piss off a buffalo."

Lexington Avenue was strangely quiet later that night as I made my way back to my brother's apartment after meeting a friend for a drink. At 10:30 p.m., the street was typically bustling. I faced the fact that in less than thirty-six hours I would be on a journey that would make this sleepy street feel like a raging nightclub. There would be no cars, no streetlights, and no paved streets where I was going. I wondered if the Maasai warriors I was going to be with spoke English. Probably not. If they didn't speak English, would the body language I experienced with Amos be sufficient to tell me if I was in danger? Fear of the unknown finally hit me. I needed another drink.

THE NEXT MORNING, a ping of an incoming text message interrupted my mild hangover. It was a message from Becca:

> Landed. Headed to your bros. Forgot some things. Do you mind
> if we run an errand or two?

The errand or two turned into a mad rush around Manhattan. Becca forgot her socks, toothbrush, and hairbrush. She insisted on replacing her lost Ray Bans with a pair of cherry-red aviators. She also forgot her drawing pencils, so we scoured seven art supply stores to locate some special van Gogh edition pencil, which to the naked eye was no different from any generic piece of lead wrapped in a wooden stick.

That evening we ordered Chinese food. As I slurped back and forth between lo mein and Corona, Becca filled me in on her life. She had just completed a two-week road trip with a friend, was working on a new graphic novel about her life with a punk band, and was thinking about joining a team of puppeteers in Nebraska.

"Don't your parents ever pressure you to go back to school or get a different, maybe more stable job?"

Without thinking twice, she responded, "Why would they do something like that? First of all, I'm an adult, so what I choose to do isn't their decision anyway. And second of all, I'm really happy with my life, and that's all they really want for me."

I caught myself envying Becca's freedom. Her family seemed to love her unconditionally. I, on the other hand, always felt like a hamster on a wheel seeking my family's approval. Becca didn't need to lie to her parents about going back to Kenya. She said they were thrilled about her upcoming adventure. They didn't ask if she was going to improve her résumé. They just told her to have fun and be as safe as possible.

Thoroughly stuffed, we evaluated each other's packing supplies:

Mindy	Becca
Chanel (Red Dragon) nail polish, avocado oil, tweezers	Ceramic bull pin (accessory)
Under Armour tops, tank tops, hats, pants (enough for Becca and me), three pairs of Under Armour boy shorts	One breezy floral cotton dress, various vintage attire
Digital camera	Old-school Canon film camera
Hiking boots, mint-colored jeweled flip-flops	Five flowery thongs, four lacy bras
Books: *Valley of the Dolls, Wilderness Survival for Dummies, Confederacy of Dunces*	Books: *Man on Wire, Persepolis* (graphic novel)
Package for Nic (tape of *The Lion King*)	Dr. Bronner's all-purpose soap
One sweater	One blue down comfy sleeping bag

"Nice packing choices," I said to Becca as we relaxed in the tent that I had set up on my brother's hardwood living-room floor (an earthy addition to his Lincoln Center apartment, which I thought would get us in the mood for the bush).

"Just the essentials, of which I noticed you forgot one."

"What?"

"Your sleeping bag."

"Yeah, I thought about that, but I really want to live as true to the tribe as possible."

Becca looked at me like I had "Idiot" written across my forehead and said, "Do what you want, but I am telling you now, you are going to be miserable."

"I may be miserable, but I will be authentic."

Becca fumbled with the envelope addressed to Nic. "Who is Nic?"

"My mom's friend from Santa Barbara asked me to deliver it to some guy involved in her nonprofit when we land in Nairobi. I think it's just a tape of *The Lion King*."

"That's random."

Rolling to her back and propping her head with a pillow, she asked, "So, how are we getting this warrior thing done?"

Trying to make my lack of travel plans sound as robust as possible, I said, "We're going to stay at the Holiday Inn for one night and then we'll go back to the volunteer center where we met Winston. We'll find him or at least find someone who knows where he is." Becca nodded, and I continued, "And I guess after we find him, he'll take us to the cave to begin the rites of passage."

Becca was silent.

"You scared?" I asked.

"Nope—just thinking that I want to be back in the US for Oktoberfest."

The next afternoon, Becca and I grossly underestimated the transit time to get to the airport. "Twenty-five minutes should be plenty of time," I said.

I was so wrong.

One and a half hours later, I found myself trying to hand cash to at least three Swiss Air employees to hold the plane and help us speed through security. Becca and I sprinted through the airport, only stopping once to ponder buying squishy neck pillows in tiger and leopard print. Deciding against the purchase, we got back to running and caught the gate door as it was closing.

Exhausted, I quickly fell into a deep sleep that lasted all the way to London, where we switched planes to Nairobi. It seemed we'd only just taken off when the flight attendant with good-morning snack packs woke me from my vegetative state. I opened my eyes to the relentless rays of sunlight at thirty-five thousand feet, my cheek stuck to the plane window as I surveyed the scene below. A feathery layer of clouds defined the horizon. The familiar trees punctuated the plains like green and brown tinsel-topped toothpicks. The valleys were parched, making it hard to believe that hundreds of thousands of wildebeests, gazelles, and buffalo are able to exist on what looked like no sustenance.

Becca was passed out, so I took the opportunity to draft my first communication with Mr. Plank on my Blackberry (see Appendix, Letter 1), which I would later copy and mail as a handwritten note.

After reviewing my letter to Mr. Plank, I chuckled. The note was short, sweet, and would surely make him smile. I fully understood that the idea of selling Under Armour to people who make less than a US$1 a day was ludicrous. But every woman had a warrior within, and I felt that if I could get Mr. Plank to become my pen pal, then maybe we could create some kind of platform that would allow women to share warrior experiences as well as do something big for Maasai women or even warrior women everywhere. Sending professional business letters was not in my mind the way to get Plank's attention. My letters would be straight from inside—straight from my warrior within.

ONCE WE LANDED in Nairobi, we hopped into a taxi and chugged along through the jam-packed streets to the Holiday Inn. A message was waiting for us when we arrived. Becca and I thought the same thing: "Winston?"

I took the envelope from the receptionist and tore it open:

> Welcome Ms. Mindy. I have been awaiting your arrival. I look forward to our meeting. Please call me when you settle.
> Ole Kamuaro – Nic

"It's not from the Chief. It's about *The Lion King* delivery."

Before going to our room, I bought a couple of stamps from the store and mailed my first letter to Mr. Plank. I wondered how I was going to send him my weekly letters from the bush. The Maasai, of course, received mail—who doesn't have a mailman?

Once in our room, I called Nic while Becca scribbled in her journal. She was writing about a relationship she was having with a guy who was a movie theater attendant by day and a singer-drummer by night—a relationship that was totally separate from the one with her other boyfriend, which we later gabbed about while sipping mimosas by the pool.

"What happens when one of them finds out that you have another boyfriend?" I asked.

"They already know about each other and are actually pretty cool with it."

She took a long sip from her drink and, while crunching on a piece of ice, said, "The only requirement is that I can't add another dude into the mix."

I nodded, "Four really is a crowd."

At 8 p.m. we met Nic in the hotel lobby. He was a dark-skinned, handsome man, around six-foot-four and forty-five years old, dressed in a navy-and-white pinstriped collared shirt, a blue blazer with big gold buttons, and khaki pants. He smiled with the biggest, whitest smile I'd ever seen. I handed him the package and invited him to dinner.

Over our second bottle of wine, we told him about our mission to become warriors. He nearly choked.

"I am sorry. Please tell me your plans again."

"We are here to become warriors. We are meeting a Chief tomorrow who is going to take us to a cave to complete the rites of passage," Becca said.

Nic dabbed the sides of his face with his napkin. "This isn't possible. Where is this Chief?"

"Somewhere around Mulot," I said.

"This is not a good idea," Nic said. "The danger is vast. I am Maasai. I know what is involved. Can I please talk you out of it?"

He was so polite that for a moment I almost agreed with him, but I stood my ground.

"No, I'm sorry, but we are committed."

Nic pleaded, "I understand that this could have a very important impact on the Maasai—especially the women—but you should leave this up to Maasai women. They have been raised in the right conditions. The Maasai way of life will be too different for you, and now that I am your host in this country, I feel responsible for your safety."

Seeing that we weren't budging, Nic tried scare tactics. "Did you know that female circumcision is a rite of passage that cannot be missed?"

"Yes, but we are not going to do that. Lots of Maasai girls aren't getting that procedure done anymore, so we should be fine," I said.

"Have you thought about getting into trouble with the men?" Nic continued, sounding almost panicked. "The elders in the community will never accept your idea to become a warrior. And even if some do accept you into the culture, then you will be the property of any man in your age group and clan. You must know that it is acceptable and very common for men to bed down with any woman in their clan even if the woman is married."

I was pondering his words when Becca broke the silence, "We'll be fine."

Nic furrowed his brow. He was not convinced but grudgingly accepted that this mission was going to happen in front of his face or behind his back. It seemed he preferred to be in the know.

"I am only concerned for your safety. Make sure you text me frequently. If there is trouble, I will try to help you. But life in the bush is not planned, so when danger occurs, it will occur instantly and there will most likely be nothing I can do," Nic said, nervously gulping his wine.

I felt bad for sharing what we were going to be doing with Nic. He didn't need the drama in his life—especially from a couple of girls he had only just met. I smiled softly and said, "We'll keep you informed as best as we possibly can, but please know that both of us are going into this knowing that the chance of making it through warrior training, being accepted into a clan, and becoming warriors is slim to none. But again, we are knowingly taking that chance."

At 9 a.m. the next morning, a driver from the volunteer organization picked us up. We were jet-lagged, so the second we hit the highway, Becca and I both fell asleep in the broken-down backseat of the Mitsubishi SUV. I woke abruptly from the vehicle bumping and clunking over rocks. We pulled over and parked on the side of the highway. As I leaned forward wondering what was going on, the driver made eye contact with me in the rear-view mirror. "I thought you would like to see the Great Rift Valley. This is the perfect viewing point."

We got out of the car and followed him to the rim of the road. In front of us was a deep, seemingly limitless carving into the earth. My eyes dove hundreds of feet, winding through the thorny acacia trees and hopping over low green and yellow brittle shrubs to the bottom of the valley. Lifting my eyes to the powder blue sky, my vision drifted forever forward, hovering over the Kenyan savanna. Bursts of green trees popped up like islands between the wispy blonde and green grass. Yes, danger was surely ahead, but at that precise moment, I couldn't have cared less.

An hour later, we pulled into the volunteer center's gravel driveway. We were escorted to our quarters—a luxurious tent as opposed to the mini-mansion we had during our previous visit. The space was compact, with two twin beds covered in red tartan Maasai blankets and a stone bathroom. We dropped our backpacks and Becca did a belly flop on the bed and went back to sleep. With adrenaline shooting through my veins, I cleaned up, grabbed a little lunch and excitedly wrote my second letter to Mr. Plank (see Appendix, Letter 2).

I gave Becca's curls a tug to wake her up. We headed out and asked the first person we saw, "Do you know where Winston is?"

The woman pointed west and said, "He should be tending to his herbs in the garden."

We followed the stone path to the garden, and that easily, we found him, his potent muscular arms glistening in the sun as he analyzed buds shooting up for their first breath of fresh air. We pummeled him with hugs and affection. Gripping his beaded bracelets I said, "We're back!"

He smiled and said, "Yes, it is good to see you." But then he extricated himself from our hands, took a step back, and gave us a confused look. "But why are you here? The clinic will not open for another year."

"We're not here for the clinic!" Becca said lightly. "We're here to become warriors!"

He scratched the tiny, tight curls on the back of his head and his smile evaporated. "No. That will not happen."

Dead silence.

I had never considered that the Chief would renege on his promise. I suddenly realized he'd thought it was a joke when I made the original deal with him. Anger steamed up from my belly into my heart and out my ears. I'd trained mentally and physically for this mission, and I was not going to turn back. I was going to follow through with this plan with or without Winston.

The Chief looked at us with eyes narrowed and lips in a hard line. "Do you have any idea how dangerous it would be for you if I allowed you to do something like this? This is not something to be taken lightly. Becoming a warrior is not simple. The two of you are not only physically inferior, but you are also *mentally* weak. Do you know that on a lion hunt, I saw a friend decapitated by one swipe of a lion's paw? His head was ripped away from his body in an instant." He snapped his fingers and carried on, "Do you know that my father's brother was rammed by a buffalo and barely survived? He wished he were dead. His whole body shattered. You want to become a warrior? You want something like that to happen to you? Because it will."

I began to panic, not from what Winston was describing, but from his increasing anger.

"Do you know that the shortage of food and water is so bad that grown adults walk like skeletons?" he continued. "Warriors are the first ones to go hungry when others don't have enough. You girls will not last one day." The Chief took three steps closer and leaned into my face like a military drill sergeant. "If you are only here to become a warrior, then you should leave now. I will not have the deaths of two Americans on my head."

"Come on . . . it's us!" Becca said. "If things get bad, then we will leave, but at least give us a chance."

He shook his head and knelt back down to his plants. He was done with us.

Dinner that night was in the gazebo. I couldn't eat, but Becca loaded her plate with the quintessential American-style meal: steak and mashed potatoes. Leaving the buffet line, we grabbed two Tuskers each. We sat quiet and still.

I had grossly misjudged Winston. Now I needed to consider our options. We could leave the volunteer center and try to find the cave on our own, but we didn't have the slightest idea as to where it was or even if anyone there would train us. What if Winston told other warriors in his tribe we needed to learn a lesson and had them injure us in some way? I didn't believe he'd do that to us, but he was very angry. Another option was to get on public transportation and go from village to village trying to find a warrior who was willing to take us under his wing. I had no idea where other Maasai villages were, but I could probably find out from someone. Then I thought about Nic, the only other person I knew in all of Kenya.

I sent him a quick text message:

Our plan with the Chief did not work out. We need another warrior to guide us. We would really appreciate it if you could point us in the right direction.

He wrote back quickly:

This doesn't surprise me. This is expected when you are dealing with a nomadic culture.

I wrote again:

Nic, please try to understand how important this mission is to me. I fully understand that we may not make it through the rites of passage, but I need to at least try.

Then it came—hope:

I know and I understand. Come back to Nairobi. I will see what I can do. I may have someone for you.

After slugging down a beer, Becca said, "Who are you texting?"

"Nic. He thinks he might know a warrior who would be willing to take us through the rites of passage." I put down my phone and continued, "We'll go to Nairobi tomorrow to meet with Nic. If he gives us a source, we'll interview the person just to make sure that we're on the same page."

Becca nodded.

"And if he doesn't come up with a good option, then we'll put an advertisement in the newspaper or go from village to village until we do find someone. I am even more committed to getting this done than I was before Winston kicked us to the curb."

6

Into the Bush

FRUSTRATED, I FLUNG the 500-thread-count sheets off the bed in our Nairobi hotel. According to my schedule, we were supposed to be far, far away from fancy linens, cushy beds, and pancake breakfasts. At this point, we were supposed to be on foot, eating only what we could kill, somewhere in the Rift Valley on our way to a cave. With energy bouncing inside me with no outlet, I decided to go on a run around downtown Nairobi. I laced up my hiking boots (the only shoes I had with me), wrapped my hair in a high bun atop my head, and hit the streets.

Jogging past government buildings, I focused on how I was going to get this warrior mission on the right track. Ideally, Nic would introduce us to the perfect person who wouldn't hold back on the rites of passage or tests of strength necessary to prove that women were strong and brave enough to become warriors, but that was a tall order. He seemed to be a very nice guy, but it was unreasonable for me to think that someone I had just met, who was connected only through a friend of the family, would go out on a limb for us, particularly one most people thought was destined to snap.

As I rounded the streets, I wove in and out of a steady flow of Kenyans on their way to work. Everyone here seemed to have a purpose. Becoming a warrior had become my purpose. My Plan A had failed. There wasn't any time to waste or any point in sulking over this fact, so I needed to think of a feasible Plan B, C, and even D. First, Plan B. I mentally crafted my "Help Wanted" ad: "Wanted: English-speaking Maasai warrior to take two untrained, white American women through the rites of passage to become a warrior."

If I saw an ad in the paper that said, "Wanted: Maasai-speaking Jewish princess to take African warriors to a bar mitzvah," I would laugh and surely not respond. But this was Kenya and I didn't have any better ideas, so I would go back to the hotel and ask some of the employees which newspaper Maasai would be most likely to read and thus where I should place the ad. I figured we'd have at least a few responses, and one might be intrigued enough to accept the challenge. But I acknowledged the risks that accompanied this plan were great. Going off with a completely random person to some unknown location to do unknown things was pretty dumb. The consequences of my lack of planning were becoming clear.

After a cold shower and a thorough lathering of avocado oil on my parched skin, I joined Becca and went to the restaurant. Nic was already sitting at the table near the pool sipping coffee and chatting softly, yet intently, with a young man. Spotting us, he put down his mug, stood up, and opened his arms wide to welcome us. Becca and I each gave him a hug and sat down.

Nic led the conversation. "Mindy and Becca, this is Danson Lanet Lekuroun, the brother of a very good friend, who has since passed."

I soon found out that this slender young man in a gray-and-black-striped Quiksilver T-shirt, tattered blue jeans, and a brightly colored bracelet in the shape of a watch was the exact "tall order" that I was looking for. Lanet, as he liked to be called, was a twenty-five-year-old, English-speaking, university-educated Maasai warrior, whose culture and family were the most important values in his life.

Warrior Princess

Elephants

Far left: Lanet. Left: Topoika.
Below: Rokoine, Leken, Magilu,
and Lanet making a fire.

With Otomoi

Maani

Magilu

Topoika
with goat meat

With my horns

Magilu drinking goat's head soup

Lanet overlooking Loita landscape

Topoika and Lanet

Otomoi's enkaji

Maasai village

The young warrior nibbled at his food while Nic explained that Lanet was from a very traditional place called Loita, which was on the border south of Nairobi and northeast of the Maasai Mara.

"What do you mean by traditional?" I asked. "What is the difference between Loita and Mulot, where Winston is?"

Lanet spoke up, "In Loita, the Maasai way of life has remained pure because we have little or no interaction with other tribes or missionaries. Our original ways of life have not been interfered with. This means that our culture, language, way of dressing, traditional foods, organizational structure, and other aspects of everyday life have not been altered. The majority of Maasai in Loita have never even seen a white person. The men herd the cattle for months at a time, the women build the homes out of cow dung and branches, the ceremonies are conducted in the traditional form, religion has not been altered, and the diet dates back thousands of years. You will find no changes due to Western influence. In Mulot, it is very difficult for the Maasai to uphold their authentic traditions due to development. Mulot has a cash crop, which made them interact with all types of people who then brought new behaviors and values. In Loita, our way of life is still based on the Maasai currency, which is a bartering system."

Loita sounded like the ultimate challenge in terms of immersing myself with the Maasai. This was exactly what I wanted—to be stripped of all that I had to lean on and be left alone with me. This was my opportunity to prove that I alone was enough.

"It sounds magnificent," I said.

Lanet nodded and asked, "So you think you can be a *moran*?"

I looked up and in a puzzled tone asked, "Moron?"

"Yes, moran. That is why we are together. Is that not correct?"

"Well, I know that what we want to do is a bit eccentric, but I wouldn't say that we want to become morons."

Lanet looked to Nic.

Nic looked to me, and they both burst out laughing.

Becca slapped my arm, "Dude. Moran is Maasai for warrior."

It finally clicked, and I felt like a true moron.

Lanet continued, "So you do want to become morans, no?"

"Yes!" I said enthusiastically. "That is exactly why we are here. Becca and I were in Kenya a couple of months ago building a clinic near Mulot and fell in love with your culture. Your deep and unfiltered relationship with the land, animals, and humanity made me recognize how disconnected I was and still am."

Lanet took a sip of his orange juice while he considered my response. Finally he said, "Yes, but why do you want to become a moran? You must know that this is not a common request. In fact, I have never heard of anyone asking for this before."

I explained my path thus far. "After I spoke with Winston, I met a Maasai woman who told me that women in her tribe have wanted to become warriors for generations."

Lanet nodded.

I continued, "She told me that if for some reason I have been given this opportunity, then I need to follow through. And I need to follow through for her, but I also need to follow through for me."

Becca nodded in agreement.

Lanet sat quietly again for at least two minutes and then excused himself to go to the men's room. When he was gone, Nic told us that he finally understood how important this was to us, but he also said that Lanet would make up his own mind and that he would not influence him in any way. I fully understood.

Lanet returned to the table and started talking, "Even though I was raised in Loita in a very traditional household, my view of women is very different than most men in my tribe. It bothered me that while my mother chopped the trees for firewood, built our homes, milked the cows, and took such great care of the children, that even after all of her contributions, my father still did not recognize her opinions. I have always wanted to help give Maasai women a voice but never had the opportunity. Maasai women deserve more respectable roles. Maybe by guiding the two of you, I will get more clarity as to how to achieve this."

My stomach fluttered with excitement. As I was about to speak, Lanet continued, "Nic prepared me for this, but I was not going to commit unless I got a feeling that the two of you were chosen for this."

I spoke gently, hoping that I was right. "Does that mean we're in this together? Are we going to Loita to become morans?"

"I can't promise you that you will become morans. You may find that you do not like our way of life and that it is too different or difficult. You may decide that becoming a moran is not important to you. I also can't tell you that my tribe will accept you even if you do everything properly. There is going to be much danger involved. I will do my best to help prepare you, but there is no way to predict the future in my world or yours. All we can do is try."

Nic bombarded Lanet with questions, "What will they do? Where will they stay? What will they eat? Are you sure that this is a good idea?"

Lanet only answered the last question, "No, I am not sure of anything, but I believe that these women came into my life for a reason that I should not fight."

Lanet folded his napkin and placed it on the table. He looked at our now bare plates and said, "We will leave within an hour to catch a *mutatu* to Narok. In Narok we will buy swords, spears, and olkarasha (which I knew was traditional Maasai clothing from my last trip). From Narok we will head to Loita."

He was speaking fast now and with a sprinkling of words that were not in my language. I asked him what a mutatu was—he told me it was a public bus. I paid the bill, and Lanet ended with, "I recommend that the two of you take a long shower because it will be the last one you will have in some time."

Nic looked at us and sighed, "I guess you are moving forward. Now all I can do is support you in the best way possible." He reached in his pocket and pulled out two beaded necklaces—one electric blue and orange with silver paillettes and the other a strand of red beads woven together with interspersing yellow beads. He handed me the blue and Becca the red and said, "I wore these necklaces when I was a moran—now they belong to you. Wear these in good health and with fierce commitment."

Later that day, Becca and I wheezed under the weight of our stuffed backpacks as we followed Lanet down the alleys of downtown Nairobi. We continued walking until we arrived at Nairobi's version of Penn Station, a small street filled with Kenyan men in front of tattered, punctured passenger vans, the matatus. The men were screaming out their destinations, "Narok?!!" "Mombasa!" "Namanga!" Lanet stopped in front of a tin box with wheels and told us to give the man with the clipboard our names.

I handed the man fare for three, which came out to about 900 shillings, or US$10. I felt a tap on the back of my head and a tugging of my backpack. Nervously turning around, I saw a boy around thirteen years old trying to pull my backpack off my back. I held on tight to my straps and pushed away from him. He continued to grab at my backpack. When I saw Lanet out of the corner of my eye, watching as I struggled, I became angry and called to him. "Are you just going to stand there, or are you going to get this guy off of me?"

He ambled over, pulled my hands from the straps, and took off my bag explaining, "This boy is only here to put your luggage in the trunk."

I exhaled, wiped my sweaty brow, and realized that even though I seemed confident and determined on the outside, internally I was a terrified mess.

With all of our bags stowed, we squeezed into the mutatu, a vehicle sized for eight but with a good fifteen stuffed in. The van was ready to burst at the seams.

"Are we going to be this cramped the entire trip?" I asked Lanet while trying to figure out where I was supposed to rest my other butt cheek.

Lanet asked if I was uncomfortable.

"Just wondering how long I should expect to be in this contraption?"

"Have you seen my watch?" Lanet asked as he yanked the mutatu door down its squeaky rails to a final close.

"You mean the bracelet that looks like a watch but is really just beads?"

Lanet nodded and said, "This watch says all you need to know about time."

Confused, I replied, "But your watch doesn't change. It says nothing."

Lanet smiled, "Exactly. And always remember, in order to be Maasai, you need to *be* Maasai. Owning our concept of time is essential."

The engine rumbled and the sound of Snoop Dogg's "Gin and Juice" blared through the speakers. The passengers in the crowded van wore a variety of expressions. Some chatted. Some laughed. Others sat with blank, somewhat depressed stares. Struggling to be heard above Snoop, I leaned in to Lanet and asked, "Are all these people coming from work?"

"Most likely, no. The unemployment rate is above 60 percent, so maybe some of these people are coming from interviews or on their way to see their families." He gazed at a group of Kenyan women in long polyester short-sleeve jackets and ankle-length skirts, "Life here has become very difficult. You will see. The unemployment rate and drought are making people scared for their lives."

The four hours to Narok were bumpy and death defying. The driver swerved in and out of lanes like a racecar driver, and with each jolt to the right or the left, I was certain that the next jerk would surely result in our tin box rolling over and over. My conversation with Lanet was limited, mainly due to pumping rap music, but I did learn that he spent two to three weeks in Nairobi every few months in order to work odd jobs to make some money. He seemed able to compartmentalize aspects of his life, which I found inspiring. My own life seemed to be lacking boundaries. The values that were instilled in him while growing up in Loita stayed with him and would not change based on new information about religion, technology, or politics he discovered while in Nairobi. He believed that many Maasai who go to the big city become hypnotized by the material life and have a very difficult time going back to the pure Maasai way of life. Kids who go to dance clubs, drive cars, and have pocket money begin to look down on their traditions. He had watched this degradation of his culture and was convinced that if the schools did not begin to respect and value the time-honored teachings of the Maasai, kids would drift farther and farther from the culture. He feared this would result in his tribe becoming nonexistent within fifty years.

I asked him if he felt that women becoming warriors was another degradation of his culture. He said that he'd thought about that long and hard before he agreed to take us to Loita and concluded that it absolutely was not. If anything, allowing women to become warriors would help keep the culture alive.

"There are certain things that the Maasai need to alter in order to survive. For example, some Maasai have started growing vegetables and fruits. In the past, we only consumed milk, meat, and blood. If we had continued to live that way, many people would have died due to the decreasing supply of cows brought on by the drought. Another way of life that should change is to allow women the right to voice and act on their own opinions. This can only lead to strengthening the culture."

The rap pumped louder in the van, so Lanet and I decided to pick up the conversation at a later time. But before we returned to the thoughts in our heads, he pointed to my T-shirt and said, "What's that symbol on every piece of your clothing? Those two shields crossing each other?"

Smiling wide and proud, I told him that I was testing the durability of the clothing and that I would soon be in direct contact with the founder and CEO. Lanet responded, "I would like to see how that clothing holds up in the forest." My mouth dropped in horror and he turned away from me and began to bob his head back and forth and side to side with the beat of the music, giving me the perfect opportunity to compose another letter to Mr. Plank (see Appendix, Letter 3).

CLOUDS OF DUST from the dried mud roads formed around the mutatu as we pulled into Narok, which means "Black Water" in Swahili.

"This is our last stop before Loita," Lanet said.

Becca and I tossed our backpacks over our shoulders and followed Lanet like two puppies through the streets.

I raised my voice so that Lanet could hear me over the city noise. "What are we going to do here?"

"You will not be able to buy anything in Loita, so we will get supplies for your training and purchase gifts for my mama."

We walked up a gravel driveway to a neon-purple, turquoise-trimmed grocery store. While distinctly different on the outside, the fluorescent lights and linoleum floors inside reminded me of every other grocery store in the United States. Lanet told us to buy only what we couldn't live without. I walked up and down the aisles, and stopped in front of the toilet paper. I scanned the individually wrapped rolls, looking for the familiar cuddly Charmin bear, which would have ensured that at least when I was relieving myself, I could do it with a little bit of comfort. But there was no bear. There was only one unknown brand. I unwrapped the packaging to feel the texture. It was rough like sandpaper. I put the roll back on the shelf, figuring that poison-ivy toilet paper would be a better option.

I continued walking the aisles, stopping momentarily in front of the row of chocolate bars. The purple Cadbury bar with almonds beckoned me from the shelf. "You know you want me," it said.

I stared at the bar, my mouth beginning to water. It spoke to me again. "Oh please. I am completely essential. Do you actually think you are going to be able to live without me for even two days?"

The bar had a point. I don't think I've ever gone longer than forty-eight hours without at least a smidge of chocolate. Even on strict diets when all calories were accounted for, I would exchange a portion of allocated calories meant for iron or protein for a chunk of chocolate. Here I was, in a purple grocery store with posters of Jesus and Elton John on the walls, face to face with my food addiction. I looked to Jesus for some support, but got no response. So I focused on Elton, who was wearing hot pink goggles and a feathery turquoise boa around his neck.

"Elton?"

All of a sudden Elton's piano began to play and he sang, "Can You Feel the Love Tonight" from *The Lion King*:

There's a calm surrender to the rush of day
Something. Something.
Yadda. Yadda.
It's enough for this restless warrior just to be with you . . .

I heard Elton loud and clear. He was telling me to abandon my addictions. I looked at the Cadbury bar one more time, then back at Elton and thought, "You would have bought the entire stock of Cadbury and had your entourage carry it for you. Total double standard." But Elton was right—it was time to recognize and say good-bye to addictions.

I finished walking up and down the aisles, deciding that all I truly needed were some Aleve and extra tampons. Becca, on the other hand, purchased two chocolate bars and a couple packs of condoms. Remembering my manners when we met Lanet at the checkout line, I told him that my mother always told me to never show up at someone's home empty-handed. What does one bring as a gift to someone in the bush? Surely not a bottle of pinot noir.

I asked Lanet, "Is it customary in your culture to bring a gift when you go to someone's home?"

Lanet took a moment to respond. He always took a moment before speaking, as if he were really thinking about all of the angles of a question. I hoped that I would pick up that habit by the end of my time with him. My tendency to speak and then think had gotten me into a lot of trouble over the years. Finally he spoke up, "You can bring sugar and rice."

We left the checkout and went to the bulk food aisle. I watched as Lanet loaded up an entire cart with ten-kilogram bags of rice and sugar. I guess he wanted more than a little box of Rice-A-Roni. I stared with mouth agape as he piled the packages high.

I turned to Becca, "Is he expecting me to buy all of this?"

She shrugged her shoulders.

I looked at the price of each package, which was less than $7, so I figured that I would keep my mouth shut for now. It was a small price to pay for a priceless experience.

After the grocery run, Lanet directed us through the hectic market. Vendors filled every square inch of space, selling everything from cell phones and Maasai jewelry to chickens and huge burlap bags of potatoes. We stopped in front of a man hunched over a package wrapped in cotton cloth. As Lanet spoke with him in Maasai, he slowly unwrapped the cotton cloth to display several iron spearheads. Lanet lifted each one, carefully analyzing its shape and construction. While feeling the weight of each lump of iron, he said something quickly to the seller. I wanted to know what I was missing. This was obviously an important decision, and I had no idea what he was looking for.

"What's going on?" I asked.

Without taking his eyes off the iron, he said, "I am asking for the history of these spearheads."

"Why do you care about that?"

"You will need your spear to protect you. If it has been used with bad intentions, then it may bring you bad luck."

"What do you mean by bad intentions?"

"If your spear was used to kill something or someone that was not meant to be killed, then your spear will only bring you darkness. These two spearheads were used by warriors for the right reasons, so you should be safe."

I had never been a big believer in superstitions, but all bets were off in the bush. I had no idea what code or laws made the world go round out here, so I took Lanet's belief as fact and began to analyze the lumps of iron myself. Even though Lanet already said that the spears were safe, I still looked for dried blood or bends, which might have come from an animal or a human fighting back.

With spearheads in hand, we walked around the corner to find a man with a dozen swords lined up and lying next to their red leather sheaths on the ground in front of him. Lanet inspected each one and then told us to choose our weapons.

"Is there a difference between the swords?" I asked.

"Not really. You will need to start with something, so you can pick whatever you like. You don't need to worry about the swords. They are all made in China, so there is no problem."

Our final stop was to buy our olkarasha. We walked from one side street to the next until we arrived at a tented market. It was packed with rows of people standing behind wooden tables selling everything from used T-shirts and jeans to blankets and various colors of the tartan sheets that I saw the warriors wear at the volunteer center. "Which one do we choose?" I asked.

"Whatever color suits you, but blues, purples, and pinks are in style."

"Colors go in and out of style in the bush?"

And with a blunt "Yes," he handed Becca and me two blue and purple olkarasha each.

After purchasing the garments, Lanet told us that he would show us how to put them on tomorrow and then led us to a nearby restaurant, a small cement building with interior aquamarine walls spotted with mold. A tarnished floor-to-ceiling metal gate divided half of the fifteen-by-fifteen-foot space. Behind the fence, legs, ribs, and other cow carcass parts hung from chain links nailed to the ceiling. Directly below the meat was what looked like a scene from my first days at New York's gritty nightclub, The Tunnel. Instead of throbbing bodies rubbing up against one another, there were pulsating insects piled on top of one another with first dibs on our lunch. As I looked back at the gate and down at the floor, my mother's firm voice resounded in my head: "This is filth. Someone needs to call the food safety inspectors. Malaria is here! And those cuts of meat have too much fat!"

We sat down on a wooden bench at the only table in the room. Lanet ordered lunch, a mixture of cow bone and meat drowned in oil. When the tin plates were set in front of us, I wanted to cry. I was starving, but there was no way in hell I was going to eat that nastiness. All I wanted was a Cadbury bar, but

I had already made the horrible decision that this was the time to end my food addictions. Not eating anything was surely one way to end a food addiction. It was also a way to end my life. My stomach growled as I watched Lanet and Becca dive face first into the trough of golden fat with chunks of bone. The protein of the meal was probably fly remnants and pieces of cow ear and tail.

"Nothing goes to waste here," Lanet said as he finished his plate and moved onto mine. He munched and munched, and each crunch of the bone in his mouth caused my throat to constrict. I needed to leave the restaurant before I started to dry-heave. Swallowing hard, I told Lanet and Becca that I was going to step outside on the pretext of making a final phone call.

When Lanet sauntered up to me after finishing his meal, he said, "Where we are going there is no use for that device. Even if you tried to use it, you wouldn't get a signal."

Relieved at the thought, I said, "Perfect."

Lanet scanned the road in front of us and said, "We must hurry. Loita is calling, and we will need to take a taxi for the rest of the trip."

"A taxi?" I asked.

"Yes. The only transport into Loita by bus happens every three days, and many times people can be stranded in Narok for a week without a way back home."

We (that is, Lanet) negotiated a fee of about US$30 for a driver to take us the remainder of the journey. He then showed us the taxi: a station wagon whose sagging frame almost skimmed the ground. Lanet was worried enough to discuss the difficult terrain between here and Loita with Paul, the driver. Paul insisted that he and his car were strong like buffalo and could easily handle the road ahead. After two hours on the paved Kenyan highway, the taxi veered right on to a dried red-mud path so rocky that every turn of the tires caused our teeth to chatter.

"Are we here?" I asked.

"Oh no, not really," Lanet replied.

"All this bumping is making me want to pee," Becca said.

"Don't worry, it will get much better when we get to the elephant path."

I laughed, glad that our guide had a sense of humor.

Feeling sincerely grateful to be alive, I rolled my window down and inhaled deep gulps of unpolluted air as I admired the natural beauty of the parched brown plains. Spotting a couple of zebras and wildebeests bounding along the side of the road, I realized that I was in the pure wild and that I had a chance to be just as pure and wild.

THROUGH THE WINDSHIELD I watched the caked mud road turn into a field of four-foot blades of elephant grass. The smacking and swishing of the grass against our car reminded me of the not-so-distant days when I would take my climate-controlled SUV to the car wash. Now, instead of soapsuds and long rubber strips, the vehicle was massaged with dust and dung.

"Time is running out. We need to be off this path at the soonest," Lanet said to Paul.

I popped my head up front between the zebra-print seats and asked, "Time is running out for what?"

"The elephants."

My stomach tightened in fear. "What about the elephants?"

"This is the elephant highway."

And just as the last words trickled out of his mouth, *BOOM!* Paul slammed on the brakes, catapulting my forehead into the back of the seat.

Unfazed, Becca took her earbuds out of her ears and asked, "What happened?"

Lanet and Paul unfastened their seatbelts and jumped out of the car. I was scared to leave the safety of the vehicle and grasped for

Becca's arm, but she peeled away from me and climbed out of the car. What happened to the strength I'd felt a few moments before? Through the windshield I could see Lanet, the driver, and Becca gazing down at the ground in front of the car. Something must be dead, but at least they didn't appear to be in danger. I opened the car door and cautiously walked to where the others were standing. There lay a gazelle, still in a prancing position, limp on a patch of dirt, its shiny black eyes reflecting the sky like a mirror. I teared up as I watched a pool of blood build around the gazelle's cracked skull. I had seen dead animals before, but there was something about the stark beauty in the face of sudden death that broke me.

Wiping my tears, I looked at Lanet. He looked back at me coldly and said, "Maasai do not cry. Those who cry are weak."

This was another side of Lanet, and suddenly I feared him. His voice raised and he spoke even more harshly, "Are you weak? Tell me, are you weak?"

Desperately, I looked around, trying to find an escape route, but there was no path charted for me. The fact that this was what I yearned for was lost in the moment. I cried harder. Lanet stepped toward me, grabbed my arms, and shook me like he was shaking out a dirty rug. He stopped and my tears ceased. He looked deep into my eyes, placed his hand gently on my head, and said, "The Maasai believe that everything is good. To become one with us, you need to believe this, too. Now you need to thank this animal and move on." He gripped me tighter and repeated himself, "Thank this animal and know that everything is good."

I nodded, looked down at the bloody gazelle, and in a faint voice asked, "How am I supposed to thank it? What am I supposed to say?"

"Provide the animal with due respect. That is thanks enough."

Focusing in on the gazelle's eyes, I thanked it for existing. My heart rate steadily slowed. I had found some peace.

I looked to Becca and Paul, who were standing silently on the sidelines.

"Let's go," Lanet said.

We climbed back into the car and continued on the elephant highway. The sky turned a deeper blue and Paul turned on his headlights.

Becca broke the silence, "Why didn't we eat the gazelle for dinner?"

Lanet answered, "Maasai don't eat wild animals."

"Why not?" I asked.

"There is a mutual respect that the Maasai and animals have for one another. We are all life forms. One is not better than another. We strive to coexist, but if either side breaks this agreement, then we will fight to the death."

"What do you mean by breaking the agreement?" I asked.

"If a lion eats our cattle or an elephant runs down our home, then we will fight back. We will protect ourselves and our community—this is the main role of the warrior."

Lanet continued, "The only time I was forced to eat gazelle was when I hadn't eaten in four days. I was so hungry that I speared one. The taste was so horrible that I vomited up the stringy, bloody bits and chunks as I ate it."

Through the dust-filled beams of light coming from the front of the car, I saw that we were leaving the tall grass and entering a dark, dense forest. Rather than add to the scorecard of paranoia that I imagined Becca was keeping on me, I remained quiet, clenching my teeth. Slipping my hand into my pocket and taking hold of my BlackBerry, I composed an e-mail to my brother—my last will and testament. Surprisingly, Becca took note of what I was doing and wrote her own "just-in-case good-bye note" to Boyfriend Number 1.

MINDY'S LETTER

To: Adam Budgor
Subject: Only Open Upon Mauling

Bro,

If you're opening this note, then I have had quite the finale . . . death by lion, or something very similar. But don't worry, I have absolutely no regrets. I am on the ultimate adventure. When you and I were talking about what I was going to do in Kenya, I somewhat skimmed over the day-to-day activities. My intention was not to be obtuse but as you know, I didn't do much due diligence. I thought that the analysis (your middle name) would paralyze me, causing me to cancel the trip. My heart made this decision, so I followed it, happily putting on my trusty blindfolds and earmuffs.

I am writing to you from a vehicle resembling the Flintstone's foot-propelling go-kart and am entering a forest that is surely filled with animals that would enjoy a plump Jewish Princess for dinner, hence the timing of this note. Since I can't hop on the Internet and download a template for a will, I thought I would send you my final wishes that I know you will execute with care, as you are such a wonderful brother. Please also bear in mind that the birthday gifts I've gotten you over the years have been better than the ones you've gotten me, so I am hoping that you will make up for the lackluster gifts by doing the following for me:

1. Liquidate all of my assets (including Chanel bags) and split the funds between a foundation that focuses on preserving the Maasai culture, some sort of scholarship for people who want to explore their mental and physical limits through mission-based adventure, and money to buy a plot of land large enough

to build the world's largest cat playground and then let the kitties roam free!

2. Sorry to bring this up again, but since my birthday presents to you really were phenomenal, can you pay off my Discover card? And please don't tell Mom I used it to pay for the plane tickets to Kenya because she thinks every swipe of the glittering piece of silver plastic is a deal with the devil.

Love you!
Donkey

BECCA'S LETTER

Hi.

So, I was mauled. Shit. I hope I survived. If I didn't—please know that I don't regret anything except leaving my parents' house a wreck before departing on this African odyssey. And I do wish I was able to be with you again, somewhere.

Baby, I was hoping my mauling letter could make you smile and giggle like when you get excited and talk sweet and call me Sweetness.

I guess I'll tell you one moment where I was mesmerized in love with you. (These moments are not infrequent, but I think this one really made a peach pit fall into my throat and for the first time, actually.)

That night we went to the Irish Fest. I'm sure you can remember because you lost your watch and your Asics got all fucked. After some light smooching in the hall I fell asleep right below William Blake's illustration. Out of nowhere things got heavy and your breathing was overwhelmingly loud. I didn't want to move, not forever.

I didn't REALLY want to get sappy but if something truly happens to me while I'm way out there in the Bush, I would like you to know that I love you.

Also, for god's sake please please make sure someone cancels the Charter Cable bill because it's a fucking fortune.

Yours,
Rebecca

When the car entered the forest, all I could see by the glow of my long-out-of-range BlackBerry were massive olive and fig trees that seemed to shoot straight up to the stars. Our vehicle climbed the forest path and soon slowed to a smooth stop. Lanet and Paul began a rapid conversation in Maasai. Paul pushed open his door and stood outside with his arms folded.

"What's happening?" I asked.

Lanet responded as he got out of the car, "There are some small rocks ahead. Paul doesn't think the car will make it."

I got out to evaluate the situation myself. Directly in front of me was a mountain of boulders.

"Lanet, there must be an alternate path. There is no way that this lowrider is going to make it up this mountain," I laughed.

Lanet paced in the headlights with his arms crossed and hand cupping his chin. "The car can make it," he announced, pointing an authoritative index finger in the air. "But not with us inside."

He turned to Paul and they continued their rapid conversation in Maa. Paul got back into the cockpit.

"I will navigate the car and you girls will push the car over the rocks," he said as he pulled our spears out of the trunk. "And you will need your spear if there is an intruder."

"Even I know this is a bad idea," Becca said as we grabbed our spears from Lanet's hands. My chest tightened as I squinted my eyes, trying (unsuccessfully) to see into the darkness of the woods surrounding us. "And I have to tell you something else . . . I have a feeling a lion is watching us."

Lanet scoffed, "There are no lions in this area. I will tell you when a lion is near. A proper Maasai can smell their odor from far, far away." He looked at me and smiled, "You will soon understand. One whiff of a lion and the smell will remain in your nose forever."

"Well, what if the lion just took a bath? They are very clean animals, constantly licking themselves."

Paul restarted the car's engine, and Lanet directed him forward. I remained behind the car, using it as my shield. The car moved faster. I quickened my pace, continuing to push with all of my might, sucking exhaust by the gallons.

The car stopped abruptly, but I didn't. I rammed headfirst into the bumper and ricocheted off like a lone ant flicked high in the sky, landing on my butt on the rocky ground.

"Ouch!" I yelped.

Rubbing my rear, I looked up to find Becca and Lanet on a higher boulder, snorting and cackling at my blunder. Eventually Lanet calmed down and said again, "I need you and Becca to push the car over the rocks." And so, exhausted, starving, covered in mud and unknown animal excrement, I helped push the lowrider up and over what looked like Mount Kenya's little sister.

At the top of the hill, everyone was allowed back in the car. I wiped the sweat from my brow and turned to Becca. "Today has been utterly exhausting, and it isn't even over yet. I wish we could sleep in the car."

Not missing a beat, Lanet said, "You never want to sleep in the car. If an elephant comes, you will not hear it until it's too late."

Then he continued, "You can rest. We are off the elephant highway and very close to home." Knowing a good idea when

I heard it, I shut my eyes and quickly drifted into a dreamless sleep, but not for long.

The car jerked to a stop and again my head flew into the seat in front of me. Through the windshield I saw three figures galloping just a few feet in front of the car.

"Were those giraffes? They are totally taller than the ones at the zoo!" I yelled.

Lanet swiveled his head to look at us and in a playful and excited tone said, "That was a close one! We would have been catapulted to another planet if one of those giraffes kicked the car." He shook his head in dismay. "We would have been kaput!"

"If it was that serious, why do you seem excited?" I asked.

"In Loita you live moment to moment and that, my dear mzungus, is real life."

As we continued to chug along, I began to suspect the reason why our trip was filled with so much drama was because Lanet didn't actually know where we were. Maybe he was accustomed to getting home by foot. Taking a car must have been a luxury.

"How do you know where you are when everything looks the same?" I probed.

"What do you mean everything is the same?"

"All the trees look the same, the fields look the same. We have been driving for a couple of hours and I don't think we left our starting position."

Lanet reached out the window and plucked a three-foot-tall piece of grass. "You see this piece of grass?" he asked.

"Yes," I responded.

He put his hand out the window again and plucked another piece. "You see this piece of grass?"

"Yes."

And then he held up both pieces of grass, one in each hand, and said, "Well, this piece is different from this one, so you see . . . nothing is the same."

"Okay, Lanet. I get the point, but tell me something—how many times have you taken a car to get home?"

"Maybe one time, but it was more of a motorbike than a car."

"And how many times have you walked home on foot?"

"Too many. I have walked since I was a small boy."

"And my last question is, do you know where we are right now?"

"Not completely."

I leaned in between the front seats and continued, "So pushing the car over the rocks and the elephant highway could have been avoided?"

"All the land is an elephant highway. The land is unpredictable. I am sure that we would have had to push the car at some point."

"And how are we supposed to find our way to your home?" I asked.

"We are near. I feel it."

"You feel it?"

"Yes. I know this land like the back of my foot."

"And tell me, Lanet, what does the back of your foot look like?"

He paused, "Well, now that I think about it, I am not really sure."

I leaned back in my seat and said, "Comforting, Lanet. Really comforting."

Just then, the car slowed to a stop. Looking out of the windshield, I could still only see rocks and tall wispy grass. "Where are we?" I asked.

"We are home," Lanet said.

Confused, I asked, "Home? What do you mean? I can't see your house."

"It is here and it is the greatest! You will see."

AS WE UNLOADED the car, I could make out two structures less than seven feet tall and thirty feet wide. No light was left on. There was a forest a few yards to the north and south and rolling hills of nothingness east and west. We unpacked the car and Lanet invited Paul to spend the night. Paul considered the option as he inhaled a Sportsman cigarette, then declined and courageously drove off on his own.

The three of us stood in the darkness with our bags at our feet. I was filled with pride as I realized that we had made it, that we were really in the middle of the bush about to begin training. The moment vanished when I shivered from the crisp night air, which reminded me that I had to pee.

"Can you show me where the bathroom is?" I asked Lanet.

He pointed to the forest and said, "Just find a tree and enjoy."

With no flashlight and still feeling that a lion was lurking, I asked Becca to escort me to a tree.

We walked to the periphery of the forest. Not wanting to publicly urinate, I asked Becca to close her eyes while I dropped my pants, but also insisted that she hold my hand just in case something in the forest tried to snatch me.

As I squatted, I heard a noise behind me, and with pants around my ankles, I hopped like a frog and grasped Becca's calves.

"Holy hell! What was that?"

Infuriated, Becca wiggled her legs to get out of my tight grip, saying, "I knew that going backpacking with a California girl was a bad idea!"

Trying to pee faster to get out of what I deemed to be immediate danger, I instinctively reached for toilet paper and remembered where I was. I grabbed a handful of leaves from a shrub next to me and cleaned up. Although the leaves were dry and scratched my skin, I was proud of my almost immediate ability to transition into bush life.

As Becca and I made our way back, we could see a little light twinkling in the darkness.

"Lanet must be building a fire," Becca said.

"Oh, that is so nice of him. We are so lucky to have found such a thoughtful guide."

"He might be thoughtful, but keeping us warm probably isn't the main objective. Many animals are afraid of fire, so he's minimizing the risk that we get eaten or trampled on night one."

Two warriors wearing *ilkarash* (plural for olkarasha) and beautiful beaded necklaces and bracelets were sitting on a log next to Lanet by the time we got to the fire. Becca and I stood a few feet away, waiting for Lanet to invite us to join them. The men's skin, jewelry, and the tops of their spears shimmered in the light of the fire. My throat clamped when I saw a thick scar running diagonally all the way across one of the warrior's cheeks. Did it come from a lion? From a human using a sword?

The Maasai I'd met at the volunteer center seemed different from these guys. The warriors at the volunteer center were easygoing—these two looked like they were on a mission to kill. When I made eye contact with one, his dark gaze made me cringe and I stepped back. Then the other warrior looked my way, and every muscle in my body tensed in fear. This feeling was totally unexpected and anything but welcoming. I got the immediate sense that we were not wanted. Was this how the rest of the Maasai were going to feel about Becca and me? What if I accidentally said or did the wrong thing? I didn't even know what was considered offensive in their culture. I was flooded with silent questions, so unlike my typically out-spoken self.

Lanet looked at the warriors and then looked at us. "Mindy and Becca, please sit down." He pointed to the space on the log next to him.

My body was stiff, but I was able to hunch over and sit next to Lanet. I knew that I was showing immediate weakness, but I couldn't put up a front in that moment. I felt limp and paralyzed.

"Mindy and Becca, this is Lesikarr." Lanet pointed to the warrior with the brutal scar. I looked at him and nodded.

"And this is Leken." When Lanet said Leken's name, he eased his hard expression to a slight smile. "Leken is my older brother."

I smiled at Leken and looked again at Lesikarr, whose face was still Terminator-ish, his eyes unblinking and seemingly focused in on me like he wanted to eat me for dinner. As our eyes locked, he whipped out his sword and slid his index and middle finger down the blade of the sword, slicing his skin. I gasped as the blood dripped down his fingers and hand. This man wanted me dead. I took a step back and hid behind Lanet, who promptly moved to the side so that I was exposed again.

Lanet spoke to them in Maa, stopping momentarily to tell us that these men didn't speak any English and that Lesikarr had never left the bush before, and thus he had never seen a white person. Leken, on the other hand, had been to Narok a few times, so we didn't look as shocking to him as we did to Lesikarr. I relaxed slightly, hoping that maybe the vibe I got from Lesikarr was less that he didn't want us there and more because we looked like aliens to him.

Listening to the men converse in their rhythmic Maasai language had a steadying effect on my nerves. My eyes moved to study their flawless physiques. By the light of the fire, I could see their muscles ripple and glisten under their maroon and green tartan olkarasha. Not an ounce of fat. Leken leaned over to adjust the logs in the fire with a stick. He twisted his torso to the right, exposing a scar that ran from the bottom of his right nipple and seemed to continue to his left clavicle. Over the course of the evening, five more warriors arrived at the campfire, each sporting various brightly colored ilkarash. As they stabbed their spears into the earth, their layers of bead necklaces danced in the air for a brief moment before landing on their rock-solid chests.

Lanet introduced us to each warrior one by one, and names such as Otumoi, Topoika, and Magilu twirled off his tongue. No one spoke English, and most of the men had only seen a white person from a distance. I was so stimulated by my environment and the interaction with the men that my physical and mental exhaustion vanished. Quietly, I watched the men take part in what Lanet called an "exchange of news," which happened any time someone left Loita. The person who traveled wanted to know what had happened while he was gone, and vice versa. Apparently word about Becca and I wanting to become morans had preceded us, but was hard to believe. So the men around the fire had walked kilometers in the dark of night to see us with their own eyes.

Hours passed and the fire's flame dimmed. The warriors got to their feet, grabbed their spears, walked down a hill, and entered a small tin building few yards away.

My curiosity was still in overdrive. "Where are they going? Do they all live in that small house?" I asked Lanet.

"No, no. That is my mama's house. They will sleep there tonight."

"How are all of those people going to fit in that little house?"

"Sleeping in tight spaces makes it warmer for everyone," he said with a smile.

"Don't their families expect them to come home tonight?"

Lanet looked at me with his dark coffee-colored eyes and grinned.

Perplexed, I asked, "Sorry—was that funny?"

"Oh Mindy, you will learn that expectations don't exist in the Maasai culture."

The depth of his statement gave me cause for pause. No expectations? My whole life was an assortment of expectations.

Lanet's eyes drooped with exhaustion. "It is very late. We need to rise early, so let's retire now."

"What are we doing tomorrow?" I asked.

"I will explain everything in the morning, but there are six Maasai men joining us tomorrow and we will journey into the forest where we will live for some time."

Lanet helped Becca and me set up our tent near the fire. We crawled in and Becca got cozy in her sleeping bag. She fell asleep right away while I rolled into the fetal position due to hunger pains and tried to get warm under my itsy-bitsy tartan sheet. By day it had seemed a romantic and authentic cape type of thing, but by night it was a pathetically inadequate blanket. I forced my eyes closed, but lay awake, ready to bolt out of the tent if any of my senses warned me that a predator was near.

7

Warrior Bootcamp

"Becca," I said as I gently knocked on her head nestled in her down sleeping bag. She looked like a blue cocoon with a face and a few curlicues popping out.

She wiggled a bit in her bag.

"Becca," I said again and continued to knock.

She wiggled and grunted.

"Becca, we are in the bush!" I said excitedly.

"No shit, Sherlock." And with a big yawn, she rolled on her side so that she was facing the wall of the tent. "Why are you up so early? We just went to sleep like ten minutes ago."

It probably had been only a couple of hours since I'd finally drifted to sleep, but I was wired and there was some animal yapping outside our tent.

"How are you able to sleep with that incessant racket?"

Becca grunted again, "You mean the monkeys?"

"Is that what that is?"

Becca rolled onto her other side so that she was facing me and said, "Dude—I know you are all Beverly Hills, but haven't you ever been to a zoo?"

"Of course I've been to a zoo, but that yapping doesn't sound like a monkey."

She rolled to her other side and mumbled, "There are lots of kinds of monkeys."

I wrapped my skimpy sheet around my shoulders and peered out of the semicircular window. With my nose skimming the mesh, I saw patches of shamrocks and emerald blades of grass. Then a pair of strong, sculpted black legs with protruding veins blocked my view, and I butt-hopped backward.

"I think we need to get up. There's a pair of beefy calves outside our tent."

"They know we're in here. They'll tell us when we need to wake up."

"Tell us how? Do you understand Maasai?"

"Okay! I'm up. I'm up. I'm up. Jesus, you're antsy," Becca said as she released the tight string of the sleeping bag and molted into her butterfly self.

When we crawled out of the tent, a happy Leken immediately greeted us. He handed each of us a cup of Kenyan coffee in chipped mugs that looked like they had been rolled in dirt. Becca put her nose into the steam, touched her lips to the cup's rim, and inhaled. With a satisfied smile she said, "If every day starts with this, I will be all good."

Leken guided us to a fallen olive tree to sit and drink our coffee. In the light of day I could evaluate my surroundings. A few yards north were two Mini Cooper–size buildings, crafted out of wooden planks and mud. Each building had a tin roof, a wooden door painted bright blue, and a small square window centered in each remaining wall. One of the buildings had clouds of smoke puffing out of the window. These structures were not the classic Maasai homes I'd seen in my father's coffee-table book, and I wondered if I was going to get an authentic Maasai experience after all. A high fence of wooden planks bordered the property, and piles of cow dung dotted the ground.

To the south stood another two structures. One was built similarly with wooden planks and a tin roof, but the other one was classic Maasai, made (I knew from the book) of a mixture of cow poop, mud, sticks, and human urine. Another small cloud of smoke was puffing out of this house. Directly east was a fenced-in plot of land with at least thirty cows mooing, roaming, and running their heads into each other's butts. Beyond the four structures and the cows' playpen, there was nothing but uninhabited land. No neighbors. No cul-de-sac. No street lights. No street signs. No streets. Besides the trees and loitering animals, we were completely isolated.

"Did you hear the colobus monkeys?" Lanet said as he walked up behind us.

"Huh?" I asked as I twisted my spine to see his face.

"The monkeys. Did you hear them singing for you this morning?"

"You mean the incessant hooting sound?"

Lanet smiled, "Indeed. The furry beasts were loud and proud this morning. The scent of a mzungu makes them go nuts."

Walking around the fallen tree in order to face us, his smile turned to a frown, "You can't wear that clothing. It is not appropriate. Where is your olkarasha?"

Becca was wearing a baby-pink tank top with a pair of canvas shorts that ended a few inches above her knees. The only things that might have been somewhat inappropriate were her lace-covered perfect Cs that you could see through her top. I, on the other hand, was wearing my Under Armour "cat suit," a black spandex tank top and black spandex pants. Confused, Becca and I looked each other up and down.

"What's wrong with what we're wearing?" I asked.

"That type of clothing is too tight to wear in front of elders. Also, if you want to be taken seriously as a moran, then you need to dress the part. Let me show you how to put on your olkarasha."

Back at the tent, Becca handed Lanet the tartan sheets that we'd bought the day before at the market. With a quick flick of his wrist, the cloth was shaken out and flying like a flag in the wind. He then folded the cloth in half lengthwise and tied a tiny, tight knot with the two ends. He performed the same action with the second cloth. After the two cloths were tied, he slipped one at a time over Becca's head so that each knot rested on Becca's shoulders.

"That is horribly unflattering," I said as I surveyed Becca's protuberance of purple.

After Lanet repeated the action for me, I could see Becca was equally horrified by my eggplant look. With our ilkarash fitted, it was time to fasten our beaded belts equipped with swords to our hips. Finally, we slipped on the necklaces given to us by Nic and we were ready to roll.

With a pep in my step, I felt equipped to start our training. Amazing how looking the part helps make you feel that you're living the part. We followed Lanet through the gated area and into the structure with a puff of smoke seeping out of the window cracks. The door was partly ajar when we arrived and made a loud creaking noise as Lanet pushed it open. We had to enter the small dark room hunched over since the ceiling was lower than our height. Almost immediately my eyes began to water from the smoke, and I almost tripped over a small child. Lanet pointed for us to sit on two low footstools. Next to the fire, we saw a woman, who I later learned was one of the wives of Lanet's brother Sankai, dripping from head to toe in stunning Maasai necklaces, bracelets, anklets, rings, and earrings. Her beautiful name, Noolamala, matched her perfectly. Bending over a big pot of steaming liquid with three small children by her side, she glanced up at us for a fleeting moment before her eyes turned back to the pot. The children took one look at Becca and me and scurried behind their mother to hide. Lanet spoke quickly in Maasai, and the children cautiously inched their way back into view.

"Great," I thought, "even the kids are terrified of us."

Lanet sat on another stool next to Noolamala's bed—a mattress made of woven branches with a large black cowhide stretched over it. I reached over to assess the comfort level of the bed and felt none. Her back must be tough as nails.

Noolamala proceeded to pour chai into one cup and then transfer the liquid from that cup to another and back and forth multiple times.

"What is she doing?" I asked Lanet.

"She is cooling the chai. If you drink it straight from the fire, you will burn your tongue off."

I looked back at the Naomi Campbell doppelganger and thought about how lucky we were to have met Lanet. He was smart, witty, and open-minded, and he didn't seem to mind explaining everything to us—a dream come true.

Noolamala handed me a cup and I took a sip. It was still quite toasty, but it was the best-tasting chai I had ever had. The milk was creamy, the tea leaves fragrant, and the sugar raw and real. I was starving, so I slurped it down without a sip to spare. As we handed our cups back to Noolamala, she lifted up a beautiful gourd embroidered with Maasai beading. She shook it up and down and left to right and then popped open the top. With one eye closed, she peered inside. Closing the top, she shook it some more and popped off the top again. She picked up a clean cup and out of the gourd poured a chunky white liquid. Just looking at it made my stomach churn. I leaned to Becca, "I can't go there."

Becca accepted a cup from Noolamala and said, "Oh please. It is just a little sour milk. It's like yogurt." She brought the cup to her lips, and I watched her chew the liquid and swallow.

Becca looked up from her cup and said, "Pretty tasty. Try it."

The chai that I thought had moved down to my stomach was now in a knot in my throat about to erupt out of my mouth and all over the small house. Chunky creamy foods were never chosen menu items for me. Something about the texture combined with the color made me nauseous, but I needed to assimilate and I was starving, so I slid a chunk of the gourd's contents into my mouth. I scrunched my nose as the slimy, lumpy sour milk (with a hint of grass, I couldn't help noticing) made its way down my throat. I forced myself to chew and then swallow the congealed milk that rolled on my tongue like large-curd cottage-cheeseish tofu. But that was it. I handed the cup, still half full, back to Noolamala. She gave Lanet a perplexed look and spoke in rapid Maasai.

"What's wrong?" I asked.

"She has never seen food left uneaten. When you never know when your next meal will come, you don't have food left over. Mindy, you need your strength. You should finish the milk."

My stomach gurgled and my nose curled. I was hungry and nauseous at the same time. "I can't have any more. Even the thought of another chew is making me sick."

Lanet motioned for Noolamala to hand him the cup, and she stared at him with a look of awe as he took gulp after gulp and then handed her the empty cup. He wiped his mouth and spoke to her in a rapid, angry tone.

"What's going on now? You sound angry," I said.

"That is because she questioned my behavior, and she should not question me. She feels uncomfortable because it is Maasai tradition for men not to eat in front of women and we never share food with a woman, so me finishing your milk shocked her. But she should never question me, and she knows that."

Lanet told us to say *"Ashe ooleng,"* or thank you in Maasai, to Noolamala, and then we hunched our way back out the door.

Walking outside, I squinted in the rush of sunlight. I saw Leken by the fence speaking with a man somewhere in his early forties and dressed in a red olkarasha with a gray fleece sweatshirt, spear in hand. As we walked over, a picture-perfect tan-colored cow with a white belly cut in front of us to pick up a lone corncob. Laughing, I asked Lanet if the cow lived in the house with them. Lanet had a look of love as the animal pooped two inches from his sandal and said, "Yes, this cow is my special old girl. The other cows are jealous of my love for her, so they kick and bite her. She is much better off living with me."

The other cows are jealous of her?! Sweet Jesus! This took being at one with nature to a new level. At least there was a fence that supposedly separated the wild animals from the humans, but by the way Lanet was talking, a happy night in the sack would be one with old girl chewing cud snuggled next to him.

Out of the corner of my eye, I saw the guy by the fence spit. "Who is that guy and what are we doing today?" I asked.

"You remind me of a kicking donkey."

I gasped. Lanet didn't know of my brother's or my Maasai nickname—peacock donkey. So what was it about me that reminded people of a donkey? Personal exploration would need to be conducted at a later time. Right now I was too anxious.

"This man will be going to *orpul* with us today."

"What is orpul?"

"It's sort of a warrior boot camp, but the direct translation means meat-eating camp. In orpul, you only eat what you can kill, and if you don't have anything to kill, then you don't eat. You will be put to the test when you are in orpul, and we will see if you can survive. It is essential for bonding as a unit through hardships and for building strength both physically and mentally. It is a time when everyone can begin to think the same about social issues like war and taking care of one another. And most important, it will teach you how to be a moran."

My jaw dropped a bit. The whole warrior thing just got really real.

"You should close your mouth unless you want to eat flies for lunch," Lanet said and smiled wide. He put his hand on my shoulder and continued, "This is what you asked for. You will get the real moran experience. You will even drink herbs that make warriors go crazy."

He continued, "The last time I was in orpul, Magilu, who you will meet today, was drinking many herbs. In the middle of the night, he started to rant, running directly through fire, spears, and straight through a gate. He had burns and was bleeding too much. When I finally caught up with him and pinned him down, he forgot what happened and said he couldn't feel any pain." Goose bumps rose up all over my body, and my mouth trembled in fear.

Lanet looked deeper into my eyes and said, "Does this scare you, Mindy? You can always turn around and go home."

That was all he needed to say to get my head back in the game. I was either going to go home a warrior or go home in a box. Nothing in between.

I took Lanet's hand off my shoulder, regripped my spear, and said, "Absolutely not. When do we go to orpul?"

Lanet looked me up and down and turned on his heel as he said, "We leave at the soonest."

"At the soonest" meant nothing to me, but I didn't question Lanet. What he'd said to me yesterday about not having expectations had stuck. His comment about living moment to moment was exactly how I was going to live.

Becca and I were introduced to the man standing with Leken. His name was Rokoine, and he would be joining us at orpul. He was a happy-looking man with light brown skin, somewhat crossed eyes, and oversize ears. I said the only Maasai greeting I knew, "*Sopa oleeng?*" meaning "How are you?"

Rokoine smiled and said, "*Saidee oleng,*" which Lanet translated as "Very good."

The three men exchanged words while Becca and I sat on our rumps. About an hour later, Lanet clapped his hands and said, "Are you morans-in-training ready to go to orpul?"

"What do we need?" I asked.

"Oh, not much."

"What does that mean?"

"Take anything you can't live without."

Becca and I climbed back into the tent and emptied the contents of our backpacks. Spread across the floor were items ranging from Dr. Bronner's all-purpose soap to lacy bras to Trojans to Chanel Red Dragon nail polish to tampons. I grabbed my BlackBerry, a bunch of tampons, tweezers, the nail polish, a few pairs of boy shorts, a tank top, a pair of black spandex tights, and a pair of socks. I didn't see everything Becca stuffed in her bag, but I did see a few Trojans slipped in at the last minute.

We took down the tent and placed what we were leaving behind in one of Lanet's tin-roofed structures. With spears in hand and backpacks on our shoulders, the five of us—Leken, Rokoine, Lanet, Becca, and I—side-stepped more piles of Ol' Girl's deposits and closed the gate behind us.

Lanet pointed north, saying, "We will walk until we stop."

Great detailed directions, I thought, but at least now I could let my mind fully soak up the experience. I was nervous, excited, scared, and thrilled all at the same time, the way I used to be before the start of an ice-hockey game in high school. I never knew what was going to happen in the rink, and I definitely didn't know what was going to happen in orpul.

"The trek is easy," Lanet explained. "It will take just a little while."

Good, I thought, that should mean less than an hour. We continued to walk and soon reached a very large hill, nothing I hadn't scaled while training in California. In a few steps, though, the panting began. Sweat bubbled up in every crevice. What was going on? I thought I was in pretty good shape, but apparently I was sorely mistaken. I wiped my brow and looked up to see Lanet, Leken, and Rokoine hiking up the hill ahead with as much ease as I would walk the mall. Their muscular quads pumped one after another and suddenly all I wanted to do was crawl into the fetal position and return to my mother's womb. I turned to Becca, who was also struggling.

"I don't feel very well," I said.

"It's the altitude," Becca replied. "We are definitely above eight thousand feet."

"Really? I don't even know if that is high. What is the altitude in California?"

"North or south?"

"I was sort of being facetious when I asked that question. Do you know the answer?"

"North or south?" she spouted out again.

"South."

"Los Angeles is probably about thirty-five hundred feet."

"I am totally impressed with your random knowledge, but I have to say that at the pace we're going, we are not going to make it up this hill until dawn." All of a sudden a wave of nausea swept over me, and I vomited up the chunks of sour milk, splattering my boots and the sides of Becca's legs.

"Gross!" Becca shrieked.

Lanet heard Becca's cry and ran back down the hill to see if we were okay. He took one look at the scene—me wiping my mouth and Becca looking at her legs in disgust—and burst out laughing. He hollered up to Leken and Rokoine in Maa, which caused some giggles from them as well.

I looked at Lanet with apologetic eyes and said, "I'm so sorry, I shouldn't have had that milk."

"Oh, don't worry. I am glad you didn't have more. Becca would have been really sour at you." He laughed at his joke.

We didn't.

I wiped my mouth again with a corner of my olkarasha and took a swig of my water bottle before Becca yanked it from my hand and used it to clean her shins and calves.

"Do you need to continue to repose?" Lanet asked. Of course, I did, but I didn't want to appear weak on my first day, so after a few deep heaves, I kept moving. Each step up the hill felt like it was going to be my last, but I put my head down and repeated, "One foot in front of the other. One foot in front of the other. One foot in front of the other," and eventually made it to level ground. Once there I planted my spear, knelt down, and comfortably rested my body weight on my heels, which allowed my quads to stretch and let my eyes roam the rolling hills of green and blonde grass.

Although the sun was strong, there was a nice breeze that helped calm my heartbeat. I pulled out my ponytail and ran my fingers through my wet-with-sweat hair. Directly south was a small pool of water about ten feet long and two feet wide. We'd climbed a great deal, so as I relaxed on the hilltop, I thought about the concepts of time and endurance in the Maasai culture.

Yesterday's trip to Loita, which Lanet had told us would not be very long, had ended up taking all day and night and was probably the most brutal traveling experience I'd undertaken. This morning Lanet had described our trek as short and easy, and already it was the most grueling hike I'd ever been on. I wondered if I would ever be able to remove the gap between our perceptions. Taking my eyes off of the vista for a moment, I looked to my right and saw the three men chatting, leaning lightly on their spears. None of them seemed to have expended a drop of sweat. The climb was like a leisurely stroll for them. I, on the other hand, was one whipped chick.

Becca was now stretched out on her back with eyes closed and arms cradling her head. Feeling self-conscious of my lack of endurance, I rose to my feet and walked over to the men.

"Do you need to continue to repose?" Lanet asked.

"We have only been reposing for thirty seconds, so yes, a few minutes would be great." From a distance I heard bells jingling. "What's that?"

"You don't recognize the sound of Ol' Girl?"

It took me a moment to remember who "Ol' Girl" was. "Your cow?"

Lanet nodded as the jingling got louder and louder. A few moments later, Ol' Girl ambled out of the forest and onto the flat grassy area where we were resting. Lanet whistled a high tune and within seconds at least twenty more cows bustled out of the woods. Becca quickly got to her feet to avoid being trampled. I dodged the cows, but whenever I thought I was in the clear, another one would come out of the forest and nearly knock me over. For some reason, the cows had a different level of respect for the Maasai—they trotted around them—but when they looked at Becca and me, it was apparent that all they wanted to do was run us over.

The cows now filled the clearing. Over the moos and jingling I hollered to Lanet, "What's going on?"

Gazing at the cows and prodding the random deviant that tried to leave the pack with a stick on the rear, he said, "This is their watering hole, which is also our watering hole."

I looked at the murky water in the hole and then at the dirty cows and nausea swept over me once again. A stray cow made its way to the watering hole and began to drink straight from the source. Swallowing hard, I said to Lanet, "We share water with the cows?"

"Yes, ma'am," Lanet replied, as calm and cool as ever. "You are lucky to have the opportunity to drink from the same place as our sacred cows."

As an overwhelming smell of cow poop filled the air, Lanet inhaled deeper while I pinched my nose. I watched as the young girl who was herding the cattle dunked a bucket into the hole, filling it with water, and then walked over to the watering trough, a twenty-foot hollowed-out log. She couldn't have been older than seven or eight, but she was already taking care of the family's most valuable asset on her own. Wearing one tartan sheet (half of a typical warrior uniform) over a white shirt gone muddy brown, she poured the water into the log as the cows rammed into one another trying to get front-row access. The girl kept filling the bucket and splashing the water into the log, every now and then slapping a cow on the butt to get him to move so that another one could take its place. I remembered Chief Winston telling us that young boys were always the ones to herd the cattle.

"I thought boys were supposed to herd cattle," I said to Lanet.

"They are, but this young girl rises earlier than her brother and takes the cows to graze. Her father tells her every day not to take the cows, but every morning she takes them again."

"What's her name?"

"Kinyi."

Kinyi was hard at work, her attention never leaving the cows. I watched her skillfully maneuver the herd. She was in her element. I liked her and already respected her for what my Nana would call her chutzpah. When one cow trotted off into the woods, she looked up and hollered something at Lanet, which Lanet told me was her "ordering" him to go and get her cow. And Lanet did go and get her cow. When he returned with the cow, Kinyi looked up and made eye contact with me. I smiled. She looked back, revealing no emotion. This girl had probably never seen a white person before and surely had never seen a woman in a moran's uniform carrying a spear and a sword. To the Western eye, I must have looked like a transvestite or, given my red nail polish and cat suit, maybe a drag queen. Yet despite

111

my shocking apparel, the little girl didn't flinch, unlike Lesikarr, a full-grown warrior, who'd lost his composure upon seeing Becca and me for the first time. Kinyi went back to work, slapping the rear ends of cows, moving them along to allow space for other cows to access water.

LANET, LEKEN, AND ROKOINE stared at the cows for close to an hour. I couldn't figure out what the fascination was all about.

"Are we going to keep hiking today?" I asked.

"Yes."

"Soon?"

Lanet created a hard line with his lips and said, "Are you in a rush?"

"No, it's not that I'm in a rush, but I guess I don't understand what we are waiting for."

"You don't find the cows beautiful?"

His question threw me off. Beautiful? I never thought of a cow as beautiful. I turned my head and saw one cow sniffing another cow's poop.

"I don't think I would describe them as beautiful."

Lanet shook his head, "Maybe you have not been opening your eyes."

Lanet called to Becca, and as we started walking again, he explained the importance and history of cattle.

"The Maasai believe that cattle possess the qualities of Ngai, which is that which began the earth. Eating meat and drinking milk is so important and essential in our culture because it represents becoming one with Ngai. At the beginning of time, when the sky and earth split, Ngai, who owned all of the cattle in the world, created a long rope and sent all of the cattle down from the sky and gave each and every beautiful cow to the Maasai. There was a group of hunters who resented the Maasai for all of their cattle, so they cut the rope, which created a divide between the heavens and earth. This stopped cattle from being transported freely to the Maasai, but since Ngai already gifted the Maasai with all of the cattle, we believe that all cows are under our ownership. This caused and still causes bloody battles between tribes, when Maasai take cattle from others. You will meet men during orpul who have been through near-death in order to claim our cattle. Never under-estimate the importance of cattle to the Maasai. We believe that when people die, they can take one of two paths. If a person is bad when on earth, then at death, that person will be sent to the desert with no water or cattle. But if the person is good, then the person will be sent to a land with endless cattle that have plenty to eat."

As Lanet concluded, he pointed to a grassy slope a few yards in front of us and exclaimed, "The campsite is just ahead, a short distance!"

I looked up and saw more of the same: another brutal hill with no signs of a campsite. So I mentally prepared myself for another "quick and easy" three hours before we would be able to take off our boots and have something to eat.

Panting, dripping with sweat, and ready to collapse, we reached the top about thirty minutes later. And what did we see? More bush. I had expected a hut or two, and I was secretly hoping for an outhouse. But then Lanet began to cut away some branches to form what he told us would be the "entrance" to camp. Becca and I watched as he masterfully swung his sword, chopping the stray branches and weeds. When he was done thrashing, the result actually *was* a nicely manicured six-foot-wide entryway. We followed him through the entry and around a bend where we were faced with Leken, Rokoine, and three other warriors in red ilkarash, squatting over a goat.

A bolt of fear ran through me. I had never seen three of these men before. Did they follow us? I yanked the back of Lanet's olkarasha and asked, "Who are they? What are they doing here?"

Lanet could hear the nervousness in my tone. "Mindy, I can't promise you that you will be safe from animals, but I can tell you that the Maasai who will be with you in orpul will be looking out for your best interests. These men volunteered to be here. They left their families and cattle because they are open-minded enough to want to see if women can be morans."

My nerves calmed as I realized that all I needed to do was choose to trust this group. My other option was to be unnecessarily uptight and on guard. My goal was to become one with the tribe, not to remain an outsider. I told myself that these men were going to become my family. We didn't share blood yet, but by the looks of what they were hunched over, we soon would.

The five men wore red tartan-patterned cotton sheets tied in tight little knots atop their sculpted black shoulders. Around each muscular waist was a two-inch, intricately beaded cowhide belt. Each warrior also wore earrings hanging low from their earlobes and string upon string of brightly colored beaded necklaces and bracelets.

Lanet motioned his hand forward and said, "Please sit down."

Becca sat next to a warrior introduced as Magilu, a small-framed, twenty-something guy who had warrior embedded in every inch of his powerful, tight body. His head was clean-shaven, and his earlobes were stretched and wrapped around the top of each ear in tiny Princess Leia–style buns. Becca, with her lily-white midwestern skin, looked almost translucent under the sun—especially next to the tribesmen. None of the men took their eyes off the twitching goat that was lying on the ground. One man was holding the goat's mouth shut while another held its front and back legs in two tight grips. It took me a moment to realize that they were in the process of suffocating the goat. My gasp got the men's attention, but they didn't let go of the goat, and within a minute or two its eyes rolled back into its head.

I'd never seen a human kill anything before except maybe an ant or a bee. While I never shy away from a good filet mignon, seeing the animal's life being taken away filled me with sadness.

"It is a very healthy goat. We will have plenty to eat for at least three days," Lanet said as he inspected the now spirit-less body. Lanet spoke with the men in Maa, and in unison, all heads turned and eyes focused in on Becca and me. With knives in hand, ready to slaughter the goat, they looked completely primal—like any other wild animal hunting for dinner. That thought allowed me to turn off my sadness and turn on survival mode. I don't feel bad when a lion hunts for its prey because the lion needs to eat. Why should I feel bad if I kill for my meal?

Lanet introduced us to one of the warriors, a lanky teenager with tightly coiled braids in his hair and a gap between his front teeth, who was busy slicing the skin of the goat's neck with his sword.

He stopped cutting and said, "Hello. I am Maani."

Shocked to hear another Maasai speak English, I responded with great exuberance, "Hi, Maani! I'm Mindy. This is Becca. It's nice to meet you."

"Hello. I am Maani," he repeated.

Puzzled, I looked at Lanet, who piped up and said, "Those are the only English words he knows, but you can teach him more. He thinks he is smart because he went to school longer than anyone else here. He made it to sixth grade, and the rest of the men here either didn't go to school or they didn't spend more than a year or two there."

"Why did Maani stop going to school?" Becca asked.

"His family needed him to take care of the cows and tend to the crops. It was unfortunate because he loved school. He was a great student—very motivated—but when his family forced him to drop out, he gave up all interest in learning. I gave him some of my old schoolbooks, but he never opened them up."

Maani pointed at the goat with his sword and motioned for us to sit with him. Wanting to be accepted as soon as possible, I knelt down next to him, pulled out my sword, and motioned for him to teach me how to hold the sword and skin the goat. But before I began, Lanet introduced us to the final warrior.

"This is Otumoi." With big brown eyes the size of jumbo jawbreakers, full lips, and long legs, this guy looked like a J. Crew model. I had to remind myself that I was not here to find a boyfriend, but it was fact that many of these men were beautiful.

Maani held my hand around the sword and guided me to the nape of the goat's neck, where he angled my sword and pushed it down until it pierced the skin.

Lanet smiled and said, "We will soon begin to enjoy."

"Enjoy what?" I asked.

"The fresh blood of this beautiful goat."

My stomach lurched. Oy vey! The time had come. I was going to have to drink blood. I wanted to be respectful of their customs, but it felt like we were jumping the gun a bit. I should have been prepared for this, and yet it surprised me that Lanet thought I was in a position to drink blood after my incident with the milk that morning.

As the words left Lanet's mouth, one of the warriors crouched down next to the neck of the goat and handed two empty mugs to Lanet. Lanet quickly slit the jugular and blood flowed in a glistening maroon stream into one cup and then the other. When the two cups were half-full, Lanet passed one to me and one to Becca. She grabbed the mug, peered down, passed the mug back, and I guess decided that she was not going to take part in drinking blood because she walked off into the forest.

"Where are you going?" I called to her as she walked away.

"I need a minute," she hollered back.

"Is she okay?" Lanet asked.

"Yeah. I am sure she will join the next time."

The warriors focused their stares on me. Drinking blood was a big step in being accepted into the tribe's culture. All the forces in the universe needed to come together for this event to go well. I looked into the mug at the thick maroon liquid with bubbles of blood on the surface while Otumoi, the J. Crew warrior, moved to the belly area of the goat. Maani placed another mug at the jugular and Otumoi began to massage various parts of the stomach and rib cage, which allowed for more blood to flow out of the vein. I knew that the longer I waited, the less likely I was going to be able to drink, so I pressed the mug to my lips, closed my eyes, pinched my nose shut with my left index finger and thumb, and took a swig.

The blood was still warm as it slid down my throat. I furrowed my brow, curled my toes, clenched my butt, and continued to drink, while holding back the vomit. It took every ounce of my being to hold back the bloody throw-up. It felt like drinking warm whole milk, which I've always refused to do not only because of the obscene amount of calories, but also because I have always had an aversion to thick liquid substances. Case in point: the morning's sour milk that I puked on the trail.

Opening my eyes, I couldn't help but laugh when I saw five sets of fearful eyeballs staring at me. I looked back at the mug, and the reality of the situation set in. I just drank goat's blood, I am surrounded by a bunch of warriors with spears, and . . . and . . . and . . . I'm going to be sick! I felt the liquid begin to travel back up my esophagus, so I quickly handed the mug to Lanet and sprinted to the nearest tree. I didn't quite make it before puking blood. Dropping to my knees, my head shot forward and I planted my face into the tall grass. Lanet and Leken were at my side seconds later. I looked up at Lanet and noticed blood on his lips.

"Did you just drink blood?" I asked.

He smiled and displayed bloodstained teeth. "Yes, and you will soon love the taste of blood. It is most nutritious, and you are very blessed to have it."

Blessed? Blessed?! Blessed would be a package of double-stuffed Oreo cookies dropping from the sky. From my stance on all fours, I slowly rose to my feet, shaking the dirt off me. Leken, Lanet, and I walked the few yards back to camp and found the rest of the crew finishing off the blood, mug by mug.

WHEN BECCA GOT BACK from her short walkabout, Lanet had already given me instructions to continue to help skinning the goat. Maani passed me a knife wrapped in leaves, which I later found out was done for sanitary reasons. Flanking Otumoi, I pulled out my sword and studied the slaughter. Magilu, the Princess Leia ear guy, sat next to Becca and took her on as his student. He grabbed her hand and molded it into the proper position on the handle of the sword, demonstrating how to grip and place her sword at a forty-five-degree angle in between the skin and flesh. He showed her how to carve with the utmost precision and she stretched the skin in one direction, not leaving a morsel of edible meat to spare.

Within a few minutes, the dead animal at my knees didn't sicken me. Soon there was no resemblance to the original goat. Its insides were exposed, with intestines, organs, skin, and bones on the ground in a bath of blood. Just as I was about to leave the scene for a breath of fresh air, Maani reached into the goat's cavity and sliced out a jellybean-shaped organ that fit neatly into the palm of his hand.

"Kidney!" Lanet exclaimed as he took it from Maani and shoved the reddish purple glistening organ up to my face. He then cut off a small bloody piece and popped it into his mouth. With a look of complete satisfaction, he cut two more bite-size slices and handed them to Becca and me. The kidney slid around in my hand and stained my palm with blood.

"The kidney is a delicacy," Lanet continued. "You need to eat it."

Motherfucker! I screamed internally. Was this slice of kidney going to go down and come up again like everything else today? No.

I can do this.

I can do this.

I can do this.

I looked at the tiny slice and figured it was about the size of a couple of almonds.

Turning to Becca, I said, "*L'chaim!*" and we popped the piece of bloody organ into our mouths at the same time. The warm, smooth, liver-like chunk reached my throat. I almost lost it, but I swallowed deep, held myself together, and it stayed down. With the morsels safely downed, Becca and I gave each other a high five.

Our celebration ended shortly after it began when Lanet guided us into a dense part of the forest and gave us our first independent warrior task: Chop branches until you can't chop anymore. Lanet explained that the Maasai will only harm nature for very specific reasons, so when it comes to chopping branches, they will only do so if they are creating camp in orpul, for bedding, for skewers for roasting food, to access herbs for medicinal purposes, and to feed animals.

Given that we were with a bunch of men with spears and swords, I decided to simply follow directions. Plus, I was beyond thrilled that we didn't have to do something else involving the consumption of another body part.

After three hours of nonstop chopping, I took a much-needed rest. Sitting on the cold dirt floor, I surveyed the scene. Rays of light seeped through breaks in the dense canopy of leaves, babbling calls of the colobus monkeys echoed in the trees, and

Becca's curly bob hopped up and down as her sword hacked at the joint of a branch. I glanced at the palms of my hands, which were burning hot. They sported blisters the size of half-dollars—the result of a two-foot metal sword with a wooden handle furiously vibrating against my formerly flawless skin. After quickly evaluating the bloody slices that my amateur sword work had left on my palms, I realized that, combined with the blisters and red nails, my hands were quite fierce. Just as I was finishing my diligent hand inspection, Becca, whose arms were now piled high with branches, said, "Of course you're inspecting your nail polish. What are you going to do when an ape eats one of those treasured thumbs?"

Heaving branches, we reentered "camp," a twenty-square-foot patch of land nestled under a seriously old oak tree with a circumference so wide, it would have taken ten of me standing with arms spread wide to encircle it. I would have happily exchanged the next hour for plucking each miniscule nose hair out one-by-one with tweezers, but with a warrior watching my every move, I did the most tedious task on the planet: removing each flimsy leaf from the branches we had just chopped and laying each piece of foliage in single-file lines on the dirt to make our community "bed." The result was a twenty-by-eight-foot rectangle, almost the entire size of our new home. The sight of a green "bed" that was one leaf thick was not at all comforting for a girl raised on pillow-top mattresses. I turned to look at Becca, who had finished making her side of the bed and was now rummaging through her backpack, exhibiting in the process the many lace bras that she brought with her.

Lanet entered camp with another new Maasai, who appeared to be seven feet tall and a close relative to Darth Vader.

"Mindy, Becca, this is Topoika Loet." I nodded with a shy smile. He immediately brought out the obedient side of me. Lanet went on, "We are very lucky to have Topoika at orpul. This man is a legend in the community and a very modern thinker. He will teach you how to protect yourself from the angriest animal in the forest—the buffalo. Topoika has killed over a hundred buffalo in his lifetime and was respected as a fearless moran."

Grabbing his spear, Lanet left us with the task of helping Topoika hang the meat to dry. This consisted of Becca and me picking up the pieces of goat and handing them to Topoika, who then punctured a hole in the intestines, the stomach, the liver, the legs, and other assorted parts, threading each piece on a four-foot-long, two-inch-diameter branch like clothes on a clothesline. When the meat was secure, he motioned for us to lift the branch and rest it between the branches of two larger trees. I took a few steps backwards and realized the meat, which was about six feet off the ground, was being placed directly over our bed.

"Becca, don't you think the position of this meat rack is potentially problematic?"

"Huh?"

"Well, it's going to be hanging over our heads while we sleep."

"So?"

"What if a leopard or hyena wants to get the meat? After the dead meat is consumed, we will be next."

She shrugged her shoulders and said, "When it's your time to go, it's your time to go."

Earlier, while Becca and I had been out gathering branches, the group of warriors had constructed a three-foot fence around camp, made of hundreds of crisscrossed branches.

"I guess this is supposed to protect us from animals," Becca said.

"Good luck to us," I said. "An elephant could tear down this piece-of-shit fence with a pinky toe."

As Becca studied our new security system, I glimpsed a patch of leaves wiggling softly about a yard in front of us. Becca shook the fence lightly, causing the entire thing to wobble. "Yeah. This is a piece of shit. But when it's your time to go, it's your time to go."

I didn't subscribe to Becca's hippy-dippy *c'est la vie* attitude. My own worldview was much more aggressive: "When death comes knocking, open the door, kick it in the nuts, and run for your life."

And that's when I saw it. Another movement in the trees. This time the leaves didn't just jiggle. An entire cluster of trees swayed like windshield wipers, right to left.

Only one day in the bush, and we were face-to-face with the enemy.

SNNNAAAAPPP!!!! SNNNNAAAAAPPPP!! We watched, with our eyes bugged out and unblinking, as branches tore from their sockets and trees toppled, fracturing trunks in half and leaving only shards of raw wood. A massive white tusk shot into the sky.

I screamed.

"Dinosaur!"

A twenty-foot-tall, hundred-ton, wrinkled gray butt appeared through the trees, and an elephant's tail angrily whipped around. Powerless, I watched the monster take a step backward, closer to camp, closer to us. I knew Operation Warrioress—and life itself—was about to come to a thunderous end.

Lanet rushed into camp, grabbed hold of our beaded belts and yanked Becca and me backward. Jolting us from our paralysis, he tossed over our spears, pushed us out of camp, and ran off to join the other warriors. Magilu, the Princess Leia warrior guy, waved his hand for us to follow him while the deep, heavy voices of the Maasai echoed through the forest, "*oooooOOOOOO!!! oooooOOOO!! oooooooOOOOO! OOO! OOO! OOOO! OOOOOOOOOO!! Sorr, HORR OLAG OLAG!!! SORR!!!!*"

With our thighs pumping and our beaded necklaces jingling, we ran after him, the tops of our spears guiding and protecting us from branches. We hopped over fallen trunks and shrubs and wove in and out like skiers gliding through trees. Ensuring that we were okay, the perfectly molded warrior turned his head and gave us a bright, encouraging smile every few seconds to make sure that we were following quickly. Seconds later, he stopped in front of a mammoth tree. He smiled, nodded his head, and pointed his spear up the trunk.

I turned to Becca, panting like a golden retriever. "He . . . he . . . wants us to climb the tree."

"Go! Go! Go! I am not going to die on day damn one! This is NOT my time to go!" she screamed, as she slapped my butt to get moving.

Needing no more encouragement, I placed my boot on the lowest notch in the tree, gripped stray branches jutting out, and used my upper body strength to pull me up until I found a secure branch to rest my rump. Becca and the warrior settled in other branches next to me. Once stabilized, we stared down at the camp. Three elephants were loitering directly outside the piece-of-shit fence.

Becca punched me in the arm. "Dude, you thought the elephant was a dinosaur!"

"Look at the size of them," I said. "They're five times bigger than any elephant I've ever seen. The tusks are the size of airplanes!"

She huffed, "Yeah, it's like a trippy version of *Jurassic Park*. But the good news is that the piece-of-shit fence is holding up quite well."

I laughed, "Doesn't it look like they're waiting to be invited inside or something? It's like the elephants have etiquette! The top of the fence doesn't even reach their ankles, but it's working!"

We watched Lanet and the rest of our new family scurry to build a fire. Within minutes, a low flame was burning. Three men ignited two sticks each and hid behind big, thick trees, taking turns making the deep, throaty *oooOOOooo* calls intended to scare off our guests. One by one, the warriors threw their torches at the elephants. The monsters didn't budge.

Becca looked at the warrior in the tree next to us. He flashed another dazzling smile. She tapped me on the shoulder, "Did you notice this hot little warrior smiling the entire time we were running? It's like he enjoyed it or something. And did you notice his ass of steel?"

"Becca, we almost got trampled by elephants and we are still in the midst of a mess, and you're looking at a warrior's butt?"

She smiled.

After what seemed like thirty minutes of hooting and flying flaming sticks, the pack of elephants decided that they were not going to be invited past the fence for tea and strolled off. Lanet walked over to our tree and called up to us.

"Whoa!" he said. "That was a close one. Those elephants were very arrogant, making us wait so long for them to move."

As the four of us walked back to camp together, Lanet smiled and said, "Today has been quite an introduction to bush life. The two of you have fended well. Now it is time to feast on that beautiful goat."

Our chores done for the day, we lodged our spears in the ground next to the entrance of camp—convenient if any unexpected animal visitors stopped by in the middle of the night. We could just grab and go.

Although beyond exhausted, I took a seat in the dinner circle as we roasted a couple of goat legs, some ribs, and liver. It was pure Atkins. My mom would have been proud. The elephant invasion brought all of us closer. While initially it felt like a pane of glass was between us, now the glass was shattered and we saw each other as fellow warriors first, not isolated by our different cultures.

Topoika was in charge of the roast. I drooled at the skewers lodged deep in the dirt, resplendent with two-foot-long cuts of meat that sizzled on the fire.

Hungry enough to eat dirt, I turned to Becca and said, "I don't think I've ever been this famished."

I watched as Topoika continually nudged and poked the meat with his fingers to check its "doneness." We learned that the Maasai love their meat either totally raw or totally over-cooked. Although both Becca and I preferred our meat medium-rare (or whatever the chef recommends), we kept quiet about our tastes, realizing this was not the time to appear fussy to our hosts. When the meat was done, Lcken took it off the roasting stick and carved little pieces using his sword. Each person around the circle received one piece at a time. In this way we all, hungry grown men included, ate tiny morsels of meat like dainty ladies, just to ensure that everyone was given a fair share. It was very democratic and very different from the overflowing plates of food served in the States.

I had never had goat before, but it was quite tasty and tender—a crispy, lean version of beef that left a thin coating of fat on the roof of my mouth. Becca watched me gobble down the goat.

"How do you like it?" she asked.

With grease dripping down my chin, I chewed on the over-cooked meat and, between bites, said, "Amazing."

Night seemed to fall quickly and completely out in the bush, the darkness flooded with millions of shiny stars and just as many creepy animal sounds. As we settled into the community bed of leaves, everyone lined up like Cuban cigars in a humidor. I was between Becca and Lanet. Magilu, of the Princess Leia earbuns, was on Becca's right. The earth floor was cold and hard as a rock. My entire being felt like one big cement block. I tried desperately to get myself a teensy bit comfortable under the one thin navy-and- burgundy blanket that Lanet gave me, but every shimmy resulted in a twig or a rock jabbing into my back.

Becca caused a lot of commotion when she crawled into her blue sleeping bag, which the morans later dubbed "the worm." None of them had ever seen such a contraption. The questions were flying and the fingers pointing. Where was that device going to take her? Could she breathe in there? Would she be able to get out? The biggest concern would be whether or not she could run from animals if she was locked in the bag. They had a point. It would take at least twenty seconds longer for Becca to get out of the worm, and in the bush you may not always have even two extra seconds to spare.

Lanet tried to calm their nerves by explaining the concept of the sleeping bag, but I could tell from their expressions that most of them didn't understand it and couldn't get over the danger it presented. Becca, cozy in her quilted bag, just smiled. She'd told me at the very beginning that the only way she was going on this mission was if she was able to bring her sleeping bag, so I was staying out of the issue altogether.

The Maasai were sound asleep in seconds. One of them was snoring like a freight train. Not me—my eyes were about to pop out of my head. With every faint rustle of leaves or yip from a forest beast that I couldn't identify, I visualized a repeat elephant drama. As a quick pitter-patter of feet traipsed by the now *respected* piece-of-shit fence, I flung my body up and forward like a jack-in-the-box and turned my head to see if a set of glowing eyes would be looking back at me. Nothing. I turned to Becca with definitely a little jealousy, seeing her bundled up like a baby in that cozy bag, buffered in goose down and looking like a miner with a headlight strapped to her forehead while reading *Man on Wire*.

"Aren't you even a little scared?" I whispered. "We're surrounded by god knows what kind of hungry beasts and you seem to be a-okay with that."

With eyes still on her book, she said, "You're forgetting that I have been camping in the backwoods since I was a young buck. Sleeping outside is second nature to me."

But I was scared. My body was tense and hard as ice, and I had the nagging feeling that something was lurking nearby. "I swear there's a lion watching us. I just feel it."

"You always think a lion is watching."

Lowering back to the ground and gripping my blanket until my knuckles turned white, I tried to settle down.

"So what did you think of our first day?" I asked.

"Pretty epic."

Becca shut off her headlamp, tucked her book on one side of her sleeping bag, and asked, "Can we talk about boys?"

Trying to get comfortable, I lifted my torso and pushed together a pile of leaves, insects, and dirt to create a cushion for my head. "I guess so."

Nuzzling her head into her bag and forming a small smile, Becca responded, "I told you that you should have brought a sleeping bag."

"Becca, it is so not cool to rub that bag in my face by continually reminding me how right you were and how wrong I was for not bringing one. I am so uncomfortable right now, I don't know how I am ever going to fall asleep, and I really get moody when I don't sleep."

"You should have brought a bag. I am so comfy."

"If you mention that bag one more time, I will take out my sword and mutilate it. You should take a lesson from the Maasai and learn to share."

Becca snuggled even deeper in her bag. "Maybe I will, but not tonight. Now, can we talk about how totally adorable the warrior sleeping next to me is? Plus, he saved our lives today, which makes him even hotter."

"His nipples are constantly erect. It's kind of odd," I noted.

Becca nodded, and I continued, "How about you take it slow with any kind of love affair and focus on becoming a warrior?"

"I *knew* you were going to say something like that. It's just that he is really cute and we made really good eye contact tonight."

"But you don't even know what eye contact means in this part of the world. It's probably very different from what it means in Chicago."

"True."

"I am not going to be a warrior-killjoy, but it's only our first day. At this rate, you are never going to leave the forest, and I will come back to find you with fifteen kids, drinking blood for breakfast."

Becca shrugged her shoulders and said, "What would be wrong with that? I wonder how they kiss."

"I wonder *if* they kiss."

A MOVEMENT IN THE TREE directly above our heads interrupted our conversation. Lying completely still, my muscles were flexed and I was ready to pounce. "What the hell was that?"

Becca didn't respond and no one else seemed to be bothered, so not knowing what else to do, I thought I'd relieve a little stress and write another letter to Mr. Plank. I slipped on my only item of unnecessary extravagance: a pair of mocha-brown flip-flops with hundreds of miniature mint-green rhinestones encrusting the thongs, and walked over to my bag, lodged in nearby tree branches. I grabbed my journal and pen and, considering the fact that I had no confidence in the bush mail system, I scrounged in my bag for my BlackBerry, so that when I was done with my handwritten letter, I could copy what I wrote and save it as a draft e-mail to myself. Warming myself by the fire, I composed my fourth letter to Mr. Plank (see Appendix, Letter 4).

8

Trekking & Target Practice

CHOMP. CHOMP. CHOMP.

With knees bent and pressed into my chest and a stiff-as-a-board spine, I reluctantly eased my eyes open to the bright blue sky seeping through the gaps in the tree branches above my damp, cold head.

Chomp. Chomp. Chomp. Chomp. Chomp. Chomp.

What was that chomping sound? I had an option: Continue to lie still on the ground and wait until whatever was chomping to chomp off my thumbs like Becca had predicted, or somehow pull myself upright and have a chance to protect myself. Picking option two, I squeezed my abdominal muscles as tight as I could, clenched my thighs together, and slowly lifted my back up like a bridge raising to allow ships to pass. The pain in my back was deep and felt permanent, well beyond what I had experienced from being slammed into the boards during ice hockey games.

Chomp. Chomp. Chomp. Chomp. Chomp. Chomp. Chomp. Chomp.

By the time I was sitting upright, I saw where the chomping was coming from: Topoika eating goat. It must have been the crack of dawn because everyone else was still tucked in his (or her!) proper position in the cigar box. Topoika glanced at me as he used his sword to slice a piece of meat off a slab from the dying fire. I smiled wearily. He didn't smile back.

Damn, these guys are intense. His expression remained hard and relentless. Maybe smiles are not as universal as I thought they were? How does one "break the ice" with a nomad? I thought the elephant attack helped, but maybe not. But maybe it did? I had no idea what being companionable looks like to a Maasai. We don't speak the same language. We don't have the same or even a similar diet. We look different (I pleasantly plump and they not at all). We sleep differently (they on a leaf bed and I on a mattress with individually wrapped inner and outer coils). From appearances, the only thing we did have in common was the fact that we were both human. Would that mere fact be enough to create a meaningful bond for both parties? I thought it would, but maybe my lack of boundaries wouldn't go down well with the Maasai.

Mesmerized by the fire, I sat in silence while Topoika continued to chomp on goat. I felt a slight poke on my upper arm and turned to find him offering me a slice. Happily accepting the meat, I gave him another smile, which he didn't return, but that was fine because I decided he was smiling from within.

The rest of camp woke up shortly after. I watched the morning scene while I nibbled on my slice of goat: The men straightened their ilkarash, went over to the tree where they hung their jewelry and swords, and put all of their accessories back on. Magilu then walked purposefully to a large oak tree at the bottom of camp and began chipping a little chunk of wood the size of a Chips Ahoy cookie out of the trunk.

Turning to Lanet, I asked what Magilu was doing.

"That is our calendar. Every morning we will chip a piece of bark from the trunk and that is how we will know how long we have been at orpul."

"Speaking of how long we will be at orpul, how long will we be out here?"

"I hope you are not ready to leave already . . ."

"No! I was just wondering what the plan is. How long will we be at orpul, what do we need to do out here, and what do we need to do to become morans?" Lanet looked at me with his mouth beginning to droop and I continued to babble.

"Becca and I booked our flights to leave in three months, but we can always change that. I guess I am really just trying to understand the process. And if we are in question-answering mode, I am also wondering if we could do something about the toilet situation."

"What toilet?"

"Exactly."

"What is the problem?"

"Well, right now it doesn't seem like there is a designated spot to relieve oneself. I never thought that we would have a proper toilet in the forest, but don't you think all of us should be pooping in the same general vicinity?"

"Do you think the animals poop in the same 'general vicinity'?"

"Of course they don't, but shouldn't there be some kind of line in the sand that we draw between us and the animals?"

"It should be your goal to mimic the animals and specifically you should learn the ways of a lion—the top of the food chain. When you act like a lion, you will have the greatest chance of survival, but in the meantime, you should know that all of us are already relieving ourselves in the same 'general vicinity.' The other Maasai took note of where you and Becca squatted, and we will stay in that area. But what you need to think about is how you are going to study the ways of the lion."

"Speaking of lions . . . I have heard conflicting information about whether a moran needs to kill a lion in order to be a true moran."

I remembered Winston proudly telling the entire group at the volunteer center that he had killed seven lions in his lifetime.

While trying to kill a lion sounded incredibly difficult—and, of course, dangerous—I wasn't scared of the hunt itself. The part that didn't sit well with me was the fact that lions were almost on the brink of extinction, plus I have an absolute obsession with cats. I figured that in some way, shape, or form the lions in the bush were related to my cats at home, and there was no way I was going to kill one of their distant cousins.

Lanet shook his head and said, "I don't know how that myth spread through the world. It is not a rite of passage to kill a lion, but it is still considered the ultimate honor by the community, so we will discuss this as time goes on to see if this is something we will do. But it is now highly illegal in Kenya to kill a lion unless it is purely for self-protection."

"So how am I supposed to study the ways of the lion if I am focused on my survival and the survival of my tribe? Wouldn't that mean that I should stay away from lions?"

"You can stay away while still keeping them close."

Lanet called for Becca, who was still in her sleeping bag, staring at Magilu as he munched on goat. Her extraction from the worm caused all of the Maasai to stop everything and watch her. With a wiggle and a kick of the bottom of the bag, she was up and out. Rokoine and Topoika whispered something in Maa and finally I saw it: Topoika cracked a smile! A rush of joy filled my heart.

With Lanet between Becca and me, he explained what we would be doing in the forest.

"There isn't a fully defined program. I spoke with Topoika and Rokoine last night about this very issue. No one has ever done this before. If you were Maasai, then you would have moved from one age group to another when you were twelve or fifteen and at that time you would have gone through rites of passage and become a moran or not. This situation is very different, so we will need to compromise. We will need to test you and as we go, we will decide what to do."

Becca and I nodded and Lanet continued, "We think we should stay in the forest for at least six weeks. If at any time we feel that you are not up for the challenge, then I will take you back to Nairobi and you can go back to America. But if you do well, then we will attempt to introduce you to the community. And it happens that there is a very big ceremony soon where thousands of Maasai from Kenya and Tanzania join together. My hope is that the two of you will be shown to all of the Maasai at that ceremony."

The thought of being included in a ceremony with thousands of Maasai filled me with excitement.

"Wow, Lanet, that would be so amazing to be included, but do you think the community will want us to be involved?" "That is what I don't know. We will have to see when the time comes."

With everyone awake, we gathered by the fire and ate breakfast (goat meat) Words were seldom spoken. This was the complete antithesis of a morning in my parents' house when I was a kid. Alarms would start blasting at 6 a.m. and a slow clomping of slippers would follow a pitter-patter of paws running down the wooden stairs. Right after my mother fed the cat, she would open my door, clap her hands like a pair of cymbals, and say in an authoritative tone, "Up and at 'em!" I would roll to my stomach and nuzzle my head in the pillow, prompting my mom to whisk the duvet and sheet off my warm body, leaving me just plain miserable. My father's voice would call from the other side of the house, "You can sleep when you're dead! Get up and be productive!"

I grew up yearning for a stack of buttermilk pancakes with maple syrup rolling down each cake, but I'd always have to settle for some low-calorie concoction. This was more often than not a cracker as dry and hard as cardboard, some low-fat cottage cheese, and a few cherry tomatoes. Conversations were always loud and animated, discussing current events or my career trajectory. Needless to say, I fully enjoyed my first breakfast in the forest.

As the last round of goat was passed, Lanet explained that we would spend the day learning how to use a spear. Given that we were complete novices in the bush, we would trek to a part of the forest animals typically do not visit, as it wasn't close to a water source and there wasn't a lot of greenery for the animals to feed on. This would allow us to focus on the training and not worry too much about an animal invading our practice.

Sparingly using my precious bottled water—I knew that when it was gone, I would be drinking cow saliva—I wet my Oral-B toothbrush with just a drop and added a dab of Tom's licorice organic toothpaste (my attempt to blend in with the earth as much as possible while on this journey). As I began to brush, Magilu handed out a few branches, which were immediately stuck into the Maasai mouths. As I stared, Lanet smiled at me as he ground the branch with his back teeth. Every so often he would spit little wood splints out of his mouth, and then manipulate the branch to pick his teeth like a toothpick.

"What is that?" I blurted out.

"Bushbrush," he replied with a wink.

"That is your toothbrush?"

When he nodded, I confessed, "I'm so confused. You guys have some of the most beautiful teeth I have ever seen, and you're telling me that you use a branch to brush your teeth?"

He continued to chew on what was now a completely frayed branch. Passing the twig to me, he told me it was an olive branch. I scrunched my nose and clamped my lips tighter than Kate Moss in the face of a cupcake.

"I don't share a toothbrush with anyone because that is just not the way I operate. I'll try an unused brush another time, but not today."

I turned and made my way to the tree that I peed next to the night before, keeping an eye out for other human excrement. While squatting, I could see camp through the branches. I cringed as Becca took the used bushbrush from Magilu. I shook my head and thought, "That could be a problem."

When I was done, I looked around for some soft leaves to wipe with. The leaves thus far were so crunchy and dry that they left my skin itchy. Hopping around the tree with pants hanging at my ankles, I finally found some soft green leaves that actually felt quite nice against my skin—still a far cry from the cuddly Charmin teddy bear, but a major improvement from wiping myself with a twig. Walking back to camp, I gave myself an imaginary pat on the back for adapting so quickly to the bush bathroom system. With a bounce in my step, I asked Lanet what was on the agenda after spear training.

"Tomorrow your hands will not be useable, so we will do hair plaiting."

"What's hair plaiting?"

He yelled to Maani, who scurried over to us. Lanet put his hand on the top of Maani's head and gently pushed it forward so that we could study the hundreds of intricate tight braids planted in right against the skull. The hairstyle was a work of art, but one that looked like it would inflict serious pain as well as take a considerable amount of time, particularly for me given my thick mane. Even as a kid, my hairdresser had to book double the time because of my abundant curls.

"Have you seen the amount of hair I have on my head?" I asked Lanet.

Lanet spoke in Maa to Maani for a minute and said, "Yes, you do have too much. The good news is that we will shave it if you become a moran."

I waved my finger in the air in a forbidding manner and said, "The shaving of the head is a deal breaker. I have seen plenty of morans with their hair still nice and full on their heads."

"When you transfer from moran to junior elder you will need to shave your head. The reason why you have seen morans with full hair is because they have not been through the rite of passage to become junior elders yet. No one who becomes a junior elder has his hair. As you say, not shaving your head is a 'deal breaker.'"

The truth was that hair was just another attachment. It was one that I would have traded in for the entire spring collection of Louis Vuitton and Chanel combined, but it was still just an attachment to the material world. If required, and if I ever even reached the lofty level of junior elder, I would shave my head. But now I needed to steer the conversation back to the bushels of hair I still possessed.

"You do realize that it is going to take four days to put all of those tiny braids in my hair."

"It needs to be done," he replied and then turned on his heel, grabbed his spear, and joined the other men outside of camp.

I looked at Becca and noted, "Well, at least we know what we are going to be busy doing for the next couple of weeks. I actually think you might have even more hair than I do."

"Did you see how tight those braids are to the skull?" she asked while biting the nails off her index and middle fingers.

I nodded.

"That is going to hurt like none other."

This time I was the calm one, as I gently reminded her that this was only day two and we needed to just go with the flow.

THE TREK TO the "safe" area was merciless. The hills weren't nearly as tough as the mountains I'd hiked in California, but the altitude was still killer. Breathing was one gasp for air after another. I wanted to ask Lanet questions about the men we would be living with in orpul, but I could hardly form a sentence because of my labored breathing.

Along the way the landscape changed from tawny rolling hills to dense green forest. As we entered the first patch of dark forest, I panicked. My breath quickened, as did my feet. I moved from second from the back to second from the front, and pushed Rokoine, the leader of our pack, to go faster. I was so close that he could probably feel my wet breath on the back of his neck.

As more light filtered through the trees, I knew that the end of the forest was near. Still fearful, I jogged past Rokoine and settled in as lead until I entered a bright grassy field. Moments later, the rest of the crew came out of the forest one by one and took time to "repose," spread out in snow angel positions on the ground. Lying with my back to the ground, I told myself that I didn't have anything to fear. Lanet sat next to me, and we relaxed in silence for a few minutes.

In a gentle voice, he said, "You were scared in the forest."

"Mmmmm hmmmm."

"Everyone and everything can sense your fear. When you are scared, you not only put yourself at greater risk, but you also put everyone else at risk. Animals can sense fear. It is when you are scared that it is the best opportunity to attack."

I swallowed deep, my throat tightening again.

"I don't know what it will take for you to stop being afraid. Do you?"

"I don't. Maybe time?"

"Time will help, but you need to figure out how to change your perception of yourself immediately. You are giving the feeling that you are not strong, and I know that is not the case. I never would have taken you to Loita if I thought you wouldn't make it. You must know that. You must know that I believe in you, but that is not enough. You need to believe in yourself. You need to believe that you have just as much reason to live as any other animal in the forest. Once you believe that, then you will be the lion."

When we continued on our trek, I tested changing my perspective about whether an animal would attack. I pretended that I was hiking in the California hills. In California, I still had to be alert, but it was an environment that was familiar. In this way, I put "fake it 'till you make it" into action. Yes, my mission out here was to quit fakin' it and believe that I was already makin' it, but I cut myself a little slack because it was only day two. Maybe around day twenty-one I would reevaluate.

After a few hours, we reached a flat grassy plateau at least eight kilometers away from camp. The "safe" zone had large mud craters in the center.

"Why are these craters here?" I asked.

"This was a former buffalo playground. The buffalo would play and roll around in the mud. If you look closely, you can see the indents from their hair," Lanet said.

"Buffalo playground? And this is supposed to be a 'safe' area?"

"They don't come here that much anymore because there is no more water nearby."

That wasn't exactly reassuring, but I repeated my mantras with a Rain Man redundancy, "Fake it 'till you make it. Fake it 'till you make it. One foot in front of the other. One foot in front of the other." In the middle of this inner pep talk, Lanet called for my attention. Our lesson was about to begin.

As Lanet instructed Becca and me in slow motion about the fine points of precision in spear throwing, Topoika and Rokoine napped on the grassy rim surrounding one of the buffalo pits. Lanet displayed his hand to us and balanced the wooden part of the spear on his palm. He pushed the spear a millimeter to the right, and the spear tipped over. He put the spear back on his palm and balanced it. He pushed the spear a millimeter to the left, and it tipped over.

"You need to find the point where the spear will balance on your palm."

I placed the spear on my palm and tried over and over to get it to balance on its own, but each time, in less than a second, the spear tipped out of my palm. Lanet finally came to my rescue and showed me that the balance point was somewhere near two-thirds down the wood toward the front blade. Becca, a gold-medal archer in high school, was a quick study. I was still at the point of balancing when she launched her spear in the air for the first time. Aim was also not my strong point. In hockey, I played defense because a human body was typically a big enough target to take down, but a puck in a goal? I left that to the center and wingers.

Lanet yelled to Topoika and Rokoine about something, and moments later Rokoine appeared with a skull in his hand.

I gasped. "What is that for?"

"That is a buffalo skull, and it will be our target for today's practice."

Rokoine jogged a few yards in front of us and placed the skull on the ground. Lanet ran forward a few steps, then sort of skip-hopped on his back leg before throwing his spear in the direction of the skull. The spear flew through the cloudless blue sky, finally landing less than a foot away from the skull. I turned to Lanet and said, "While that was quite impressive, I am wondering how that would help if a buffalo was barreling toward us. I mean . . . you did miss the target."

Lanet smiled, "If it was a real buffalo, I would have hit it. My throw accounted for the movement of the beast if it were alive."

Something didn't make sense. Scratching my now wet and filthy head, I continued, "Don't you have to hit its heart or leg or in a specific place to make the buffalo stop or die?"

Lanet nodded, "You are right, but that is the reason we typically never travel alone. If any of us is going on a long trek, then it will be with other warriors or elders. We travel in packs, just like the animals."

Soon Becca and Lanet were having a grand time throwing spears, Rokoine and Topoika were asleep, and I was standing still, getting frustrated with my lack of spear skills.

I watched as Becca's next shot ended up a few feet shy, but directly in line with the target. Lanet told her she needed to work on power but her form was good. Determined, I did a hop, skip, and jump and released. My spear flew straight up in the air and came plummeting right back down only a few feet away from my feet. As the spear landed on the grass, the spearhead popped off. With a feeling of disappointment, I said, "I killed the spear," and turned to see Lanet's reaction.

"You have work to do," Lanet said and shook his head. "Precision will save your life. Power will only speed up your death. Practice your form."

We spent hours practicing, until my mouth was parched from dehydration, my palms bled from the friction, my forearms and shoulders cramped from the repetitive motion, and my face burnt from the full day in the sun. I was ready to collapse, but I didn't see much improvement in my spear throwing. One out of fifty throws would be judged decent if I had been a kindergartner in some fully protected buffalo-free environment. The rest were, in a word . . . pathetic.

Lanet initially spent a lot of time with me trying to get my form right, but the motion wasn't clicking into my brain, so he moved on to the more talented Becca. By the end of the day, I was ready to leave the spear behind and hope that my karate skills from age six to twelve would suffice if faced with a lion. All I really wanted was a glass of ice water with a squeeze of lemon. Anything short of that was just not okay with me. After a frustrating day of making no progress, my inner warrior was losing out to my inner child and it was dangerously close to throwing a tantrum.

ON THE TREK BACK to camp, I asked Lanet to explain the age groups in more detail. "Young boys take care of the lambs and calves, but boyhood is mainly the time when the kids can play wild. Young girls cook, clean, and milk cows. Every fifteen or so years a new generation of morans is named. These are boys who have reached puberty and can range in age from eleven to twenty-seven. To become a moran, each man has to go through circumcision. The circumcision defines if a man will become a warrior or not."

Becca chirped in, "That is what the Jews do too—but we circumcise our boys at birth."

"We don't circumcise at birth," Lanet interjected. "We circumcise only after fifteen years of age because it is only then that men are able to withstand the pain. At the ceremony, the boy wears the headdress of an innocent. After the penis is skinned . . ."

I stopped in my tracks. After the penis is skinned? I didn't even have a penis and I could feel the pain.

"Did you just say after the penis is skinned?" I called up to Lanet who was already several paces ahead.

"Yes. The penis is skinned from the top to the bottom with a sword." Although I was horrified, Lanet was able to discuss the process freely. "Once the circumcision is complete, milk is poured on the bloody penis to help it heal. It is mandatory during this time for the boy undergoing the circumcision not to show any emotion. If the boy winces from the pain, then he will not become a warrior and will be considered weak for the rest of his lifetime."

I wanted to scream.

"Well, given that we don't have penises, how are we supposed to make it through that rite of passage?" Becca asked.

"You will always have the choice to get a clitorectemy."

"I already told you that is *not* going to happen," I blurted out angrily.

"I heard you say no, but you should talk with some Maasai women. I do not think it is something that a woman has to do, but many women see it as a major honor."

This was one thing that I knew I was absolutely not going to do. I had researched this and was very familiar with the procedure. If saying no to it meant I would not become a warrior, I was okay with that. But I did wonder about the future.

"Lanet, I can tell you with full confidence that I will not get that procedure done, but do you think that in the future women will need to undergo this circumcision in order to become morans?"

Lanet was silent for a few moments. Then he spoke with Topoika and Rokoine for a great deal of time. By the time he came back to us, I had almost forgotten what we were talking about in the first place.

"I have consulted with the elders on the topic of female circumcision and they do not have an answer, but they will think about it and let us know. It is a very good question, and I am inclined to say that it will not be a formal rite of passage because we are already moving away from conducting that procedure. But we need to see what the elders say."

As we continued to hike, Lanet explained the progression of the warrior groups. First after moran is senior moran and then that age group graduates to junior elders and then senior elders. The ceremony from senior warrior to junior elder is a big event called *eunoto*. This is the ceremony where the warrior's hair is shaved off to signify his moving into the next level of adulthood.

When I spotted the entrance to camp in the distance, I was surprised by a nice feeling of familiarity. I didn't know how long we would be at this site, but for all intents and purposes, this little nook was now our home. I was thrilled to see that our community bed was already made, with a new sheet of shiny green leaves. Lanet told me that Maani and Magilu were out fetching water from the watering hole from the day before. Sidling up to Lanet, I asked him if he found it healthy to be drinking from the same place where the cows slobber.

"As I said yesterday, you are blessed to be drinking the same water as the cows. You have nothing to be concerned about. The water is boiled before we drink it. This water is clean and fresh. You will not get sick."

I felt better knowing that all of the water was going to be boiled, but what we would be drinking still seemed pretty vile. Then I remembered Lanet's advice to change my perspective and be like a lion. A lion would not have trouble drinking this water.

As I rested in camp, I prayed to the powers above that we would not need to do any chores that night, that we would just eat dinner and go to sleep. But within seconds of my plunking down on the bed and taking a few sips of water, Lanet pointed to a fallen olive tree a few yards out of camp and told Becca and me to find wood that was dry and make the fire. I groaned and moaned as we picked branches. Lanet stood watching and ordering like a drill sergeant, instructing us how to decipher whether an elephant or buffalo had knocked down a tree. It was actually quite simple: If a tree was broken or cracked at a higher point, it had to be an elephant, since it would be taller than a buffalo.

With what felt like a hundred pounds of lumber in our arms, we made our way back to camp. Panting and stopping every few steps, I asked Lanet how Maasai men could possibly think that women were not strong enough to be warriors, given that they lugged vast quantities of wood using only a leather strap from their foreheads.

He responded, "Women are very strong. What we need to prove here is that women are also able to protect their communities."

Becca and I watched and listened as the fire got started. Matches were obviously a no-no; the Maasai started fires the old-fashioned way, with friction. With a pointed dowel from a fig tree and a flat piece of cedar, this method of creating fire was effective and mystical at the same time. Rubbing your hands together creates heat. Rubbing your hands together with a stick between one's palms over a dab of dung on metal creates fire. We watched as Lanet, Leken, Magilu, and Maani went to work. Lanet pierced a hole near the edge of the flat wooden slab and placed it over his sword. A bit of elephant dung was put on the metal. Magilu began a frantic twisting motion, rubbing his hands up and down the stick from top to bottom and back again. The stick spun in the hole in the plank, pressing on the dung smear on Lanet's blade. Next to him, Leken's palms cupped a nest of two types of dried moss. Magilu transferred the task to Maani, who without a word continued the intense motion without missing a beat. As the spinning stick went back to Magilu, smoke began to appear on the spot of poop. He picked up the sword and pushed the smoking substance with his finger into the moss. Leken blew on the smoke and a tiny gorgeous fire ignited in the nest between his hands. He put the flame on the ground, which began the blaze that would cook our dinner, keep us warm, and, most importantly, keep away wild animals.

As we rested by the fire eating goat, Lanet told us more about the forest we would be living in during orpul. It was called *Naimina Enkiyio*, which translated as The Forest of the Lost Child. This was a sacred place of worship for the Maasai, home to many of their deities. I wondered aloud how it got its name.

"There are many stories," Lanet said as he chomped on his meat. "But the one I believe is that there was a mysterious disappearance of a greedy boy who disrespected the forest by eating too many *nityook* berries. He took advantage of the forest, so the forest swallowed him whole. That is what happens when you don't respect nature."

With tummies full, one by one we lay down next to each other on the cold ground topped by an unyielding bed of leaves. The pain from the day's work vanished and settled into numbness. I wrapped my makeshift blanket/cape around me and turned to my right to see that Becca was already passed out in her worm. My last thought before sleep was one of desire for her sleeping bag. Not good.

9

Braiding Hair & Drinking Blood

CHOMP. CHOMP. CHOMP. CHOMP.

I knew the sound by now, but there was no way that it was morning already. I'd swear I'd just laid down on the stiff leaf-bed less than an hour ago.

Chomp. Chomp. Chomp. Chomp. Chomp. Chomp. Chomp. Chomp.

Sweet Jesus! I was so exhausted and my body . . . oh, my body. My hands felt like claws with bubbles all over them from the intense friction from the spear training. Even my Red Dragon nail polish was chipped.

Chomp. Chomp. Chomp. Chomp.

I opened my eyes and, just as I suspected, the sky was still black velvet speckled with a million little lights. Who in the world would be chomping in the middle of the night? A pang of fear shot through me. "It's an animal and when that beast is done chomping whatever it is chomping right now, it's going to move on to one of my thick thighs!"

I slowly and quietly turned my head from right to left to see if the cigar bodies next to me were still unsmoked. Both were there, but the chomping continued. Lifting my neck just a tad, I was able to see the fire below me. I couldn't see anything else. I lifted my neck a bit more and turned to the right, where I saw Leken taking a big hunk of a bite out of a rib—*chomp chomp.*

Thank goodness it was only Leken. But why was he eating now? We'd just had dinner.

I sat up and Leken made eye contact with me. He gave a big greasy smile, offered me a piece of goat, and squeaked out, "Hiyeeee."

I smiled back, glad that at least one of us was learning the other's language, and said, "Hi." Then I laid down, closed my eyelids, and went back to sleep.

The next time I opened my eyes, there were no cigars packed in next to me. Under the bright blue sky the camp was empty— everyone was gone. Not cool. My heart started to beat fast. Did they leave me here alone? Even though I felt safer in camp than on a long trek, that didn't mean that I was ready to be left to fend for myself. I hopped to my feet, flinching from the soreness in my quads, shoulders, hands, back, and eyelids. Looking at the calendar, I noticed another chip carved out of the trunk, marking the completion of night number two.

I ran out of camp and turned in a big circle to see if I could spot anyone in the periphery. No one in sight. Walking back into camp, I sat alone. I examined my hands. They looked like they belonged to Freddy Krueger's sister: blister after blister on top of blister. In some places the skin was torn off and all that was left was dried blood and dirt. My quads and shoulders burned, but in a strange way I enjoyed the pain. It proved I'd worked hard. I rolled to my back and fell asleep again to the sound of the leaves rustling in the wind.

I woke to an incessant tapping on my head and Magilu leaning over me, up close and personal. He stared at me for a few moments, and I stared right back. In a slow drawl and with a shrug of my shoulders, I said, "Whhhheeerrrre iiiisss evveeeerrrreeeeyyyyoooonnne?"

He stared at me. As I got to my feet, Magilu stood up straight and walked out the gate. Was I supposed to follow him? My decision was made moments later when he returned and stood outside of the gate with his spear up on his shoulder. I grabbed my spear, adjusted my sword, and walked beside him, down the hill and to the watering hole. There, Lanet was knee-deep in the muddy water dunking a bucket in and filling it up with water, then passing the full bucket to Becca, who placed it on the grass next to three other full buckets before handing Lanet an empty one.

"Hey!" I called to Becca and Lanet.

"Good afternoon," Becca responded. "You came just in time. We have to take all of these buckets up the hill to camp."

My thighs twitched, cursing me in their own way at the thought of lugging the heavy buckets up the mountain. But this is what I signed up for, so I told myself, "One foot in front of the other. One foot in front of another."

Lanet dunked another bucket into the muddy pit and smiled. "Today you will go to a very different type of hair salon."

Taking down my ponytail, I tried to run my fingers through my hair, but within seconds my fingers got stuck in a crunchy, filthy rat's nest. Carefully, and exceedingly slowly, I lifted my hand to the sky, exposing my armpit, and took a whiff. Miraculously, there was still a hint of my Donna Karan Cashmere deodorant, but the vast majority of my being smelled like an aromatic blend of buffalo excrement, burnt twigs, goat meat, and layer upon layer of sweat. It was invigorating as another reminder that I was fully in the bush, but as a "Warrior in the Savanna" scent it was making my stomach turn.

"Lanet, when do we get to shower?"

"Shower?"

"Okay, maybe not shower in the technical sense, but when are we going to clean ourselves?"

"In some time. It is very important to conserve water. It is common to go longer than two weeks without a bath. And you and Becca smell different to us. You should go longer so that you fit in better."

Holy hell. I could go a day or two without cleaning myself, but two weeks or more? No, no, no. I would have layers of dirt and dead skin, and I didn't even bring my loofah! Feeling myself getting worked up, I remembered that I had chosen this and that the Maasai way was just different. It wasn't bad, just different.

As we hauled the buckets of water up the hill, my muscles screamed and the metal from the handles dug into the open wounds on my hands. I tried to tap into my inner donkey, but all it released was an angry kick. The good news was that I was not gasping for breath the same way I did days before. My system was adjusting to the altitude, and I knew my body would only get stronger with each step.

We dropped the buckets at the base of camp and followed Lanet to a shaded area where we found Rokoine, Leken, Otumoi, and Maani lounging in the grass. Lanet pointed his spear in front of the men and said, "Ladies, please sit. Mindy, Rokoine and Otumoi will work on your hair, and Magilu will work on Becca's."

We followed orders.

Rokoine leaned over the top of my head, tugged at my hair band, and said something in Maa. Lanet told me to take the band out. I did, but my ponytail stayed in the same position, like a marble statue. Rokoine produced a small blue plastic comb and dove into the nest. With one tug, the comb was entangled. He tried to yank it a couple of times, but all I experienced was a minor feeling of whiplash. I asked Lanet to tell Rokoine that I very much appreciated his efforts, but that I would comb out my own hair. I ran back to camp, wet my hair with some of the muddy water, and slowly but surely combed out the nest.

When I returned, I noted Becca appeared to be really enjoying the tug of the comb being pulled through her hair by Magilu.

"Your head looks like a furry pyramid," she told me. "I have no idea how these guys think they are going to get through two Jewfros in one day. An hour has probably passed, and they haven't even started the braiding."

Rokoine dug back into my hair with a pointed stick, making a part across my head from ear to ear. After he tied the bottom of my hair with a string, Otumoi leaned in and started twisting a small section of my hair between his fingers. He spoke softly to Rokoine, and Rokoine grunted after each statement. Lanet was no longer in sight, busy boiling the water that we'd brought from the cow hole. The men twisted and twisted my hair between their fingers. I looked over at Becca, who was undergoing the same treatment, but with Magilu's strong chest and pointy nipples directly in her line of sight. Becca and I made eye contact and she shrugged. After another ten minutes, I finally yelled for Lanet, who came running.

"What is wrong?"

"What are these guys doing? They haven't even made one braid."

Lanet spoke, then Rokoine. Lanet grunted. Rokoine spoke. Lanet grunted. Rokoine spoke. And over and over.

"Uhhh . . . Hello? What's the deal?" I asked.

"They have never seen hair like this before." Lanet took a small section of my hair and began twisting the strands between his fingers and continued, "It is very soft and smooth. They think the braids will not stay."

Lanet walked over to Becca's hair, grunted, and spoke in Maa. All five men grunted simultaneously, making me smile.

"They will try," Lanet said and walked away.

Rokoine dug back in my skull with the stick, and the gates of pain opened as he sectioned off a few strands of hair and twisted them between his palms for about ninety seconds. Clenching my teeth and closing my eyes so tight that I could see stars, I tried to divert my attention to the pain in my palms or my back or my shoulders, but the pain on my scalp was too intense to ignore. Then it doubled as Rokoine and Otumoi each took a section and twisted at the same time. I heard Becca yelp and looked over to see her furiously punching the ground.

"Hurt much?" I asked.

"Hurt much? Hurt much?! This is obscene. I would rather get stabbed with a kitchen knife over and over!"

But we endured the pain, and eventually Lanet came back to inspect the work. He grunted as he poked around my skull. Rokoine spoke, and then there was silence as Lanet inspected Becca's head.

He came back to my head and said, "No, I don't think this will work yet. Your hair needs to adapt more. We will give you a classic moran hair style, but the hair plaiting will have to wait."

Becca yelped again, this time in joy. Rokoine and Otumoi went back to work, untwisting the strands and sectioning off the top of my head in three portions, which they wrapped around and around and around with a string. They took the back portion of my hair and wrapped the string from root to ends. Finally, Otumoi produced a tiny pink hand mirror and showed me the end product: three horns pointing to the sky on top of my head and one hanging down in the back. Lanet appeared in the mirror as I examined the hairdo, and I watched as he placed a huge brown and white feather in the back horn—the perfect accessory.

"Now you look like a real moran," Lanet said.

Lanet called out something loud in Maa, and the entire group of Maasai gathered around. They spoke to one another and smiled or grunted as each one touched my horns. Seeing the men smile with approval made me happy. Based on their response, this was a very important step in them accepting me. Maybe they were also happy when I drank the blood or ate the kidney, but then I was too wrapped up in my own horror to pay attention to their reactions.

Becca's hair, on the other hand, remained untouched. "Why didn't they do your hair?" I asked.

"I think they knew it would take them a month to get through my hair and gave up."

With the hair session complete, Lanet told Becca and me to gather leaves to make the bed.

"You want us to go alone?" I asked.

"Why not?" he responded.

"It seems a little soon to let us go off on our own."

"Do you doubt yourself, Mindy?" Lanet asked.

I shook my head, "No. Not at all."

"Good."

Becca and I grabbed our spears and headed back into the forest where we'd gathered leaves the first day. Hacking at the branches with my torn palms caused the scabbed areas to open up, and fresh blood soon painted the handle of my sword. Blisters popped, but I worked through the pain.

"This is pretty amazing, isn't it?" I asked Becca.

"It sure is. You know, I really didn't think you were going to be able to pull this whole warrior thing off. I thought the idea was wild when you proposed it to Winston, but really, I never thought it was going to happen."

"I told you that it was do or die for me."

"Yeah, but you're also a California girl, so I didn't know how much to believe." We chopped for a moment in silence and Becca said, "This is no doubt the hardest thing I have ever done, but we are fucking doing it!"

I was so pleased that Becca was pumped. I continued to chop, happy that I had such an easygoing travel partner. Becca's slight jokes and playfulness eased the intensity of the experience and brought the perfect amount of levity when needed.

LUGGING THE BRANCHES back to camp, we saw Otumoi, Maani, and Magilu huddled over something. Magilu took his spear and poked at whatever they were looking at. He then flipped his spear upside down and closely examined the blade.

"I wonder what they are up to now," I said.

"It's probably a dead animal," Becca replied.

"Gosh, I hope not. I still have visions of the gazelle and the goat. They come back in my dreams prancing together."

"Ridiculous," was all Becca said, and soon enough we were peering over the warrior's shoulders. It wasn't a dead animal. It just looked like a pile of poop. Mystified by their fascination, Becca and I walked back into camp and dropped off the branches.

Lanet was watching the water boil, and in normal circumstances, I would have made some flip comment, but I held back and instead asked about the poop. He got to his feet, and I followed him out of camp to the huddle. Lanet poked his spear in the poop and inspected the blade, just as Magilu had done moments before.

"What's going on?" I asked.

"A lion is near," Lanet responded as he looked even closer at the poop.

"How do you know that is lion poop?"

"You see the color? This poop is red from the blood in the lion's diet. Lions go straight for the jugular when on a kill. They drink the blood and then eat the meat. They have the most efficient killing technique of any of the animals"

I took a closer look at his blade. He was right. The poop was a deep burgundy.

"How far away do you think the lion is?" I asked.

Lanet poked the poop again and said, "You can tell how far an animal is by the softness or hardness of the poop. If it is soft and warm, then the animal is near. If it is cold and hard, then it has been some time since the animal was here."

"So what's the deal with this poop?"

"You tell me."

"Huh?"

"You tell me," he repeated. "Since this is the first time you will do this, you need to put your finger in."

I took a step back, horrified. "You have lost your mind."

He gave me a stern look. "This is the only way you will truly learn. Put your finger in the poop now."

The other warriors watched me with blank stares. I knelt down, my throat constricting as I got closer and closer to the pile.

"This is absolutely the most revolting thing I have ever done," I said as my index finger made contact.

"Put your finger all the way in the poop. You need to ensure accuracy."

I poked my finger through the poop. "Lukewarm and sort of hard," I said.

"Good. If it is completely hard, then you are in no danger, but since this is still slightly soft, that means a lion was here within the past day . . . maybe last night."

I flinched as Lanet continued, "We will need to keep watch tonight."

Magilu spoke and pointed his spear north toward the hills. Maani faced the same direction and lightly nodded his head in agreement.

"Is the lion in that direction?" I asked.

"It is possible. Otumoi thinks he can smell it, but he must be far now because the scent is not clear. If he was close, then we would all smell him."

"What does a lion smell like?"

"They stink very bad, and the smell of their urine will make you wish your nose was broken."

"Good to know," I said and jogged back to camp to share the news with Becca.

Interrupting her from sketching, I told her what happened while waving my poopy finger in her face.

"You did what?" she asked.

"I stuck my finger in lion poop."

She burst into laughter, "That must have been some kind of prank."

"I don't think so. Lanet told me that I had to do it to fully understand how far away an animal is. If I were you I wouldn't be so smug—you are definitely going to need to do the same thing." Suddenly I realized we weren't even talking about the crux of the information: the fact that a lion was around the corner. Feeling like my heart had dropped to my stomach, I grabbed Becca by the shoulders and said, "Did you hear what I said?! A lion is nearby, and all you care about is the fact that I put my finger in poop."

"I heard you, but if we were in real danger, don't you think the Maasai would look a bit more concerned?"

"Tell me, Becca, what does a concerned warrior look like?"

"Good point."

I paced in front of the leaf bed, thinking about what we should do. Looking at Becca, who went back to drawing, I wondered how much responsibility I should take for her being in a life-threatening situation. Yes, she was an adult and she could make her own decisions, but I can be pretty convincing if I want to be and maybe my inherent super salesman skills worked too well? If something happened to her, I didn't think I would ever be able to forgive myself. Her parents and family would be devastated. I looked down at what she was sketching—the start of some kind of animal. Maybe we could move to a different area that wasn't so dangerous? Maybe we needed to go back to Lanet's home. If we left the forest, our warrior mission would be over, and if we moved to a different part of the forest because we were scared, the Maasai we were with would probably never respect us and our chances of being accepted as warriors would be slim to none. The last thing a warrior does is run from danger.

Continuing to pace, I wondered if there was something that lions didn't like . . . something that would keep them away. A sound? A smell? Given my impending monthly female visit, my smell was probably what attracted the lion in the first place. I remembered my *Wilderness for Dummies* book. I pulled it out of my backpack and cracked it open for the first time. I scanned through the topics: how to make a fire, how to navigate, how to signal for rescue. Useless. I wanted this author to explain to me how sending out a smoke signal was going to help me when even a massive forest fire wouldn't be noticed for days. Looking through the rest of the book, I saw there was nothing about how to protect yourself from animals.

Becca interrupted my thoughts, "You need to calm your ass down. When it is your time to go . . ."

"Yeah, yeah, yeah. It is your time to go. But just as you knew it wasn't your time to go when we were almost trampled by an elephant, I know it is not our time to go on day three by a lion."

She shrugged her shoulders and I noticed what she was drawing: a lion with exaggerated (or maybe not) fangs. "How can you draw at a time like this?"

She dropped her pen. "A time like what?" Before I could respond, she said, "This is the wild, Mindy. I know what I signed up for. If this experience leads to the end of me, then it leads to the end of me. That is fact."

I stopped pacing. I didn't need to protect this girl. Based on what she was saying to me, she was better prepared mentally than I was. Settling on the "bed" next to Becca, I remembered Lanet telling me to change my perspective. If I had my choice

156

of thoughts, I would want to believe that whatever trouble came our way, we (as a family) would make it through unharmed. It was all about training my brain with new messages. It was about being faced with a problem and having my first thought be that I was going to succeed rather than jumping to the conclusion that I was going to fail.

WE ATE DINNER EARLY. As I munched on a slab of goat, I watched Rokoine grind something in the big cauldron of water that Lanet was heating earlier. Over the rim rose big gray bubbles of foam. I looked at my lone bottle of water with only one good gulp left and wondered if I could survive all of orpul without water.

"Becca, do you know how long a human can live without water?"

"With food or without food?"

"With."

"Well, I guess it depends on how much water is in the food, but I would say about a week. Why do you ask?"

"Have you seen the water that we are supposed to consume?"

"You mean the stuff that Rokoine is stirring?"

I nodded and she continued, "I don't think that's just water. I've had to boil water when camping before, and I don't ever remember foam being involved."

As Becca finished speaking, Rokoine handed each of us a cup filled with the concoction from the pot.

"Pewww!" I said. "What is this?"

"This is a delicacy, and it will make you strong," Lanet said as he guzzled his cup of the foul-smelling liquid. I went back in for another whiff and felt the goat chunks rise in my throat. I thought I was done throwing up in the bush, but maybe not.

"Drink it," Lanet demanded, shoving the cup to my lips and then doing the same to Becca.

I looked down at the murky gray liquid and consumed it just like I drank the blood—pinching my nose and opening my throat. The aftertaste was bitter, and it left a slimy texture on the roof of my mouth. I felt the liquid burble in my stomach, and then I felt the chunks rise again. I bolted out of camp and puked the nastiest puke I had ever puked before: gray liquid with goat chunks, which made me vomit even more. My face and body were cold but sweating, and I heard a voice within tell me that the end was near. Crawling on all fours away from the putrid mess, I prayed to all of the deities for some Gatorade or even a piece of mint gum.

With horns still in the grass, I felt the earth vibrate and wished for a buffalo to ram me to another planet where the taste would vanish, but it was only Becca.

"Mindy!" she called. "Mindy! You are not going to believe this!"

I grunted.

"Mindy! We just drank goat head soup!"

"Huh?" I said as I lifted my neck just enough so that my face was not planted in the mud.

I looked up and saw her laughing hysterically, squeezing her thighs together and holding her vagina.

"What . . . did . . . you say?"

"That stuff that we just drank has goat brains in it! We just drank goat head soup!"

"Shoot me," I said and rolled onto my back. Just the thought of seeing or smelling the "soup" made my stomach turn. Rokoine must have been grinding the goat head earlier. Lanet thinks that stuff is a delicacy? I got to my feet slowly, smacked the grass and mud out of my olkarasha, wiped off my face, straightened my horns, and walked back to camp. A burst of anger filled my body, and with my voice at least two octaves too high, I hollered at Lanet, "I am willing to drink blood, eat raw kidney, and drink cow saliva water, but I am never ever going to drink goat head soup again! That is where I draw the line!"

"So you did not enjoy?" he asked laughingly.

I wanted to punch him in the mouth, "No, I did not enjoy!"

"You must drink this soup. It will make you and Becca strong. The head is the best. Tomorrow we will have stomach, which is also good, but the head is the best." He brought a mug to his lips, and without taking a break to breathe, he finished the mug. "You will get used to it and soon grow to love it."

Infuriated, I said, "You said the same thing about drinking blood. You really believe that? I have never tasted anything so gross in my life."

"Gross?" Lanet asked.

"Yes, gross!" I replied.

"Gross. I like that word." He smiled and repeated the word over and over, "Gross . . . Gross." Magilu apparently liked the word as well because he blurted out, "Gross!" and doubled over laughing.

I was getting nowhere with these guys. No sympathy, no nothing, so with a pair of desperate eyes, I asked Becca if she had any snacks. "A piece of gum? A mint? Something from the convenience store?"

Sneakily, she dug into her tomato-red leather purse, looking around to see if any of the Maasai were watching. Feeling comfortable that the coast was clear, she revealed a shiny purple package of Cadbury chocolate. To my eyes, it glowed like a gift from God. With saliva pooling to the front of my mouth, I could already taste the chocolate on my tongue.

"Calm down, lady," Becca said. "You look like you are about to start foaming at the mouth."

I swallowed and sat with legs crossed and hands placed neatly on my lap—Emily Post would have been proud. I watched as Becca opened the package and broke off two out of three squares that were in a row before blurting out, "How about you give me the entire row? You can't just leave one alone like that. It will be lonely."

Becca laughed, "I'm already being generous by giving you two pieces. Tuck your tongue back in your mouth and be grateful." She handed me the chocolate and continued, "Also, we need this to last. We have no idea how long we are going to be out here."

She was right, of course, so I took my two pieces and ran behind a tree, afraid that someone or something would see my treasure and ask for a morsel.

I broke off one square, placed it on the center of my tongue, and closed my mouth. Nothing had ever tasted so good. I rolled the block of chocolate around, savoring every moment, but also getting more and more anxious as the square got smaller and smaller. I unfolded my olkarasha and looked at the other square. The next piece needed to last much longer.

With the first square deep in my stomach, I took a nibble out of the next square and decided nibbling was the right course of action. It allowed me to get the sweet, milky taste over and over and over again. I looked at the piece in my dirty, bloody palm and was so disgusted by the sight and so exhausted by the energy expelled that I popped the remaining 99 percent of the square— the very same piece I'd intended to cherish—in my mouth and with one, two, three chews, I swallowed and the chocolate was gone.

FEELING INFINITELY BETTER, I joined the tribe by the fire, sitting next to Rokoine. While I didn't feel a strong bond with any of the Maasai yet except for Lanet, I had felt an aloofness from Rokoine. But now I felt a new and different energy radiating off of him. What once felt like a brick wall between us was now a free exchange of positive energy. In acknowledgement, we turned to one another, looked deep into each other's eyes, and simultaneously smiled.

Everyone seemed worn out. Maani and Otumoi were already asleep, and Becca was snuggled in her worm next to Magilu. Lanet, however, was still eating and every few seconds tried to shove more meat in my face.

"You are not eating enough. You need your strength. Goat is good," he'd say.

I asked Lanet if there was anything special we needed to do to protect ourselves tonight from the lion. He explained that Topoika would stay awake that night and that for the next few nights, each one of us would rotate keeping watch. It was the responsibility of the one on guard to wake the others if there was even a hint of danger.

"So, just to manage expectations, am I going to be on guard one of these nights?"

He replied, "Indeed."

Using humor to mask my fear, I said, "But of course! Three days under my belt and everyone's lives are under my watch." Lanet nodded and I continued, "Just so you know, even at the age of twenty-two my parents didn't trust that I could take care of their cat, so they hired a cat sitter when they went out of town. And it was a good thing they did because the cat got stuck in a food cabinet and ended up eating all of the bagels."

"What's a bagel?" Lanet asked.

"Damn, I forgot. You don't have those out here. A bagel is this chewy, doughy bread thing shaped in a circle with a hole in the middle."

"Why is there a hole?"

Taking a moment to think about it, I came up with nothing. "I have no clue."

"Seems like a waste."

Back on my completely uncomfortable leaf bed with three of my horns pointing to the stars, I thought about the amazing ability of humans to adapt. Only a week ago, I slept under a sparkling crystal chandelier and sat on a heated toilet seat. I had never peed in a bush, and I certainly had never been without a shower for more than twenty-four hours. Just a week ago, I had access to plenty of food. I had money, so I could and would buy much more than I ever needed. Now, I was in a situation where waste was a sin, where wealth was measured in cows, not cash. Just six days had gone by, and I had already settled into a routine that would have seemed preposterous to the old me and, of course, to my friends and family at home:

- Wake up to chomping and a stiff back.
- Mark new day by a chip in tree trunk.
- Brush teeth with a twig—and then sneak behind a tree to re-brush teeth with Oral-B brush and Tom's toothpaste.
- Trek for a few hours to new locations for spear training.
- Trek a few hours back to camp.
- Force goat soup down my throat.
- Perform daily chores: hauling cow-saliva water up a hill and then boiling it, cutting branches and laying leaves to make the bed, getting materials for and then making the fire, chopping and heaving firewood, going on long treks to find herbs that were supposedly going to alter our minds.
- Share stories.
- Sleep / listen to Rokoine snore.
- Write letters to Mr. Plank.

Four mornings later, I snuggled under my blanket for a few extra moments and ran my fingers over my palms. They had basically healed and were now covered in calluses. My hands were any-thing but feminine, but I was proud of them. I hoped this work would leave a scar so that anytime I looked at my hands, I would be reminded of my life with the Maasai: pure and in the present.

My mind skipped to wondering why we hadn't seen any animals since the first day at camp. When I asked Lanet, he told me that the area we were in was known as one of the safer spots in the forest and not a frequent place for animals to visit. In time, as Becca and I were showing great improvement in our spear throwing and not putting up a fight or throwing up after drink-ing the goat soup, we would soon move to a more dangerous location where we could prove our courage.

Based on the bark calendar, it was day seven. Food was getting scarce, and our portions were smaller and smaller. We hadn't discussed what we would do when we ran out of goat. My stomach was shrinking, but I was still hungry all the time.

During a trek to spear training, I finally asked Lanet what we were going to do about the food situation.

"What food situation?" he asked.

"Based on our rate of consumption, I estimate that all of the meat and even the hooves of the goat will be eaten within a day."

"Oh, yes. We have another goat on the way."

"Where is the goat coming from?"

"This goat is one of my own. You will need this food to keep you strong, but there will be a time when we will go with-out. I told you that morans are the first members of the tribe to go hungry during unfortunate times. You and Becca will need to prove that you can survive maybe three days without food."

Lanet explained that morans are viewed as a communal asset, thus the community contributes goats, sheep, and cows to morans during their time of service, including orpul. The first goat was given to us from select people in the community as a sign of support and respect. Morans don't pay for food or other supplies—everything is provided by the tribe because morans protect them. It was even acceptable until recently for morans to steal and raid if members of the community did not give them what they requested. A moran's family is also looked after by older generations so the moran is free to do what is needed to protect the group. The particular goat en route was coming from Lanet's father. Lanet suspected that his father did not yet approve of our goal to increase women's rights, but he did respect his son and the goat was proof.

By the time Maani escorted the sleek gray goat up the hill, I was salivating. Lanet instantly recognized the goat, just as I would know if someone came walking in with one of my Louis Vuitton bags. The thought of crispy ribs was turning me on. Maybe Lanet was right. Maybe I would begin to love the taste of blood. Then, just as the thought hit my consciousness, my stomach responded with a painful cramp. My menstrual cycle was late due to the change in diet and environment, but the cramp was a sign that it was about to begin.

The goat had been happily trotting around, but with one look at me and the team of warriors, he began to jump, buck, and bleat.

"Becca, it is your turn to bless this goat and put him to rest. All you have to do is hold down its mouth until it stops breathing."

Gingerly Becca walked over as Magilu caught the goat and held his legs—a pair in each hand.

"How am I supposed to know when it stops breathing?" she asked.

"When it is dead."

"Duh! But how do I know when it is dead?"

"It will stop breathing."

Becca spit in her palms and rubbed them together, getting herself prepared for the task at hand. Magilu continued to hold down the goat as it squirmed with all of its might. I was starving and could already taste the cooked ribs in my mouth, but I still thought this process was miserable. Becca kept her hand on the goat's mouth for a minute or two before she looked at Lanet, let go of the goat's mouth, and asked, "Am I done?"

Lanet jumped forward and yelled, "NO!" but he was too late. The goat was conscious again. My heart fell to my feet, and it took everything in me to hold back the tears. I felt so horrible for the goat—this was no way to die. Frantically, I searched the vicinity for something to knock it out of its misery. My eyes locked on a log and I bolted off and came quickly back with the log in hand. Maani saw me and before I got to the goat, he knocked into me, taking me down instantly. Screaming to Lanet to put the goat out of its misery, I wiggled my way out of Maani's grip and ran back to the goat. By the time I got to the scene, Lanet was gently coaching Becca on how to make sure that the goat was dead. This time it worked. Later, Lanet explained that a very important part of the Maasai culture was in respecting and showing gratitude for the animals that feed us, and that hitting the animal with a log would have provided the animal with unnecessary pain. Maani understood this even if I did not.

With the goat dead, Lanet sliced the skin and nicked the jugular. The blood gushed and formed a little pool in the nook created between the goat's insides and his skin. Magilu brought his mouth to this makeshift cup and took a gulp. Topoika and Rokoine went next. When it was my turn, there wasn't much blood left in the nook, but Lanet wanted me to do exactly as the others, so I knelt down, put my face centimeters from the car-cass, and dove in. My nose was pressed against the goat's warm flesh as I slurped up the remaining blood in the nook. It was only a small bit this time, so the warm, thick feeling of the liquid slid-ing down my throat was not nearly as intense, and I managed not to vomit. The metallic taste of the blood gave me goose bumps, though, as I ran my tongue across the tops of my teeth.

I watched Becca go next. She had come a long way in terms of adapting to the Maasai lifestyle since the last time we were put to this task. Without any fuss, she got down on one knee, applied pressure to the stomach area of the goat so that more blood would drain from the jugular, and when a small bloody pool formed, her curly bob plunged and she sucked it down.

Everyone took part in skinning the goat and cutting its flesh into pieces. These were then hung on a branch and again placed above our bed. Otumoi cut up the kidney in equal slices and handed each person their portion. As before, I pinched my nose, opened my mouth wide, and swallowed it without chewing.

LATER, SITTING ON the leaf bed, I took my hiking boots off, a rarer and rarer occurrence. Some nights I would sleep with them on because I wanted to be prepared for a quick getaway if an animal invaded or I needed the extra warmth. It had been a good two or three days since I last removed my boots, so it shouldn't have been a surprise that I got a whiff of something horrible as I picked off the dry mud that was caked on my laces. I smelled it again and looked around to see if an animal was dead nearby. I even stood up and walked out of camp to a fallen oak tree, where the smell seemed to be gone—until I bent forward and was hit again with the offensive odor.

Then I realized that the stench was coming from my feet. Pinching my nose and turning to the side to breathe in fresh air, I gingerly removed my socks. My feet were dark brown and covered in mud and grime. Even the little bitty crevices between my toes were filled with crunchy black dirt mixed with who-knows-what foot gunk. I was sure Lanet would say some crap about me needing to smell more like the bush, but enough was enough.

I stomped over to Lanet, who was busy making the fire, and said, "I need to clean myself with soap and water."

He looked down at my feet and then up at me, "What happened to your feet? You look like a monkey."

"My feet are dirty, my entire body is filthy and smelly, and I am ready to go swimming in the cow-saliva water." He called for Otumoi, who always seemed to appear instantly, and after a few words, Otumoi was off fetching a few buckets and his small plastic comb.

"Get Becca and we'll go to bathe," Lanet said.

I grabbed my plastic leopard-print toiletry kit containing a razor, tweezers, avocado oil, and a travel set of Frederic Fekkai shampoo and conditioner, and ran off to find Becca, who was reading under the afternoon sun. When I told her we were going to bathe, she hopped to her feet and grabbed her neon-purple kit, and we followed Lanet and Otumoi back down to the cow-saliva watering hole.

Lanet showed us where we would bathe, a tiny patch of flat land behind a sparse set of trees.

"Isn't there a place where we are a little more hidden?" I asked.

"You have nothing to fear. No one will look at you."

Becca and I dipped our buckets into the brown water and set up shop behind the trees. We were limited to one bucket each due to the water shortage in the area, so we discussed strategies on how to properly clean ourselves in the most efficient manner.

"Maybe you should dunk your head in while I wash and shave my legs?" I said. "No, wait, that won't work. I don't want your hair on my legs."

"I have a better idea," Becca said. "How about I wash my body first and you hold the bucket to catch the water and then you can use that water to wash your body?"

"Absolutely not. I think we're just going to have to use whatever we have in our own buckets and be very careful not to waste a single drop."

Becca and I undressed with backs facing one another. Besides changing underwear and sports bras every now and then, this was the first time that I had been fully naked in eight days. Examining my body for the first time, I noticed that I was a full shade darker from dirt and grime. I also noticed that I had lost quite a bit of weight. My stomach, which even after my P3 training had sported a slight pouch, was now almost flat, leaving me with more direct contact with my abdominal muscles.

Deciding to first wash my chest, midsection, and female parts, I dunked my hands in the cold water. Goose bumps sprang up all over my body as I lathered my hands with soap and worked my way from top to bottom, watching the dirt wash off and my olive-colored skin reappear. Half the bucket of water remained after I finished cleaning and shaving. That left the horns on my head. Standing clean but still naked and back-to-back with Becca, I asked her if she would undo my horns and wash my hair.

"Only if you wash mine," she said.

"Deal." And with that, I walked over to my pile of clothing and slipped on a brand spanking new sports bra and boy shorts.

Five seconds later I turned around. Becca was in a turquoise lace bra and a pair of silver lamé bike shorts.

"You are ridiculous," I said with a chuckle.

With a look up and down, Becca said, "You think I look funny? You look like a reindeer in underwear."

"And you look like Madonna in the eighties."

"That is the best compliment I've ever received," she said as she walked over and began unleashing my horns. As my hair was brought down by gravity, I ran my fingers through it, scratched my scalp, and tossed it from side to side, up and down.

Becca and I washed each other's hair, spending a little extra time and effort on the scalp massages. We deserved them. I tried with all of my might to transport myself to the Peninsula Hotel Spa in Chicago. What I would give to climb into the cozy and oh-so-warm and cushy bed, flip to my stomach, and let the masseuse rub a blend of sweet orange, rose geranium, and lavender oils deep in my skin. My body swayed forward and back as I was lost deep in mental bliss, until the freezing cold cow-saliva water was poured on my head to wash out the soapsuds.

CLEAN, CLOTHED, and back at camp, I relaxed by the fire. As I munched on a fresh piece of meat, I let my mind drift. The Maasai had become family. For the past five nights, each Maasai had shared a story with us about being a moran. Leken began. He told us that after he was circumcised, the older morans took him on a raid as a way of congratulating him. The raid was far away and in order to reach the village, they needed to cross a small stream. Rain began to pour down in buckets, and in between bolts of lightning, the men took the cows from the enemies. They made it out of the village without getting caught, but by the time they arrived back at the stream, it had turned into a deep river. Crossing the river with the cows took extra time, so it gave their enemies time to catch up with them. As they drew closer, Leken saw that they had guns.

"Four people were killed that night, and my only age mate and closest friend was shot. He was screaming, 'Please don't leave me. Don't let me die here alone. Let me die on your shoulder.' My heart broke that day." The other men took Leken's hand and told him that he needed to keep moving forward. He needed to leave his best friend. His best friend died, and still today he is haunted by his voice.

The next night Topoika shared his story. His father was known throughout the land as one of the bravest warriors of all time. He lived during a time when the forest was bursting at the seams with lions, elephants, buffalo, and hippos. His father had told him how once, after a long day of herding cattle, he settled for the night deep in the forest and lit a fire. Out of the corner of his eye he could see a cow stray from the herd. He chased after the cow with spear and sword in hand. Upon his return to the fire, the only other light was radiating from the moon. After planting his spear in the ground, he looked up to the fire and directly across from him was not a man and not a monkey, but both at once. The monkeyman was warming his half fur/half skin hands by the same fire. They locked eyes, and within moments, the monkeyman scooped up his shield and unplanted his spear from the earth and disappeared deep into the forest.

Everyone sat in silence a while after that story, shuddering at the thought of the monkeyman.

The next night Rokoine shared his story. Many years ago when poaching was accepted and very popular, he went on a long raid for cows with four other morans. They would need to trek for days to an area near the border of Tanzania and would go without food to reach the location where they had heard a rumor that someone who was not Maasai had many cows.

"God gave the Maasai all of the cows, so this person stole from us. We were claiming back what was ours," Lanet translated for Rokoine. "One afternoon, we went to sleep under a tree because we trekked all night and were very tired. One moran stayed awake to keep watch because we were in an area known to have many elephants. But when I woke up, I was alone and the tree I was sleeping under was on fire. I quickly got to my feet and then heard gunshots. When I spotted the shooter, I could see that he was not alone —there were three white men with guns. I knew that they were poachers looking for elephants, and I knew that they thought that I was their competition. At that time, some tribesmen were paid by the white man to bring back ivory. These men were after my life. I ran, dodging bullets, until I was safe in a dense part of the forest.

"When I arrived back home, I found the morans who had left me. They were shocked to see that I was alive. Even my mother cried when I came home because she was sure I was dead. I was very angry at the morans and wouldn't let them speak to me. But my mother told me I needed to listen to them. It turns out they had tried to wake me up when the shooting started, but because I was in such a deep sleep, they were unable to rouse me. They even carried me to another tree because the first tree went up in flames when bullets hit it. When they reached another tree and I still was not awake, they thought I was dead. The guns started again and they needed to protect themselves, so everyone separated. By the time I woke up, the second tree was on fire."

When Rokoine finished talking, Lanet shook his head and said, "I heard this story when I was a young boy. It is so much worse when you hear it directly from Rokoine." Rokoine interrupted Lanet, and he translated, "He said that he was unable to sleep for a month after he heard the truth. To this day, he is still nervous to fall asleep because he is afraid that he will not wake up if an animal attacks.

THE FOLLOWING NIGHT was Lanet's turn to share. "It was one of those good days when there was plenty of rain, milk and honey, and the cows had enough to eat. I was relaxing on the green lawns outside my house along with many other morans who came to visit. 'Let's go on a trek,' my good friend Santiya, who was four to five years older than me, said. We said yes and set off toward one of the densest parts of the forest where a huge river drains its water to the lakes Magadi and Natron. Before we reached the river, we could hear the hippos slurping water. I was busy making fun of my cousin Otumoi for eating honey that made him act very crazy and break out in hives all over his body. I now know that he probably is allergic to honey, even though he still eats it. He was so lazy after he ate the honey that he couldn't even carry his own spear. All of a sudden, I heard another moran, Ole Karasha, whistling to notify us that there was danger. Otumoi summoned all his strength and went to the highest point of a tree, and Ole Karasha came face to face with the hippo."

With his teeth clenched, Lanet shook his head and continued, "I can't possibly describe the size, but in an instant Ole Karasha speared the hippo and it went wild chasing him! He was calling for backup, and soon six of us went to his rescue. I threw my spear and got the hippo right between its ears, but it didn't stop the beast. Now my spear was only acting like a horn in the hippo's neck muscles."

My back tensed as I listened to Lanet. "Santiya was the last to arrive, and when he threw his spear, the hippo concentrated all its attention on him. It looked like he was not going to stop until Santiya was dead. The hippo chased him toward a tall, thin tree. He rushed atop the tree with the hippo hot on his heels. I was hidden nearby mourning my spear, which was now broken in half. Santiya was up the tree, but the tree looked as appetizing to the hippo as a milk-soaked loaf of bread would for our teeth! The hippo opened its mouth and closed his jaw on the tree trunk. The trunk snapped and Santiya began his plead for help: 'Don't let me die! I don't even have a single child who belongs to my clan. Doesn't anyone remember that I am my mother's last born? Where are the warriors who shared milk from the same gourd? Oh God! I don't have children yet. Save me!'

"Ole Karasha got so furious about his cries that he started ranting—jumping and screaming on his own, not helping the situation at all. I then realized the tree was almost falling. I rushed with what I had—my sword—but then Otumoi shouted down from his perch that his spear was under the tree. I grabbed the spear and delivered the last blow to the hippo. I hit him with such heft that he ran toward the river, bypassing the ranting Ole Karasha and splashing into the water. And just as the hippo was out of the way, the tree fell completely and Santiya came crashing down. Santiya broke his leg, which he was fine with because he still had his life and thus time to bring children into the world."

I think everyone dreamt of Santiya that night, but I laid awake for hours worrying about the danger that was to come.

The next night everyone was tired from a long day of trekking and spear practicing, but Otumoi had a story he was anxious to tell. When he was a young moran, he was out herding cattle. He trekked to an area where he had never been before to find fresh grass. While the cows were happily eating grass, a buffalo showed up. The ugly snorting black monster stared at him, and Otumoi lost his nerve. He knew that he was never supposed to leave his cattle, but he also knew that his life would be over in a few short seconds if he didn't run. So he did. He ran and ran, but the buffalo was right behind. While Otumoi was sprinting and looking over his shoulder to see where the buffalo was, he tripped and fell into a ditch. The buffalo caught up to him in a few short moments, got hold of his olkarasha, and ripped it off his body.

"I think God was with me because he got me out of the ditch and away from the buffalo," Lanet translated and continued. "He ran home naked to his mother, and when he got home, his mother was so angry that his olkarasha was gone that she told his father to whip him for losing it."

And then Magilu's turn was up, with Lanet translating. "One time at orpul, we slaughtered two cows and created a home for the other five because we had seven in number. On the third day, we started having unwelcome visitors. You would think life was perfect with two cows to slaughter, but it was not. After enduring the rain for close to three hours, we tried to have a short sleep, but we were invaded by ants."

Lanet stopped for a moment to describe the ants. "You have never seen ants like these before. They are nicknamed by the Maasai as buffalo ants because they are ruthless."

Lanet continued Magilu's story, "We spent another hour burning herbs to chase the ants away. I was at the far end of the bed about to fall asleep when I heard a small crack-like noise from the other end of our camp. Our meat was hanging using long poles crisscrossed over the bed." As Lanet finished his sentence, I looked at our meat, which was also hanging over our bed. I looked at Becca and said, "I told you that meat hanging over our bed was a bad idea. We haven't even heard the end of this story, but I already know where this is going."

Becca rolled her eyes, "Calm down."

Lanet continued translating for Magilu. "As you can see, the poles are only strong enough to hold the meat, and that is done on purpose because if an animal tries to get the meat, the poles will break and that will wake up the morans if they are sleeping. As I lay awake waiting to get the exact position of the noise, the two poles that ran across our bed came down. As quickly as possible I grabbed a branch and lit it on fire. There was an extra noise like a growl mixed with the shouting and screaming of the morans. Then by the light of my flame, I saw a beautifully printed mass of a thing jumping up to the nearest branches. It was a leopard stealing our meat. No one was hurt that night, but the leopard did fall on top of a moran, and he stood shaking by a tree before breaking into an uncontrollable rant. He screamed and jumped for an hour and ran off into the forest. When he returned, he was not any calmer. He ran through the sticks of the gate and through our spears, knocking everything over and only stopping because he had huge gashes all over his body."

I knew this setup of the meat over our sleeping heads thing was insane. I jumped to my feet and scanned the small plot of land for a more suitable location. I pointed simultaneously to the intestines and slabs of meat hanging above our bed and at a tree at the bottom of camp, "Why don't we hang the meat in that tree? It is far enough away, but close enough so that if an animal tries to steal our food, we can react quickly enough." Lanet shook his head, which infuriated me. "Lanet! A leopard falling on your head is NOT an experience that should be repeated." He looked at me blankly. I wasn't getting through to him. "I am serious Lanet! We could easily make sure it never happens again by simply moving the meat branch."

"We are not moving the branch. That tree that you suggest is too far away. Every second counts. The problem is that you do not know what it is like to go without food. When you know hunger, then you will happily do anything to protect your food."

I took a deep breath, accepted that he had a point, and said, "You're right."

THE LAST STORY was Maani's. While he was a moran, he accepted work for a safari company. He was responsible for driving the jeep while another Maasai, who spoke English, talked with the white tourists. With a full capacity of clients aboard, he set out in the morning for a game drive. He was looking for a pack of cheetahs in the vast reserve when suddenly he came across a herd of elephants grazing with young ones.

Lanet interrupted Maani and said, "As you and Becca know, families of elephants are very dangerous to anything or anyone who would seem a threat to the young ones. Elephants are very protective and organize in a manner that in case there is danger, there is always one in charge."

Lanet motioned for Maani to continue. Then he translated, "On seeing the herd of elephants, the tourists got on top of their seats, and since most white people think that the elephants are funny and will actually not hurt them, they did not listen to the safari guide and used their cameras, clicking for pictures. The other guide immediately warned them that noise was not tolerated at the park and, of course, told them about other rules including not getting out of the car, but they did not listen. One elephant that was visibly disturbed by the noise and the intrusion stood in their way and brought the car to a stop, which caused the engine to turn off. This was very dangerous, considering that the elephant expected the intruder, the vehicle, to move away. The tourists finally understood their dangerous position, so they got back in the car and held their breath, waiting for the worst to happen. As Maani tried to start the engine, the added noise increased the elephant's anger and soon the herd turned toward the group and trumpeted, making very scary noises."

Maani spoke again, via Lanet: "I have had many experiences with elephants. I was not scared, but the problem was that the car refused to start."

Lanet continued. "The elephant that was supposedly the leader and the one charged with taking care of the rest came forward hurriedly, with his big ears raised. The tourists started screaming. Maani, being a Maasai moran and a professional, leaped out of the car, raising his hands and shouting. This was meant to attract the elephant's attention toward himself and thus reduce the danger to the clients. Immediately, the beast saw him—and he also lost his professionalism and ran back to the car. The elephant came toward him and plunged his tusks into the car. One tusk went behind the driver's seat while the other one went between Maani and the front of the car. It was a close shave and when the elephant withdrew his tusks, Maani lurched toward the ignition and with a newly acquired energy, the car came to life. He saved lives, but the management fired him because they didn't understand why the car was turned off."

The stories brought us together and helped us form a more cohesive unit. Everyone shared something close to his heart, and we agreed that at the end of our time in orpul, if Becca and I made it through alive and successfully, then we would share a story about being a moran.

As we sat around the campfire, I asked Lanet if the other men thought we were improving. Lanet asked them, and as the men paused to reflect on his question, I gazed at the crackling blood-orange flame. The eldest, Topoika, broke the silence first. Lanet translated in bits and pieces.

"You have come not knowing anything about the Maasai life. You are slow on treks, your aim of the spear needs to be improved a lot, but you have made progress. I am surprised that you have made it this long. I did not think the two of you would want to stay in orpul, not because of the danger, but because we are so different. We can teach you the physical, but only you can teach your mind."

As Topoika spoke more, Lanet sat still as a statue.

"What's wrong?" I asked.

Lanet looked up, his eyes telling me that he was still deep in thought. "I didn't realize this would happen so quickly. I am so very happy. This man just said that he believes the two of you just might have a chance. You just might have a chance to be the first female morans. This is a very great sign."

A bolt of energy ran down my spine and, like a slingshot, rocketed back up to my skull. I knew that we were getting stronger and that our bush smarts were improving exponentially, but I had no clue this was how Topoika felt. I made eye contact with Topoika and bowed my head in his honor.

LATER, WITH BECCA snug as a bug in her worm and me not, we spoke for the first time about how much we wanted to call our loved ones back home. Becca wanted to tell her parents all about the journey to Loita, the Maasai we were living with, and the blood that we drank. She also wanted to call her boyfriends to shoot the breeze. "That's one thing that I miss the most," she said. "I spent hours on the phone every day just chatting with my guys."

I, on the other hand, really wanted to check my e-mail to see if Mr. Plank had responded to the letter I sent from the Holiday Inn. I was still holding three letters that I needed to somehow figure out how to work into a proper mail system because there sure as hell weren't any mail trucks out here. Hell, there wasn't even a place to buy stamps. Hell squared, the Maasai don't have a written language, so there isn't even a need for paper and pen.

I noticed that Lanet, Leken, and Rokoine were talking more than usual that night as Becca and I playfully discussed a plan to break out of camp to use our cell phones.

"You tie Lanet to a tree with his olkarasha," she said.

"And you flash a boob. The rest of the team will be so shocked by seeing a white tit for the first time in their lives that they will surely be paralyzed." We laughed ourselves to sleep that night.

"Mindy! Becca! Wake up! Wake up! Wake up!"

Startled into consciousness, I opened my eyes and realized that the sky was still a deep blue. It was way too early to be awake, which made me think, "Animal!" Wild-eyed, I flung my torso up and cried, "What happened?"

Lanet didn't respond immediately, so I hopped to my feet and saw that Topoika and Otumoi were the only other warriors remaining in camp. Something was terribly wrong.

"Where is everyone?" Lanet was still silent. Grabbing his shoulders and shaking him furiously, I asked again, but this time much louder, "What is going on? Lanet! Is there an animal? What happened? Talk to me!"

He stepped back and out of my grip, "You and Becca will go on a trek now." I shot a terrified look at Becca, still in her sleeping bag, with eyes bugged and lips pinched together. Lanet continued, "This is a test. Grab your spears. Everyone else is outside of camp."

It was one thing to trek in daylight when you maybe had a second to react if you saw an animal charging. But the key word was "saw." The only sense that I could use in the dark was my hearing because my sense of smell wasn't keen enough yet to warn of danger.

"Warriors work at all hours," Lanet replied with no sympathy to my trepidation. "I know you're scared, and for that reason alone we need to practice."

With spears in hand, we walked out of the gate. Outside of camp was a wide, open field. With the help of light from the stars, my eyes gradually adjusted and I was able to see a step or two in front of me, but no more. In that way, Becca and I dutifully followed Lanet and Topoika (the leaders) with the rest of the crew trailing behind us into the forest where, within one stride, complete darkness dropped like a curtain. My heart went into triple time. I couldn't see a thing, but I could feel Becca and the presence of the other Maasai behind me. I had no idea if I was going to trip over a log or a lion. My teeth chattered uncontrollably. All I could think about was fleeing back to camp, or at least back to the field where there was a hint of light. But it was as if I was getting mixed messages, with part of my mind and body pushing me forward and the other part holding me back. Thankfully, the parts pushing me forward made up at least 51 percent of me.

The trek got harder and harder as we climbed up steep inclines. I tripped over and over again but was always able to catch myself on the descent—until I didn't. My ankle buckled and on the way down, I felt something pierce my shin. But there was no time to focus on the pain because seconds later a deep grunting sound reverberated through the forest from a tree above.

Springing to my feet, I called out, "Lanet! What is that?"

There was a crunching of twigs and leaves, and all of a sudden I felt a hand on my shoulder. I gasped as Lanet whispered in my ear, "You need to be quiet. There are other animals in this forest that you don't want to bother."

"But what was that sound?" I whispered back. "It's coming from the trees right above us."

"A leopard," he said with a solid, steady voice. My heart beat even faster, and my breath shortened. With a panic attack forming, I could feel a full-blown breakdown with tears and sobbing creeping on. This warrior thing wasn't worth it. I couldn't protect myself from a leopard and neither could Lanet or Topoika or all of the men combined. Should I just play dead or run? My sprint was more like a geriatric stroll compared to a leopard. And where would I run? I didn't know this forest—especially not in the dark— and if a leopard wanted to kill me, a leopard would kill me.

Then my mind shifted to a more discouraged place. What was I trying to prove out here? If Maasai women wanted to become morans, then they would figure out how to get it done. A Jewish American Princess wasn't going to prove anything other than reinforce the belief that women are not as strong or brave as men. Living in the United States was hard enough—I didn't need to increase the danger by being here. As we stood still, I came up with excuse after excuse about why it would be okay for me to go back to my pecan-encrusted sea bass with roasted potatoes and a glass of pinot noir.

Lanet sensed my meltdown and said, "This mission is bigger than you. And you are bigger than you think. React only when a reaction is needed. The leopard is timid. More afraid of you than you are of it. The leopard does want to prey on you—the human is too big. Let's keep moving, but very quietly."

And with that, all I heard were his feet crunching the leaves as he walked away. I swallowed hard, pushing the panic down and out of me, regripped my spear, lifted my head high, and continued to follow in Lanet's footsteps with Becca and the crew close behind me.

The next thing I knew, we were back in the open field and then at camp. Feeling instantaneously and irrationally safer, I could feel a dampness and stickiness where my shin met my leggings, and the pain in my ankle returned in force. Hobbling a bit, I dumped my body on the bed and took a look. My leggings were torn down the front, but the material was stuck to my skin with dried blood. I could tell by the light of the fire that the gash wasn't too deep. If I were back home, I wouldn't even think of going to the hospital for stitches for a wound like this, and my ankle was going to be okay, too. I could differentiate between actually spraining an ankle, which I did while playing ice hockey, and a mere roll of the ankle, which I experienced on multiple occasions while strutting in four-and-a-half-inch heels.

Pulling at the fabric would only reopen the wound, bringing about fresh blood, so I asked Becca to get me some drinking water and a clean tank top from my bag. I poured the water on my leg, gently rubbing the wounded area with a portion of my shirt. This action released the fabric from the skin, and I slowly removed my leggings from under my olkarasha. Blood was trickling out of the wound, but at least I knew that it was relatively clean. Pulling my sword out of its holster, I sliced off a clean piece of the tank top and created a tourniquet for my leg.

Becca watched in amazement, "How did you know how to do that?" I told her that in high school I became an emergency medical technician. I didn't think I remembered anything, but apparently I was wrong.

No one felt the need to discuss the surprise trek. Back in camp as one unit, we climbed into the cigar box and slept hard.

10

Playing Hooky

ANOTHER FIFTEEN CHIPS in the bark marked a total of twenty-two days in orpul. While my cravings for Western food and conveniences had mostly faded, my addiction to sending and receiving e-mail remained strong. Sure, when it came time to wash my underwear and olkarasha, I wished I had a washing machine and some Tide soap. But applying a positive perspective, I found that washing by hand provided a nice break in routine. When breakfast came along, I pretended that I was eating cinnamon and sugar French toast and scrambled eggs instead of goat.

I even got through a full menstrual cycle without being hunted by a lion. The men knew when Becca and I menstruated because of our smell. Maasai women traditionally went in the woods alone and sat over a hole until their cycle was complete, but since we were training to become morans, we assured the group that we needed to carry out our day-to-day activities no matter what. Becca and I knew it was not going to be a problem, but proving it shocked the men even more than a surprise elephant attack, which now occurred every three to five days. Becca and I had become accustomed to elephants and rather than running up a tree, we were part of the front line making *OOO! oooOOOO! oooooOOOO oooooooooo OOOOOO!!!* calls and throwing sticks of fire. And while it became somewhat routine for an elephant to come around, the presence of one was never to be taken lightly. Also, since we had learned how to build a fire, Becca and I were now the ones in charge of that.

Lanet taught us to use our senses to determine which animals were near. When we saw tree trunks broken, we knew to look for *where* they were broken. The height of the break would warn us whether a buffalo or an elephant had done the damage. We learned which poop came from which animal and were tested when we went on treks. The buffalo and elephant ate grass, shrubs, and leaves, so their poop was primarily green. The main difference between the two was the size of the pile. The hyena ate meat and bone, so their poop was gray, and since the lion ate mainly meat and blood, their poop was a dark red.

We also could tell where animals rested by the hair they left behind. Lanet taught us to lick our palms and place them on the ground where we saw hair. The hair would stick to our palms, making it easier to examine. Based on the color of the hair, we knew which animal was near. The buffalo's hair was short, coarse, and dark brown or black. The long blonde hairs were always the lion's, but we could even tell whether a lion was healthy depending on the color of the mane. The darker and fuller the mane, the healthier the lion.

The poop identification I got down, but I was a bit slow at noticing animal prints in the ground. When I was finally alert enough to notice a print, I could usually figure out what had left it. The elephant was easy because it was the largest print in the forest. I could fit both of my feet in one elephant footprint. Identifying the lion footprint versus the leopard footprint was difficult not only because it was so rare to see these prints, but also because they looked very similar: four toe prints (typically with claw marks coming out of the top) above a larger oval section. The differentiating factors were that the leopard's toe prints are a bit rounder than the lion's, and the lion's overall print is larger than the leopard's. The hyena's footprints also looked similar to the lion's and the leopard's—with four toes on top of a larger oval pad—but the two outside toes of the hyena are curved like kidney beans and the prints are the smallest of the three. Finally, the buffalo print looked like a heart divided down the center.

We went on longer and longer treks to build endurance and get our bodies accustomed to going longer and longer without food. We rarely saw anyone who didn't sleep in the cigar box, but on the rare occasion that we passed an *enkaji,* we would stop in to say "Ashe Ooleng." And while I never thought that I would tolerate goat (fill in body part) soup, I was now drinking it by the mug. I even thought that I could tell the difference between goat-stomach and goat-head soup, but apparently only the most delicate of Maasai palates could differentiate between the two, so the Maasai thought I was full of it.

On our twenty-second night, Lanet told us that we would be leaving camp in two days to make our way to a more danger-ous area, where we would encounter buffalo, hippos, and even more elephants. We would go hungry for two or three days, and our daily treks would be significantly longer and harder. We had stayed at our present camp for an extended period of time because we needed to learn the ways of the forest and the ani-mals and we needed to build a bond with the other Maasai. We'd accomplished all of those goals and were ready to take on a more difficult challenge. Since we were going to be on the move soon, I wrote another letter to Mr. Plank (see Appendix, Letter 5).

THE NEXT AFTERNOON Becca and I decided that, since we were moving to an unknown location for an unknown period of time, we should take the opportunity to make a couple of phone calls and check e-mail. Becca wanted to speak with her boyfriends and parents, and I really wanted to know if I got into business school and if Mr. Plank had responded to my letters. At this point

I had written a number of letters to the Under Armour corporate headquarters and even managed to send some via the bush mail "system," consisting of handing a letter to a boy herding cattle. Assuming that (a) the boy was going in the direction of Narok, the closest city; (b) was willing to walk about thirty kilometers; and (c) a lion or hyena didn't eat the letter or the boy for lunch then my letter may have a chance of getting out of Loita. And then another journey would begin in Narok. I had visions of my letter crammed in the pocket of someone on a local mutatu (bus) to Nairobi who, instead of respectfully placing the letter in a mailbox, would open it, find someone that could read, and the two of them would laugh hysterically at my attempts to gain a pen pal.

"Who is this Mr. Plank and a female moran? Never!" one of them would say, waving the letter in the air like a white flag.

The other guy would agree, "This girl has lost her brain! This Mr. Plank doesn't want to get a letter from a crazy girl." They would make the decision to spare Mr. Plank hearing from a crazy girl, and together they would crumple the letter and throw it out the window, at which point it would be eaten by a lion. But there was still a chance that Mr. Plank received one of my letters, which meant that he may have sent me an e-mail. And I may have heard about my status on the business school wait-list. That minute possibility was enough to take the risk: I was going to smuggle my BlackBerry out of camp, find reception somewhere, and check in.

"I know there's a place north of the cow-saliva watering hole that has cell phone reception. I overheard Lanet mention it the first day we came to orpul," I said to Becca.

"Perfect. Should we ask Lanet if we can use our phones, or do you think that's a bad idea?"

"Why would it be a bad idea?"

"I don't know . . . maybe it goes against some kind of orpul rule."

I thought about it. There was a fifty-fifty chance that she was right, but now that I had the idea to use my phone, I had to make it happen.

"You have a really good point. I don't think we should say anything. Let's take the cell phones when everyone is sleeping and head out."

"This will be the first time we're alone on a night trek. Are you cool with that?" Becca asked.

Without a second thought, I said "Sure. We know how to use our spears, we are in much better physical shape than when we arrived, and night doesn't scare me anymore." As the words flowed out of my mouth, I knew that I was putting up a slight front, but I was getting good at the "act as if" act. Also, Lanet told us that this area was not as dangerous as where we were going, so I thought that it would be our last chance of getting this breakout done somewhat safely.

Becca, with her usual breezy outlook, agreed that tonight was the night, so we went into strategic planning mode. We would try our best to get Lanet to tell us in more detail where the cell phone reception could be found. If that failed, we knew the general direction and we would continue to circle the area until the little bars of reception appeared on our screens. We would sleep with boots and swords on so that we wouldn't make any additional noise, and we would tuck our cell phones in our bras at some point before bed.

Becca and I made the bed, which seemed increasingly ludicrous as each day passed. Even though it would seem that heaping more leaves on top of each other would add comfort, it didn't help one iota; by the time we woke up in the morning, the once-soft leaves were crispy, torn to shreds, and piled by our feet due to gravity dragging our bodies down.

Becca and I were not great at maintaining good poker faces. At dinner, Lanet even commented on how happy we looked.

"It must be the goat-head soup," he said.

After dinner, the gathering around the fire was unusually energetic. Magilu told Lanet that he never thought a woman could be so strong.

"Mindy is too strong even for a man. Maybe she is part animal," he said to Lanet. Magilu's comment opened up the floodgates, and one after another the Maasai said something about Becca or me.

Rokoine spoke next, "Mindy has a lightness of heart, but anger in her eyes. Even a buffalo would run away in fear. And Becca brings fun to all. You must smile when Becca is near."

Topoika chimed in, "These girls are heaven-sent because they bring happiness and show us something different. Maybe as a tribe we will do something new because of what we learned here, and maybe we won't, but at least these girls have the interest to show us something new."

Leken added, "You and Becca are courageous. You came very far from a place where you can get everything to a place full of problems."

Finally Otumoi observed, "Mindy looked too round to run from a buffalo or climb a tree, but she has proven to be much stronger than she looks."

His words stung a little, because he touched upon an issue that I had struggled with all my life: never totally looking the part I wanted to play. In gymnastics, I was a brute. In figure skating, I was too fat to be graceful. In ice hockey, I was the wrong sex. When starting my business, I was too young and supposedly too "inexperienced." And now here in the bush, I was both the wrong sex and too fat. Then, with a change in perspective, I found a common theme—other people's perceptions of my abilities did not stop me, and I often changed their minds.

Lanet finished by telling us that a *laibon,* or fortune-teller, told him that two mzungus would bring him significant joy and hardship. "And I have found every day there is a balance—either Mindy brings the joy and Becca the hardship or vice versa."

As the stars faded and the moon took control of the sky, I knew the time to seek the signal was closely approaching. The snoring was loud and proud, and Magilu and Leken's middle-of-the-night snack came and went. Once I was sure everyone was in a deep meat coma, it was time to go. I poked Becca's worm, and she silently slid out.

With our gear already in place and cell phones tucked in our bras, we grabbed our spears and headed in the general direction Lanet had pointed out on day one. We climbed over a few boulders and into the dense forest. As we walked, we continued to check our phones for reception. Their manufactured glow felt foreign. We had been one with nature for twenty-three days. While the prospect of hearing from business school was incredibly tempting, it didn't feel right. My gut told me clearly that the phone didn't belong in this environment, but within twenty minutes, we found service. It was just too tempting to ignore.

"I got it. Vodacom." I said.

I looked ahead and noticed a clearing just beyond a group of trees that seemed safer than where we were. We headed toward a small mound in its midst, and sitting on the hill, we checked our devices. Nothing from Mr. Plank, but there *was* an e-mail from the head of admissions at the school I was wait-listed for: The University of Chicago Booth School of Business. She wanted to have a chat. Since it was 1 a.m. in Kenya, it was 5 p.m. in Chicago, and I decided to make the call.

"Hello, this is Mindy Budgor."

She recognized me immediately. "Hi, Mindy, how are you?" she asked. "I understand that you're having a very interesting trip."

"Indeed."

"You're exactly the type of student we're looking for at Chicago Booth to continue our efforts to diversify our student body. You're on a short list of students to come here in the fall, but if we don't have space this year, please know that we want you here next year. So please keep in close touch with me."

Twenty-two days ago, I would have taken her response as a personal failure, but not any more. This was great news. I was going to attend the school of my dreams—maybe not at the time I expected, but I'm one with the Maasai now, and in Maasailand expectations are a waste of time.

"Thank you! I'll be in touch."

"Come back alive! We want you at Chicago Booth!"

"And Chicago Booth is exactly where I want to be. I will see you soon. Thanks again." I hung up the phone and turned to Becca, who was on the phone with her parents. "Dad, you would totally love it out here. We are on the ultimate safari!" She looked up at me and held her phone between her ear and shoulder, freeing her hands to give me a thumbs-up with her left hand and a palm to the sky with the other. I grabbed her thumb and she smiled, the whites of her eyes almost glowing in the dark.

Directly south there was a crunching of leaves. Becca and I looked at each other with eyes bugged.

"Hey, Dad, I got to go. I'll bring you a lion's mane headdress."

Then there was a snapping of tree branches, and we heard the very distinct laughing and screaming combination that only comes from the bone-crushing hyena. The hair on my forearms spiked, and all my senses seemed to focus and tune in.

"Hyena," I whispered.

"Hyena," Becca confirmed.

Many people think of hyenas as not much of a threat because they're known for being timid, but they become significantly more aggressive at night, killing 95 percent of their food and able to end a gazelle's life with a single bite to the neck.

As we jumped to our feet and grabbed our spears, I said, "In case of hyena, scream."

"Scream, don't show a hyena fear. They will eat us alive if . . ." her voice trailed off and I finished the statement, ". . . they sense a hint of fear."

My entire body was so rigid that my butt muscles began to twitch. Leaves on the periphery of the forest were quivering.

"Screw this, I am a warrior," I told myself and from the depths of my lungs out came *"rrrrraaaaaahhhhhhOOOOOOOOO!! OOOOO, OOOOOO!! Sorr, HORR OLAG OLAG!!! SORR!!!!"*—a half-growl, half-hoot meant to cause the hyena to run away from us. It seemed to work, but Becca and I stood listening to the silence for a good three minutes before trusting that we were in the clear. Then, with one nod of our heads, we bolted back to camp.

"Motherfucker! Motherfucker! Motherfucker!" My voice rang in my head as my knees were pumping so hard and so high that with each step forward the bottom of my boobs felt like a punching bag. *Left, right. Pow! Pow! Ouch. Ouch. Left, right. Pow! Pow! Ouch. Ouch.* But this was not the time to be thinking about my boobs. I shone the light from my BlackBerry on the ground directly in front of me to help me keep up a quick pace and not trip, but it was too weak to be of use and I returned to my instincts. They told me a hyena was south of us and either the same hyena or some other beast was to our west. This was bad. I wished I could use my cell phone and call the camp for backup, but no one would pick up because no one else had a phone! And even if they had cell phones, they wouldn't have service.

Becca and I continued to sprint, lungs now burning with every breath. I could see the end of the forest quickly approaching. Then, out in the clearing, I saw six Maasai men standing with spears cocked, ready to kill. They were much scarier than the hyena, and I was tempted to turn around and go back in the forest to face whatever animals were now awake as they would surely be easier to deal with than a bunch of pissed-off warriors. Deciding that I would treat the morans the way that I treated the hyena, I barreled toward them with spear ready to fly and out came the same growl/hoot:

"*rrrrraaaaahhhhhhOOOOOOOOO!! OOOOO, OOOOOO!! Sorr, HORR OLAG OLAG!!! SORR!!!!,*" I screamed and ran right past my fellow morans and into camp, where I lodged my spear in the earth and promptly returned to my bed as if nothing had happened. With chest heaving up and down, still desperate for oxygen and sweat dripping down my cheeks and rolling into my ears, I wondered if I could pretend that they were hallucinating, that Becca and I had never broken out of camp like convicts to use our cell phones. Coming down from the shock, I laughed to myself until I felt multiple sets of eyes blazing down on me.

"Mindy, I think you and Becca are now morans," Lanet said and smiled.

In between laughs, I asked him why. He said, "Because you have fully lost your minds. You should go look at Becca."

"Why? Where is she?"

"She took it upon herself to find firewood. I never thought I would see the day when she would take it upon herself to do tasks without someone telling her what was needed. Now she is a moran thinking of the community, not just of herself."

Becca returned with two hunks of wood under her armpits. After she maneuvered them onto the low flame, she wrapped her olkarasha around her shoulders, and we both sat with looks on our faces like two naughty children who got caught doing something we knew we should not have done. I waited for the parental lecture to begin, but it never did. Rather, Lanet was proud of us for showing courage and independence. He also told us that we were morons (not morans) for not telling him that we wanted to call home, as there was no orpul rule that we couldn't use our cell phones. He said that the preference was for everyone to live without material possessions, but of course we should notify our families that we are okay.

Thinking it over later that night, what I found most interesting was that the Maasai were not angry with us for purposely being devious. They didn't see it that way because they knew who we were—good people at a core level. It made me think of the times I acted out as a kid by coming home past curfew, or doing something that resulted in a phone call from the principal, and how each and every time my parents would respond with anger rather than respect. When I finally drifted off, the black sky had turned a navy blue, and I didn't wake until the sun was out in full force, baking the land.

THE NEXT DAY was a lazy but full one. The following morning we would leave camp and head to unknown and dangerous territory. So this day Lanet was basically force-feeding us, telling us that we would not eat for days and now was the time to fill our stomachs. In addition, we didn't want to take the remaining parts of the goat with us. And since the Maasai don't believe in waste, the only place for the meat to go was down the proverbial hatch.

That afternoon Lanet took us on a trek. Just as the sun was setting, he perched on a boulder overlooking the hills and forests of Loita, pointed in the distance, and explained that from where we were sitting you could see Mount Kilimanjaro and Mount Lenkai on a clear day. The sky glowed like the inside of a peach: gold on top with the maroon and mauve of a pit peeping up from the hills. The magical sunset inspired a conversation about faith. Lanet explained that the Maasai religion is not typically defined, because it has no regimented or written creed or

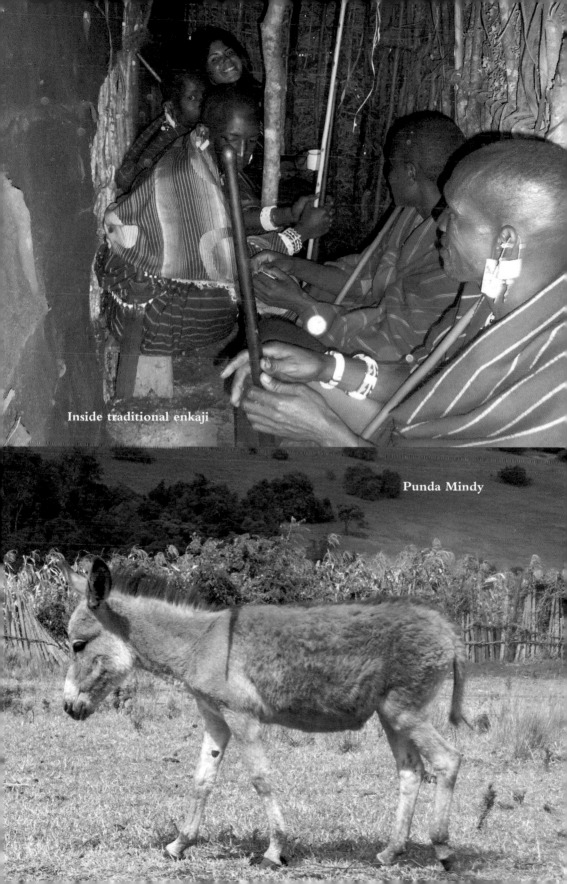

Inside traditional enkaji

Punda Mindy

The ceremonial manyatta

Thousands of Warriors marching to ceremonial manyatta

Marching to ceremonial manyatta for wedding

With Magilu and Topoika at manyatta

Maasai women

At Lesikarr's wedding

Lesikarr and bride

Noolamala

Jumping competition

My
hair-smacking
opponent

Eating goat's
ear at wedding

Younger warrior group

Kinyi and friends—future warriors?

code as in other religions, like Christianity or Islam. The Maasai believe in their god, Enkai, as supreme in all ways: giver of life, children, and wealth in terms of cows, wives, and basically everything that makes a Maasai life complete. Their god has a dual nature, the black (benevolent) side and the red (vengeful) side. Enkai's two faces are responsible for the good and the bad, as well as punishment of the wrongs committed by the people. The black God represents the blue sky that brings rain that gives life to everything—plants, animals, and people—while the red God represents death and misfortunes through lightning and thunderstorms.

Laibons are the tribe's spiritual leaders, living mediators, go-betweens, and representatives of the Maasai to God. They are not worshipped but very much respected. The Maasai totally believe in their god because their god gives unconditionally except in times of drought. Then the intervention of sacrifices by laibons is required, and normally the answers are immediate. The sacrifices are offered to seek forgiveness for unknown or known wrongs done.

By the end of the day, my stomach was convex. I stroked my belly like an expecting mother and said, "Becca, meet my baby goat."

"For real. I think we are due at the same time." We smiled and she continued, "I have never eaten so much meat in my life."

The hours passed quickly, and soon the stars sprinkled the sky. Once again we were together as a unit—as a family—sitting around the fire. The Maasai were unusually animated, telling stories about one another. It felt like Becca and I were even more in the fold with the tribe.

Everyone was laughing when Topoika got to his feet and started to sing, which cued the rest of us to rise. His throaty grunt woke up the trees, giving them a heartbeat that pulsed from their trunks. The last time I'd heard the Maasai sing was back at the volunteer center, and while that experience brought the gazebo to life, there was something deeper happening inside me now. Feeling my heartbeat thump in my ears, my body joined the rhythm, gently rocking back and forth. Topoika's grunt was then joined by Rokoine's and overlapped by Leken's, and soon the rest of the men had joined in, their voices creating a sonic base. Each man's chest lifted up and released like a mermaid flapping her fin in the water. Exhaling, their necks thrust forward; inhaling, their necks recoiled. Their breathing was also in rhythm with their pelvises, lunging forward and backward, over and over again. Topoika chanted a solo while the rest of the men created a continuous buzz for the base. Then Rokoine sang, ending with a hearty laugh, which made way for Leken, who chanted like Topoika. The sound appeared to be improvised, which added playfulness to the hypnotic rhythm.

I felt the urge to join in, but didn't want to disrupt the flow. With the singing still in full force twenty minutes later, I figured that a minor disruption wouldn't be such a big issue, so I began. Mimicking came naturally because the vibration from their singing was already deep in my memory. Topoika shot an approving glance my direction and nodded to Becca to add her voice, which she did. After a few guttural noises from me, Otumoi stepped toward the fire, leaping up in the air over and over again. As his feet planted into the ground, Magilu took off like a rocket. I watched them both carefully, trying to break down their movements into simple steps that my muscles could remember: knees bent at a forty-five-degree angle, arms laid flat against sides, and in perfect harmony with the beat, spring quads and hamstrings to propel high into the star-studded sky. When each came back down to earth, I could see by the light of the fire that the impact from the landing swelled the muscles in their calves, and the veins under their deep brown skin seemed as though they were about to burst.

Lanet leaned over and whispered, "They are jumping because they are very happy you are singing."

Topoika eyed me, and I knew he wanted me to jump, but I didn't want to look like an ass. I would be lucky if I could heave myself up more than three inches off the ground. I continued on as a backup singer while Magilu sang and Maani jumped.

The singing and jumping continued in full force for at least another thirty minutes. My body and soul were owned by the music. Feeling as if the ground was coming to life and telling me to jump, I replayed the step-by-step muscular movement and went for it. My knees bent and my legs reacted, allowing me to soar in the air. As my feet hit the ground, the earth and I exchanged energy while billows of dust formed around my boots. I was part of the dance, and the dance was part of me. And while I was only airborne for a moment, for that brief moment my inner warrior was leaping out of me. It gave me faith that I was on the right path.

11

Hunger

Our trek to Olasurr Falls, a waterfall deep in the forest at least thirty miles away, would take three days from start to finish. For those three days we would go hungry. Lanet announced the no-eating thing while we were finishing breakfast. Upon hearing the news, I stuffed my face with more and more goat and searched my clothing and accessories for places to store food. My boot wouldn't work. How about in my bra? Again, gross.

"So how exactly are we supposed to trek for thirty miles without food?" I asked Lanet. "That's a really long distance up and down mountains. I just want you to think in advance what it will feel like to drag or carry me."

"The tribe takes care of one another, but that is because each person gains respect by doing his share. We don't have sympathy for those who are weak because of laziness." Lanet then told us that we would have a small ceremony, called *ormayian,* which is done every time morans leave orpul. As we packed for the journey, Lanet explained that leaving home is very common for Maasai men.

"We leave our families for days and maybe weeks and months if there is not enough grass and water for the cattle and goats to feed on. We must always take the animals to the best grazing areas. We need our cattle healthy, not emaciated. If they are too thin, we will not be able to sell them for good money when we need it."

"So basically the men go on business trips," I said. "People do that all over the world."

Lanet processed this information a few minutes.

"Yes, exactly, but things are changing. I have been telling many people in Loita that their lives would be easier if they let their wives leave home to work. The problem is men do not want women to have power."

Leken walked into camp just then with a bunch of olive tree branches. He threw the branches, mixed with a slab of goat fat, into the fire. We gathered in a circle around the fire and chanted our prayer: *Enkai! Ai! Ai ai ekop!* (God! God! God mine!) Exiting the camp we chanted *Kipuo kiitu*, which is the Maasai way of telling the orpul they are going to return safely.

As we hiked in the blazing sun, Maani piped out a strong melodic tone, and my heart was soon in sync with the beat of his voice. Otumoi, Rokoine, and the rest of the men joined in one by one, and as the sound strengthened, my heart beat stronger and stronger. Becca and I didn't know what we were singing, but we picked up a couple of verses and joined in. As the first guttural sound streamed out of my lungs, I felt my energy once again join forces with the land and the animals. There was something magical about the combination of the tone, the beat, and the pace that made it seem as if everything on earth became one.

As we trekked, every now and then a spear would glide above our heads and we would know that a spear-throwing competition was about to begin. Everyone took part, from Topoika all the way down the generational chain to Otumoi and Maani, including Becca and me. Watching my spear tear through the air and land close to the intended target inspired me to improve still more. Proof again that it was only a matter of practice to turn what was formerly a miserable activity into one that was inspiring.

As WE WALKED down a rocky hill and through a swamp with tall wispy blades of grass, we approached a plot of land with two traditional Maasai homes next to a gated area for cows. At the sight, Rokoine picked up his pace.

"That is Rokoine's home," Lanet told us. "We will stop for chai and meet his wives and children." My stomach sprang back to life when it found out it would be consuming something other than sips of murky water.

Crossing the swamp required strategic foot placement. I knew this from experience, for while the Maasai seemingly walked on water, my clumsy steps landed my boots, socks, and shins in lukewarm blackish gunk over and over with each step. A suction-cup effect between the bottom of my boots and the slime seemed to get stronger and stronger the longer my foot was in the mud. Sticky blades of grass acted as my lifesaver as I pulled them in handfuls and hoisted myself out of the mire. Why I kept getting stuck while everyone else, including Becca, was able to figure out how to navigate the swamp without getting sucked in was beyond me.

Thus far, we hadn't been without food. I wasn't close to starving, and even now I was about to be fed a mug of chai, which contained significant nutrients. Something didn't feel right about that. If I were a moran during a difficult time, I would be the first person to go without. Chai was a luxury. So with my stomach protesting, I decided that I was going to make it the three days with only water.

It was only when I saw the Maasai women that I remembered I hadn't been with anyone outside our little family for close to a month. As I settled next to Topoika, one of Rokoine's wives scurried over to us with hot cups of chai. Lanet had objected to my water-only plan, telling me that drinking chai should not be considered eating food and warning me of the grueling terrain ahead of us. But my mind was made up.

While the rest sipped chai, I listened as Lanet told us that Rokoine's first wife had been unable to conceive during their first fifteen years of marriage. They went to a laibon for help, hoping that he would tell them to keep trying, that a child was on the way, but he didn't. To the Maasai, not having children was basically seen as a failing. Children and cows were the sign of a man's wealth, and with hardly any cows and no children, Rokoine was somewhat of an outcast. While having multiple wives was fully acceptable in the Maasai culture, Rokoine preferred to have only one, but he and his wife made the joint decision to take on a second wife. His second wife became pregnant very quickly, and within eleven chips in the bark, his first wife announced that she was pregnant as well. Nine months later, two sons were brought into the world: Panin, born on Thursday, and Oloserian, born on Sunday.

Rokoine's little boys—one in a tattered red fleece onesie and the other in a Winnie the Pooh T-shirt and black stone-washed jean shorts at least three sizes too big—hid behind their mothers, peering at Becca and me only for a second before recoiling again. "These young boys have never seen a mzungu," Lanet explained.

Rokoine's first wife, a slender woman with a meek demeanor, spoke in a surprisingly bold tone. Lanet explained that she'd heard about us and was so pleased for us to be at her home. Lanet listened while she continued to talk, her voice growing louder and her facial expression turning stern.

"She is saying that she was always a strong girl. She'd herd the cattle for her brother when she was young, and she could protect the family from animals."

She got to her feet and walked outside. Lanet gestured and Becca and I followed. As she pointed to the swamp area, he continued to translate for her.

"Look at where we live. Elephants and buffalo are here all day because of the watering hole. The elephants and monkeys try to eat my corn and I fight them off. Why aren't I a moran?" Reaching behind her, scooping up her son, and placing him on her hip, she continued, "I don't have girls. I will not have more children, but I believe that women should be given the right to protect the tribe. I know that if I had a daughter, she would be as strong as I. There is no reason why she couldn't be a moran."

She continued to tell us that she knew that morans have opportunity to see more, do more, and even go to school.

"I am not any different from all Maasai women—we all want our children to experience more. Rokoine tells me Lanet's stories of Nairobi and university, and even though I don't want to visit Nairobi, I want my children to have options like Lanet. If they want to live the traditional Maasai life, then they will get married to a young girl of twelve or thirteen and soon after have children. But what if their children are girls and they want to be morans, go to school, or work just like the boys? They should have choices."

Rokoine's second wife was quiet while his first wife spoke. I asked Lanet to find out if she agreed with the first wife. Her voice was deep and strong, "We don't need girl morans. There are plenty of boys, and the girls need to help with other chores."

I was glad the woman was honest with me, and she brought up a good point, that the young girls filled a very important role in society. If all the young girls became morans, then who would take over chores such as fetching water and getting firewood? I didn't know and wasn't likely to solve that thorny problem for the tribe. I could see that opening warrior status to Maasai women wasn't quite as simple an issue as I had thought when I embarked on this mission.

WE LEFT SOON AFTER the last cup of chai was drunk but kept trekking much later in the day than usual because we couldn't find a safe enough area to sleep in.

"We are less than a kilometer from a hippo pool," Lanet said as the sun began to dip lower and lower in the sky. He continued, "And after the hippo pool, we will not find a place to sleep for many kilometers. We need to make camp here."

"Here" was a small patch of flat land. Tonight would be the first time in a month that we didn't sleep on an incline—I could actually lie flat. With eyes drooping, we built a fire and gathered some leaves to make a bed. The ritual of making the leaf bed still didn't make any sense to me, as it provided no additional comfort, but it seemed the Maasai believed that not sleeping on a proper bed was "undignified."

Given my hunger level, which directly related to my moodiness, I felt the need for some space, so I planned to sleep a little outside of the cigar box. I curled up at the base of a massive old fig tree instead. It had only been approximately eighteen hours since my last meal, but already I was experiencing a painful headache. I ground my teeth and dug my nails into the top of head to try and take my mind off the hunger pains. It didn't work. I pressed my palms firmly into my forehead, hoping relief would soon come. Unable to rest, I sat up and drank big gulps of water. Lanet and Topoika were still awake and sitting by the fire.

"Are you okay?" Lanet asked.

"I have a horrible headache."

"Yes. It is because you did not drink the chai."

I responded grumpily, "Listen, Lanet, I wanted to be as authentic as possible. I assume that real morans don't relax and drink a cup of chai—or two or three—when children don't have enough food."

"You are taking this to too much of an extreme. Do you know it has been years and years since the last morans were not able to eat anything because of shortages?"

I threw my hands up in exasperation. "Why didn't you tell me that earlier?"

"Because you are stiff-headed."

"Stiff-headed?"

"Yes! You act like a buffalo. I figured that you would learn after going hungry."

"Well, do you have anything I can eat now?"

"No. You need to wait for another day and a half. Now there really is nothing except water. Maybe tomorrow morning I can find you some herbs to cure your head." He turned to Topoika and said something in Maa. After Topoika's response, Lanet told me that the herbs they need are nowhere near.

The pain worsened over the next couple of hours, then suddenly with a feeling of extreme nausea, I hopped to my feet and fled to the closest area that was hidden and far enough away from camp so that no one could hear what I knew was going to be explosive diarrhea. Overcome with chills and then sweat and then chills and then both at the same time, tears rolled down my cheeks. I needed some Advil, saltines, peanut butter, and a bottle of Smartwater, *stat*. With my quads quivering but not even close to being "done," I heard a crunch of branches Seconds later, another crunch—I yanked whatever leaves were near to clean myself up, kicked some dirt over the mess, and ran to camp to find everyone asleep.

"Lanet," I whispered. No movement from the red and green tartan mound.

"Lanet," I whispered a little louder, but nothing.

Another crunch and I blurted out, "Lanet! Animal!"

Everyone sprang up, alerted by my shriek. With eyes bulging, Lanet asked me what was going on. All of the Maasai stared at Lanet, eagerly waiting for my reason for waking everyone up.

Feeling guilty because I knew how tired everyone was, I said sheepishly, "I . . . I . . . I think there is an animal."

Lanet got to his feet and spoke rapidly in Maa. With spears in hand, Lanet told Becca and me to join them. We waited and waited for another crunch, but there was nothing. Soon the group relaxed again by the fire. Feeling like an ass and totally strung out from lack of food and sheer exhaustion, I inched toward the edge of camp and poked my spear into the trees. Almost immediately there was a swishing of leaves and a loud cracking of branches only feet in front of me.

I screamed and ran back to camp. "Animal! I told you—animal!"

Everyone bounded to his feet except Becca, who mumbled from her sleeping bag, "She's crying wolf again."

"Get out of your worm!" Lanet yelled.

Magilu escorted her to a fig tree, and they proceeded to climb. I looked up into the tree and all I could see was a hint of her silver lamé bike shorts. With spears cocked, we formed a semicircle, facing the area where I heard the animal.

"Uh . . . uh . . . uh uh uh uh . . .," Topoika grunted.

A trumpet-like sound reverberated through the forest, scaring me so much that a trickle of pee dripped down my leg. Tusks and trunk thrust straight into the air, and the call indicated that the elephant was mad. We gathered sticks and set fire to them. Then there was a loud crash.

In a rushed voice, Lanet said, "He knocked down a tree. He should not be so close to the fire, but he is angry."

As we ran back to our positions in the semicircle, Lanet told me not to throw the fire until he gave the signal.

I held the fire high above my head. The bright orange and yellow light in the blackness provided a halo of light that gave me a perfect view of the elephants—plural. My heart raced.

"Lanet!" I hollered over the grunting. Lanet scurried to me and I pointed. Expressionless, he rushed to Topoika and spoke loudly. Unperturbed, Topoika nodded his head and continued grunting. When Magilu hollered something from the tree above, Lanet nodded.

Becca yelled down to me, "Four elephants! There are four elephants!" A cold sweat developed at my temples.

"Lanet!" I screamed. Then, in an extraordinarily polite manner (because for some reason, in times of great danger, I become quite the lady), I yelled, "Can I please throw this?"

"Yes! Let it fly!" I chucked the fiery sticks at the elephant nearest me. It took a step, causing branches to break and the ground to rumble, which was enough to make me retreat, plant my spear in the ground, and climb the fig tree that Magilu and Becca were sitting in. By the time I got myself up the tree, I could see the elephants lumbering away. They looked magnificent as their tails swayed from side to side, and I acknowledged that for all my terror, there was a gentleness in their nature that could not be overlooked.

Within a few minutes, everyone was packed tight in bed. We chatted briefly about the invasion, and Topoika told us that we would meet many animals in this part of the forest.

"Never leave your spear behind," he said. Even I knew that was Maasai moran Rule Number 1.

I was sleeping between Otumoi and Becca. Magilu and Becca had an instant connection from glance one, and I could tell they had been getting closer over the past few days. Touching was more frequent. She would grab his beaded wrist, or he would squeeze in next to her on an already crowded log. After this last elephant event, Becca snuggled up to Magilu, wrapping her worm around his sinewy body.

Good for her, I thought as I composed a status report to Mr. Plank (see Appendix, Letter 6).

WE AWOKE EARLY the following morning, anticipating a long and dangerous trek. We were to reach the waterfall and return to this same camp by day's end. My head was still pounding, but at least I was no longer sick to my stomach. I drank a few gulps of water and ventured out for a short walk before we left as a team.

The trek started in a very dense, steep, and narrow part of the forest. We walked in a line, one behind the other. About a kilometer in, I heard a whooshing of water below us. Peering through the trees and down at least a hundred feet, I could see a stream perhaps thirty feet wide. The water looked so clean, I wanted to dunk my body in it and drink gallons—well, actually drink gallons and then dunk my body in it—so I asked Lanet if we could climb down and get some fresh water.

"That is a hippo pool," he replied, "so unless you want to get eaten whole, stay up here."

All I knew about hippos, besides the carcass I met earlier, was from cartoons, so I said, "Oh please. Hippos wouldn't hurt a thing."

Near the front of the line, Becca stopped short in her tracks, almost causing a pileup of Maasai.

"A hippo will eat you whole with no problem," she said with surprising authority. "The hippo is absolutely the most danger-ous animal in Africa, and it is responsible for the most deaths in Africa."

Lanet chimed in, "The last time I was in this exact area, a moran taunted a hippo and was chased up a tree. The hippo was so determined to kill the moran that it rammed into the tree over and over until the moran dangled from the branches, screaming like a little girl. The moran survived, but he has never been the same since. Don't ever underestimate a hippo, and whatever you do, don't ever make a hippo angry."

The only other time that Lanet gave me such a serious look was when I freaked out when our car killed a gazelle. I got the point: Don't fuck with hippos.

Once we reached a shallow area of the river, we trekked on a ledge that was only twenty feet up.

"Go with light feet," Leken warned us.

Since it was still very early in the morning, the chance of seeing a hippo was high. As quietly as possible, I straddled over trunks and shimmied around trees. Rokoine, who was leading, suddenly stopped. Leken sped up from the back of the line to the front, and Rokoine whispered in his ear. Topoika and Maani stayed behind while Lanet and Otumoi stepped up to join Rokoine and Leken. Huddled together, they stood in silence for at least ten minutes before I decided to join the front line and find out what was going on. I took one step toward them, and Topoika pulled me back. He had never done that before, so I knew something serious was ahead.

Finally Lanet told us, in a soft-as-silk voice, that two hippos were sleeping about twenty feet ahead, and that since this was the only route to the waterfall, we had to wait until they moved.

"We could be waiting for hours. How long does a hippo sleep?" Becca asked.

"Could be all day," Lanet replied.

"Can't you grunt or throw fire at them to get them to move?"

"They are too close and too dangerous."

"So now we are just going to wait? That seems kind of unmoran-ish," I said.

"Unmoran-ish?"

"Yeah. Morans are supposed to be fearless. Are hippos the exception?"

"Above all, morans are not stupid. If we retreat, they might hear us, and then it is over. If we try to wake them up with calls, they could get angry, and then it is over. If we throw sticks at them and we are not far enough away, then it is over. You see the result in all of those cases? Our life is over. So you are right, morans need to be fearless, but they also need to not be stupid."

Lanet walked back to the huddle, and Rokoine whispered something in his ear, which Lanet then whispered to Leken, and the game of telephone continued down the line to Maani. Otumoi then guided us to a huge fir tree. He pointed his spear up the tree, which we knew meant "climb." Becca and I followed orders, and Otumoi joined us on an adjacent branch. Below, Topoika stood guard with Maani now at his side. Just ahead Lanet, Leken, and Rokoine scattered to gather sticks and rocks.

It took me a moment to locate the hippos because they blended in so well with the bark and the muddy ground, but after scanning over them at least three times, my eyes kept returning to a couple of shiny brown blobs on the edge of the trail. Hippos.

"I know Lanet told us that hippos are dangerous, but look at them. They are so tired and fat. We could probably step on them and they wouldn't care or be able to move."

Becca rolled her eyes and said, "Yeah, go try it."

Maybe an hour later, after I had picked all of the Red Dragon nail polish off my dirt-lined fingernails, and, without a mirror, plucked all of my stray eyebrow hairs using my fingernails as tweezers, I decided to act. I shimmied down the tree and took a couple of steps forward, where the huddle of men used to be, but they were gone. Unfortunately, just when I was only a few feet away from the hippos, Magilu hurled a massive stick at them, striking one of the hippos on the head. The monstrous blubbery beast swiveled its tiny, ballet slipper–pink ears in my direction, turned its head, and opened its mammoth pink mouth 180 degrees. My body froze as I stared at its freakishly large incisors and wrinkled tongue—one that could easily wrap around my waist and yank me in.

All I could hear was my heartbeat in my ears as I bolted toward the fir tree. Almost airborne, I climbed the tree and grasped onto Otumoi. I squeezed my eyelids shut as if getting eaten would be better without looking. Then I could hear Becca laughing and the crunching of leaves and branches. I opened one eye and saw the hippos making their way down the ledge and into the water.

Becca lightly punched my arm, saying, "Dude, I thought you were going to poop your pants when that hippo opened its mouth."

"Me too," I said.

Once the hippos were back in the water, we climbed down the tree, where I was greeted by a stone-faced Lanet, "Why do you continue to test the limits?"

"I didn't mean to. I just wanted to be part of the solution."

"Part of the solution? You were almost killed. Do you understand that? And if you don't care about your life, think about others. All of us would have tried to save you, which would have put our lives in danger. We work as a unit. We don't do anything independently." He was furious. "You were stupid. You were not brave. You were stupid."

As we continued our trek, I thought about Lanet's comment. I very much valued my life, and didn't put myself in danger on purpose. In this situation, I hadn't known that Magilu was ready to throw a stick just as I was in the hippo's line of sight. If I was honest, I could admit I hadn't really believed the hippos were that dangerous. But what really hit home was what Lanet said about endangering the others. They could have been injured or even killed as a result of my rogue move. He was right—I had been stupid. The Maasai are always thinking of one another. Lanet's words, "We work as a unit. We don't do anything independently," played over and over in my head. While my own family was certainly a top priority, my brother and I had been raised to be independent. The decisions that we were taught to make were based on what would maximize our personal benefit, assuming ethical standards were met. Of course I valued my life, but acting solo was ingrained in me. I needed to convert my thinking to being on an organized team, where you win as a team or lose as a team. And in the bush you lived as a team or died as a team.

Lanet mentioned that the last hill was going to be "trying." During most of the climb, I was on all fours praying to make it one more inch. The rock was slippery gravel, making it impossible for me to feel secure at any moment. There was no opportunity to falter and no room for insecurities. Each inch up resulted in hundreds of small rocks tumbling down what eventually became hundreds of feet.

On the verge of tears, I lost my grip and slid down the mountain, desperately trying to stop myself by digging my nails and toes into the earth. After sliding at least twenty feet, my boots hit a ledge and I grabbed onto an exposed root. Lanet called down to see if I was okay. After a few deep breaths, I responded with my heart banging in my chest, "Yup! All good. Be right up."

"One step must be planted before taking another."

"Got it," I replied and closed my eyes to gather myself before attempting to climb again. I was not going to give up this fight. "One foot planted and then another" I told myself as I vigilantly made my way to the peak. Once at the top, I found everyone relaxing on flat ground, but still breathing heavily.

With parched lips and with sweat bubbling down my face and between my breasts, I made my way to a patch of land under an olive tree. I dropped to my knees and twisted around to lie on my back. One good thing about keeping busy was that I hadn't had time to focus on how hungry I was, but now with time to relax, my stomach growled and my headache returned. On a typical day we would have had our fill of goat, and now I had missed one breakfast, two lunches, and soon to be two dinners. My stomach gurgled, so I loosened my belt and gently rubbed my now concave belly. No pouch left.

After a short rest, we continued our trek to the waterfall. The downward slope was just as steep as hiking up, but on this side the terrain was filled with exposed, muddy roots, footholds that made the mountain easier to descend. A few steps in and with the sounds of rushing water below, I mentally thanked my parents for all the years of ski lessons as I alternated left and right, left and right, rolling my knees from side to side with my upper body facing downhill. I was mogul skiing without snow, using broken tree branches as poles.

In this way, I was first down the hill, and once the last member of the team caught up, we climbed rocks. The boulders we couldn't hoist ourselves over, we shimmied around, knowing that one false step would pitch us into the ravine. But one after another we made it, and then we were there—in front of a magnificent waterfall. Mist from the crashing water blanketed my face. Without hesitating, I took off my boots, socks, and olkarasha and jumped in the water. The water was icy cold, but felt divine. I slapped the water and splashed it at all of the Maasai like a giddy little kid.

Moving to a more secluded area, I took off my tank top, sports bra, underwear, and leggings. The water felt so clean. I scrubbed every inch of my body with my sports bra and then did my best to clean my clothing before putting everything on again. I looked at my team staring at the water. Becca was sunbathing on a rock next to Magilu. The only person who had ever been here before was Lanet, so the look on the Maasai faces was one of astonishment. Coming from a place that experienced many droughts, to see water in such abundance for the first time must have been quite a shock. Maybe they were thinking about how to move their families closer to this water source? I would have. I was already trying to think of how to convince Lanet to make this spot our home for the rest of orpul. It was more like a spa in Switzerland than the bush in Kenya. I got out of the water and spread myself out on a rock in direct sunlight to dry off. We could only stay a few hours, as we needed to get back to camp before dark.

The trek back felt slower than the way up, but thankfully— with one foot planted and then another—I made it without any life-threatening spills. Once we safely passed the hippo pool, Magilu began chopping at trees, looking, I learned later, for a special herb to cure my headache. Then suddenly, with one swing at the bark, his sword sliced his shin. Blood flowed all over his leg and began to drip to the ground. Standing next to him, it took my brain a few moments to figure out what to do. Again, my experience as an emergency medical technician came back to me. Whipping out my sword, I cut a swath from my olkarasha and tied a tourniquet around the wound. I called for Lanet, who ran over with Leken, and calmly explained the situation. Leken took one look at Magilu's shin and ran to get what I later learned was an herb called *enabooi,* a white sap that stops bleeding. Lanet removed the tourniquet, cleaned the wound, and put the sap on it as I cut another swath from my olkarasha and tied another tourniquet. It felt like we were a well-oiled machine—a unit working together, never leaving one person behind.

Becca and I trailed the group on the way back to camp.

"Did you see Magilu's wound?" I asked her. She nodded. "There was no fat on his shin. When I looked at the cut, all I could see was muscle and bone."

"He's hot," she said. "I'm really starting to like him."

"Helen Keller could see that," I said.

She smiled and said, "I'm serious, Mindy. I have strong feelings for him."

"So what are you going to do about it?" I asked.

"I don't know, but I have to do something."

When we arrived at camp, the warriors were huddled in a circle, and I sensed a feeling of uneasiness.

"What's wrong?" I asked Lanet.

"They are very concerned about staying here tonight. The elephants are near, and we want to trek to another camp, but everyone is too tired."

Somehow I found the strength to respond: "You told me Maasai are not stupid. If it's dangerous to stay here, then let's go to another location."

And with that we walked to what we deemed was a safe spot. Beyond exhausted, the last trek of the day was a blur to me. I didn't even remember getting into bed that night, but I did wake up the next afternoon groggy and starving.

12

The Rhino Clan

TWO BREAKFASTS, two lunches, and two dinners without food and my bitchiness factor was off the charts. As we sat around the fire, I painted and repainted my fingernails and toenails three times, wiping each imperfect coat away with a wet leaf. The thought of slaughtering and eating another goat was making my stomach churn, so I asked Lanet if there was anything else besides goat on the Maasai menu, and if so, could we please order it for our next meal. He told me that we could eat a cow, but getting one would be asking too much of the community. The asset was too valuable.

"Well, how much does it cost to buy one?" I asked.

He spoke with Topoika and Leken at length until, in a completely unnecessarily snarky manner, I broke in. "The prices are that volatile, huh?"

Lanet gave me a blank stare and said, "Are you proposing to purchase a cow?"

I thought about it. I only had about $50 on me, but with one phone call, my brother could send money via Western Union. And at this point, I was willing to pay $1,000 for a juicy hamburger. I knew that my desire to be authentic was flip-flopping all of the time. This originally upset and confused me because I couldn't understand why I wasn't able to stick to a path. It reminded me of my father's concern that I wasn't able to focus and that this lack of focus would lead to a life full of unnecessary struggle. But with a shift of perspective, I realized I liked that I was curious. I liked trying new things, and the fact that my personality allowed me to be able to enjoy eating a hamburger in the bush just as much as The Ritz. I answered, "Depending on the cost, yes."

Lanet's response was typical Maasai: "We need to consult with the elders. This is a very large purchase, and we need to make sure to spread any money that comes in to Loita throughout the community."

"Well, how large of a purchase do you think it will be?" While I would spend a thousand dollars to buy a cow, if I told my brother that I needed a grand to buy one, he would tell me to go back to goat and hang up.

Lanet got to his feet and paced in front of the fire, every now and then saying something to Topoika or Rokoine. Finally he said to me, "Maybe 16,000 shillings?"

"Is that 200 dollars?"

Lanet shrugged and said, "Something like that."

With a tingle of excitement, I said, "Done deal!"

"How will you get the money?" Becca asked.

"I was thinking that my brother could wire the money by Western Union, and the next time someone goes to Narok, they could pick it up and bring it back to Loita."

Lanet nodded, "Yes, this is possible. When do you want the cow?"

"When are we going to eat again?"

"Topoika thinks you have gone long enough without food. Both of you have proven that you are able to go without."

"So when can we eat?" I asked hungrily.

"Tomorrow morning should be fine."

"Then tomorrow morning we should have our cow."

Lanet discussed with Topoika and Leken how we would get the cow and from whom. Becca used the planning time to take a nap, and when she woke up, she had developed a bad cold. Every thirty seconds she was either sneezing or coughing, with snot pouring out of her nose like a running faucet.

"I don't think I can go anywhere today," she groaned.

"Becca," I said, "you are definitely going wherever we need to go because tomorrow we are going to eat a real cow for breakfast."

"Is that actually happening?" she asked.

"It is! My brother owes me a birthday present, so I am going to ask him to pay for the cow."

Becca, nodding, said "Sounds good!" and again blew her nose in her olkarasha. I took advantage of my happy mood to update Mr. Plank (see Appendix, Letter 7).

The trek to the next camp took half the day. It would have taken less time, but Becca really was ill, so we not only went slowly, but also stopped frequently. Otumoi and Maani ran ahead to procure the cow from a local. I couldn't get hamburger off my mind. I was in such a deep dream that I had to remind myself that I hadn't actually eaten the cow yet. While we were away, the calendar continued—twenty-six chips, but twenty-seven days in the forest.

Our new camp featured trees with exposed roots and inter-twined branches, making it look like Alice's alternative hangout once she left Wonderland. We went through our typical routine of clearing the camp of debris, making our leaf bed, building a fire, and constructing the gate. Becca went straight to sleep in her worm, with just her grayish-colored face popping out of the blue cocoon. As Lanet and I gathered leaves for the bed, we talked about Becca's illness.

"She will need to drink many herbs," Lanet said.

"I bet she's sick because she didn't eat. She's probably just dehydrated and completely exhausted."

"She could have malaria."

"Seriously?"

"Well, yes. The incidence of malaria is very low in Loita, but you never know. We will need to watch her carefully over the next couple of days."

"How much longer do you think we'll be in the forest?"

"Not long. Topoika told me yesterday that it is time to bring the two of you into the community and see how you fit in."

While the majority of the time in the forest was enjoyable, I was ready to experience the other part of being a moran: the community involvement.

"That is great news!" I said.

"It is. It means that Topoika is proud of your work and believes that you will do fine in the community. He would never put you in a position where he thought you would fail, so this is really very good. You will soon see the power that Topoika has in the community. He is a very respected elder, so if he believes that girls should have the right to become morans, then people will listen to him."

"Lanet, I know you risked losing respect from many in the community by teaching us. Please know that I appreciate you."

"I know. Even if I can't get girls the official right to become morans, I have started the process or at least showed people something different. It will be up to the tribe to decide if girls becoming morans is a worthy initiative."

By the time we arrived back at camp, Magilu and Maani had also arrived, covered with wounds and swelling on various parts of their bodies. Maani handed me a honeycomb with a big smile on his swollen face. Horrified by the look of them, I asked Lanet what happened. Before speaking, he popped a honeycomb in his mouth, sucked the honey out, chewed, and spit out the wax. Then he explained the logistics involved in a honey hunt.

"During the dry season there are a lot of bees. To harvest the honey, the morans enlarge the hole where the bees live and then fan smoke in, which chokes the bees. When the honey can be seen, it is collected. Usually the moran comes back with many stings, but the taste is worth the pain. And honey is very important because of its antibacterial properties."

The honey looked like the perfect food to end my fast on. I broke off a piece of the comb and stuffed it into my mouth. The gooey, golden goodness covered my tongue, and the rush of sugar tasted oh so good. I licked my lips, chewed the comb until every last bit of sweetness was soaked up, and then tossed the wax out of camp. My appetite was back. I needed more, and with one look of desperation, Magilu handed me two more pieces of honeycomb, which I tossed in my mouth without a second thought.

Lanet continued, "First we eat the bee larvae."

With wax in my mouth, I mumbled, "The baby bees?"

He nodded. I looked at Becca, who looked like a blue sarcophagus, and asked Lanet if we should give her some honey. Even though Magilu didn't understand my words, he understood what I meant, as he told Lanet that he'd already woken Becca up and given her some honey. I smiled at Magilu and told Lanet that this was not the first time one of the non-English-speaking Maa (everyone except Lanet and Maani, with his limited vocabulary of "hello") read my mind or answered my question without Lanet interpreting.

"I have also been amazed by their intuition," he said. "There have been many times when one of the men understood what you or Becca were feeling or needing without me telling them. For example, everyone knew yesterday that you were ill and it was actually Magilu acting on his own without instructions who sought to get you herbs for your head."

"Yes, but I was also grabbing my head and moaning, so I don't know how intuitive he would need to be. But I get what you're saying. The other day when I was feeling particularly dirty, Otumoi brought me my soap and a bucket of water without me saying anything." Lanet smiled, and with a few moments to think, I continued. "But he could have just brought me the soap because I smelled bad and he wanted to save his nose."

With more than six pieces of honeycomb consumed, I relaxed in bed and fell asleep with mouth-watering dreams of a juicy hamburger. Otumoi returned to camp with a black-and-white-speckled beauty trotting through the gate beside him. My birthday dinner had arrived.

In response to my loud "good looking" whistle, Lanet said, "Yes, she is beautiful, but she is going blind, so her days are done."

As Leken guided the cow to an open patch of land at the back of the camp, Otumoi and Maani got busy creating a bed of leaves to make the slaughtering area sanitary. Rokoine blessed the cow as we surrounded her. With a few short moves, Magilu, Otumoi, and Maani pushed the animal to the ground and tied and held her legs. Lanet grabbed her head by the horns, and Topoika, in perfect form, jabbed a sword into the back of her skull. Within seconds, the cow was dead.

The slaughter continued with Magilu and Otumoi sitting on the cow's side, so that when the jugular was severed, the blood would continue to spew out. Lanet showed me where to cut the skin, so that I would expose the main vein. Rokoine made one tiny incision and the blood spurted out like a fountain, splashing into a big metal pot Maani held a few feet from the source. When it was half full of blood, Topoika dunked a mug into the pot and took a gulp. With a satisfied, bloodstained smile, he passed the mug to me. I tentatively took a small swig; not only did I never want to throw up blood again, I also knew that my stomach was smaller from fasting, so I needed to take it easy. This time I didn't pinch my nose and actually tasted the blood, which was bold, salty, and metallic.

As we skinned the cow, a lanky six-foot-five, twenty-some-thing man with a six-inch scar across his left cheek sauntered into our grassy nook. Everyone greeted him with nods of the head or a couple of words. Lanet introduced me to Simel, Otu-moi's older brother. I asked if he was allowed to join orpul, and Lanet explained that on the first day of a slaughtering, people from the village are allowed to visit orpul to eat certain parts of the animal—a custom known as *ilkurisha*. Simel brought us news from the tribe, which included two invitations to Maasai weddings that would take place in a few days. Topoika thought the weddings would be the perfect opportunity to introduce us to the community.

After we shared blood and ate kidney, I asked Lanet to ask Simel if he knew about our mission and what he thought of girls wanting to become morans. Simel laughed and said, "Everyone in Loita knows about you girls in orpul. Everyone thought you would not last one night, and we are surprised. You will have a great welcome when you return."

"Yes, but what do you think of girls becoming morans?"

"I don't mind it. I would rather have my sister become a moran than get married at twelve, but there are some things that should stay under a man's control."

"Like what?"

"Women can't own cows."

"Why not?"

"Because they would become arrogant."

"Do you think men become arrogant because they own cows?"

"Yes, but that is okay."

"But why?"

Simel turned to Lanet and spoke in Maa. Lanet reminded me that my way of thinking was not the way Maasai men or women were raised to think. Introducing something new would be a long process.

That night we feasted on ribs at least two and a half feet long. Becca remained in her cocoon, too sick to eat.

"I am very concerned about Becca," Lanet said.

I placed the back of my hand on her forehead. "She has a fever."

"We will need to get her special herbs tomorrow. The trek will be long, but necessary."

That night I fell asleep full and happy and dreamt of cows.

Noompopong, the area where we would find herbs for Becca, also happened to be a common place to find buffalo grazing, so we needed to bring as much support with us as possible, leaving only Magilu and Maani behind to watch over her. A few hours later, as we scaled the side of a hill, Lanet warned, "Tread lightly, buffalo are near." Down the hill was an open patch of land that looked like it had been mowed to about the size of a football field. To the north and south of the field was tall elephant grass as far as the eye could see, and to the east and west was forest. We were west and needed to go east, which would involve crossing the field to access the area where we would find the herbs. The potential problem was that the open field was known as buffalo territory.

We stood at the edge of the forest with eyes continually scanning the field for the sign of a buffalo. Nothing, so we crossed to the other side. Along the way, I noticed a pile of buffalo dung. I put my spear in the pile—still soft from the outside in. We knew that buffalo were near, but this just made that fact more real.

Lanet noticed me poke the pile and said, "We are close to the herbs now. We will be gone from this area at the soonest."

Within a couple of kilometers, Lanet identified the herbs he was after. All of us chopped tree trunks and stuffed chunks of root in between the sheets of our ilkarash. On the way back, we engaged in a deep conversation about the current drought, one of the worst in Kenya's history. They helped me understand that when there is a drought, there is no good grass, which means the cows have nothing to graze on, which results in reducing the Maasai's main source of income. To make matters worse, the Kenyan government was systematically making constitutional changes to encroach upon the vast lands that the Maasai had used for generations of grazing, ceremonial activities, and raising their families. These were the reasons why the Maasai worried about their future and the fate of their way of life.

As we made our way onto the field, everyone instinctively stopped. Something was wrong. I looked to the left and then the right—nothing in sight, but there was definitely something near. We could all feel it. Then in the distance, tall blades of grass began to sway. And just as Moses parted the Red Sea, the grass parted to reveal a happy, two-hundred-pound baby buffalo ambling onto the open field. He was still at one end of the football field and we were at the other, but it was already too late to turn back. We each had the same thought: *Put a spear in us, we are done.* Whenever there is a baby, a mother will be near. The second the mother shows up and sees us, she will think her baby is in danger and will put us in orbit to another planet. If a worst-case scenario existed, this was it.

"Find a tree!" Lanet yelled.

I stood petrified, as the ground started to rumble. The baby buffalo trotted to the edge of the field, and the sea of green parted again to reveal the meanest animal I had ever seen. I could feel her glare from yards away. She had a big, fierce brown face with horns pointing to the sky like the devil's.

"Oh shhhhhhiiiitttttt!" I screamed as the snorting, slobbering, raging buffalo charged in my direction. Then Lanet's teaching replayed itself in my head: "If the enemy is stronger than you, you must attack first," and that is what I did. Grunting and howling, I sprinted down the football field, and with a quick request to the powers above, I released my spear. As it rocketed through the air, the other Maasai released their spears, but mine landed first, in the very edge of the buffalo's right butt cheek. Unfortunately, since my aim and strength were still not stellar, my spear hardly scratched the big bitch. I sprinted east across the field and up the side of the hill, jumping and climbing over fallen trees and weaving through branches that jutted out of the ground like little spikes. With lungs burning, I stopped at the top of the hill and peered back to the field. Lanet, Leken, Oltomoi, and Rokoine were visible and not running. But what about the buffalo? And Topoika? I retraced my steps immediately.

"Lanet!" I screamed as I made my way back to the field. "Lanet! Where is Topoika?" The men were in a huddle by the time I joined them. With tears ready to flow and with labored breath, I asked again, "Where is Topoika?"

"With the buffalo," Lanet answered, and he smiled.

His words made me think he was dead, but Lanet was smiling.

"What are you talking about 'with the buffalo'? Where the hell is he?"

"He is in the forest with the buffalo making sure she is dead." Relieved, my heart rate slowed and Lanet continued, "That man has probably killed over one hundred buffalo in his days. And again he has proven that his aim is just as precise even though many years have passed."

We walked into the forest to find Topoika, who was standing next to the buffalo.

"She is a small one," Lanet said. "Maybe only six hundred kilos."

I knew that the buffalo was big, but up close, her bulk astounded me. "She's the size of an industrial laundry machine. I am surprised that a spear could kill an animal this large."

"It is all about aim and power," Lanet said and continued, "We should leave this animal. We will bless it and let it feed other animals in the forest tonight." And with a silent prayer, we left the mound of brown fur and continued our trek home.

When we arrived back at camp, our focus was placed on Becca. We would tell her about the buffalo when she was well again. Rokoine threw the herbs in a pot with a few liters of water and boiled the mixture. Otumoi gathered all of the blankets and ilkarash while Maani guided Becca out of her worm and onto a stump. Rokoine placed the pot of boiling water and herbs between Becca's feet and then pushed her back and neck forward so that her face was almost in the pot.

"Just breathe in, Becca, until we tell you to stop," Lanet said. She nodded and Otumoi piled blanket upon blanket over her. Becca inhaled the steam for at least forty minutes, and when Rokoine finally lifted the blankets, sweat poured off her face and a blend of snot and phlegm dripped down her chin. She reached for a few stray leaves on the ground, cleaned her face, and said in her regular lighthearted voice, "I feel so much better!"

Looking around the camp with a renewed spirit, she asked, "Did we get a cow or was that a dream?"

I laughed, "Yes, we sure did get a cow, and it tastes wonderful. I'll go get you a piece."

Once Becca was fed, I told her about the buffalo. With her sense of humor back intact, she honed in on the important part.

"You hit the buffalo in the butt?"

I smiled and Lanet, who was eavesdropping, said, "It was quite a sight. I have never seen something like that before. I almost couldn't throw my spear because it was too funny. But she is able to claim the kill because her spear hit the buffalo first."

With pride overflowing, I said, "I get to claim the kill?"

"Indeed."

The achievement was bittersweet. I never wanted to kill an animal that was not meant to feed us, but this was purely self-protection. "Not exactly something I will add on my résumé, but it is . . . something."

"It is quite the accomplishment. Topoika couldn't believe his eyes. He is very proud."

THAT NIGHT, after a session of singing and dancing, Topoika sat on the top of the tallest stump and gave a very long speech in Maa. Once he finished, there were a couple of head nods, and all eyes turned to Lanet. As his lips were set in a hard line, I knew that whatever Lanet was going to say would be serious.

"Topoika has just told everyone that he will induct the two of you into his clan—the *ilaisarr* clan."

Remembering some of the clan names and their translations, I said, "The rhino clan?"

Lanet nodded, "Yes, the rhino clan. You will have responsibilities and rules to follow, but Topoika has just made this induction public, a great honor. And now that the two of you are in a clan, Topoika says that you are officially morans. You will be a part of Magilu's and my age group, and within a few years we will graduate from morans to junior elders."

I couldn't believe it. Not being able to hold back my excitement, I shrieked like a little girl, hopped to my feet, and did a little jig. I turned to Becca, who was hugging Magilu, and said, "Pinch me."

She did . . . hard, so I knew she was feeling better. Just to be sure, I asked Lanet, "Did you really just say that we are morans?" He smiled and nodded and I nearly knocked him off the log with a bulldozer hug. Then I went down the line, hugging each and every Maasai. I knew that hugging wasn't a typical Maasai custom, but when I'm happy I hug—that would never change. I scanned the faces of my new family, all smiling.

"So what exactly does this mean?" I asked.

"Well, we will need to discuss what it means, but we know that you will go back to the United States, so your responsibilities will be very different than what they would be if you stayed here. If Maasai girls are ever allowed to become morans, which we hope will happen at the soonest, then they will have the same responsibilities as the typical morans, but it is not realistic to impose those rules on you and Becca. However, if there is a tribal war while you are still morans, then we expect that you will come back to protect the community. Likewise, if there are other significant decisions that we need you to be involved in, we expect you will be available. As elders, you will have different responsibilities, and we will discuss what they will be as time goes on. And until the time comes that you go back to the United States, you will take on all of the responsibilities of a moran. You will dance and sing at the upcoming weddings, you will protect the community if there is an animal invasion, and when you are away from the tribe, you will continue to live by our principles and values, which we believe you have already taken on as your own."

Packed tight in the cigar box, I was filled with happiness, but I also knew that my time with the Maasai would soon come to an end. Our next step was to be introduced to the community. With visions of a grand wedding and dancing and singing with hundreds of morans, I fell into a deep sleep.

13

The Tribes Gather

ANOTHER FOUR DAYS PASSED, and the tree trunk looked like it had chicken pox. I added one more pockmark and counted: thirty-one days in total. How we'd keep track of the days in the village was unknown to me. What our diet would be in the village was also unknown. What the mornings and evenings would sound like, where I would sleep, how people would receive us were all unknown. I realized that with each day the forest had become known—and with that familiarity had come comfort in the danger.

The morning and afternoon were silent. No one wanted to leave orpul. The fact that our verbal communication was still at an infantile level didn't matter. We had learned to allow our energy to convey what was needed. I had witnessed how the tingle that starts from the tip of your skull and rolls down your neck and shoulders from pure happiness could be transmitted to all around you in the pureness of the wild. The signal itself was strong and clear; it wasn't disrupted or faded by thoughts of the past or future. This is what Lanet meant when he told us that in order to be a Maasai, you needed to be Maasai and a key element of being Maasai was living in the now. I wondered if I would be able to take this feeling with me when I returned to my world.

AFTER A LARGE LUNCH of the remaining parts of the cow, we blessed our campsite by burning a blend of olive branches. As morans, our first responsibility after leaving orpul was to visit the enkaji of every person we had lived with in orpul and celebrate their safe homecoming by drinking milk with family members. First stop was Magilu's *enkang.*

It took us a few hours to make our way across the plains to Magilu's. Since he wasn't married, he still lived with his mother. As I planted my spear in the ground and crouched to enter the four-and-a-half-foot-tall cow-dung structure, Becca called my name.

"How do I look?" she asked. She slapped some dirt off her olkarasha and said, "I want to make a good impression on Mama Magilu."

"You have turned out to be quite a beautiful bush woman, Becca."

She smiled, swatted a couple of flies off her face, and said, "Okay, good."

Magilu's mother was a pint-size version of him with the same round face, cheeks, and eyes. When we hunched in, chai was boiling on the fire. Her hospitality couldn't have been better, but going from the clear air of the forest to a smoke-filled Maasai dwelling was too much for me. I quickly drank my steaming cup of chai, scorching my tongue in the process, and politely excused myself from the enkaji, my eyes stinging from the smoke.

Outside, the blinding sun made my eyes hurt even more. I plopped down on a small mound of grass in front of the enkaji and began to drift to sleep when suddenly the sunlight that was warming my forehead and cheeks vanished. With lids at half-mast, I could make out a tall-as-heavens man swaying above my head. Using my arms as a kickstand, I propped up my torso and stared. The man was at least sixty years old, and lacked the typical peaceful Maasai smile I was accustomed to. He wore a red and green tartan olkarasha under a black wool tux jacket with silk lapels, and his bald head was capped by a blue knit beanie (which I later found out covered four claw scars across the top of his skull, courtesy of a leopard who visited as he slept snoring one night). He suddenly was screaming at me in Maa. My body tensed. I didn't know what this man wanted. The man kneeled and put his face only a few millimeters away from mine and yelled something even louder in Maa. Just then, Lanet appeared and yanked the man away from me.

"What's his problem?" I asked in a rushed, scared voice. Lanet said something to the man and the man abruptly turned his head causing the blue beanie to fall to the ground. There they were—the claw marks deep in his skull. With death in his eyes, he glared at me and yelled again. This time I responded with anger, "What the hell is his problem?"

Lanet successfully pushed the man a few feet away from me, which led him to walk off in the direction of the other enkaji. Without taking his eyes off the man, Lanet told me that the man was very angry that two girls became morans. "He doesn't believe it," Lanet said and continued, "He said that women have no right to become morans and especially two mzungus." If this was to be the representative greeting Becca and I were going to get from the greater Maasai community, it would take women a lot longer to have the freedom of choice to become morans.

"What did you tell him?" I asked.

"I said that the process was already in motion and that if a woman wants to become a moran, she should have the choice. Then I told him to speak with Topoika."

"Why Topoika?"

"Because this man will not give us a problem if he knows that Topoika supports the mission."

Lanet and I took a seat on the ground and waited until the group emerged from Magilu's enkaji. One by one, each person gathered his or her spear. Still utterly shocked that so many people could fit in a hut the size of a hundred-calorie Nabisco snack pack, I said to Becca, "You missed some serious drama."

"I heard the yelling and wanted to come out, but Lanet told me to wait. What happened?"

"I met the first man who is seriously against girls becoming morans."

Becca nodded, "Can't say that I am surprised."

I nodded and changed the subject, "Good meeting with Mama Magilu?"

She gushed, "It was so great. She gave me a cup of chai the size of my head. Probably expecting that a mzungu couldn't finish it, but I showed her what was up!"

Lanet pointed to our next stop, literally fifteen steps away—Otumoi's enkaji. While Magilu lived in a traditional Maasai home, Otumoi and Simel lived in a seven- or eight-foot-tall cow-dung home built with wooden planks—similar to two of the structures on Lanet's plot of land. We planted our spears in the ground again to mark our territory and entered the enkaji. Although significantly more spacious than Magilu's, it was still less than two hundred square feet in total. I breathed easier, however, as there was room for oxygen and seven people to coexist. On the inside, the homes were very similar: a mud floor, a cowhide bed built on sticks, a fire in the center of the room, and a corner set aside for ceramic cups, plates, cutlery, and a small stock of beans, sugar, tea, and maybe rice. The only visible factor of wealth was evident in the number of cows and goats a family owned. Magilu had nine cows, Otumoi had two, and Lanet had forty-seven—a fact that Lanet stated whenever possible.

At Otumoi's we had another cup of chai, and then we had another at Leken's and another at Topoika's and another at Maani's and another at Lanet's. Even though the women hadn't seen their husbands or children for more than thirty days, they didn't say much. I asked Lanet why the women weren't talking.

"Some of these women are intimidated by you and Becca," he explained. "They are very curious about you, but this is the first time that white people have been in their homes. Plus, word has already spread that Topoika inducted you into his clan, and because no white person has ever been part of a clan and no woman has ever been a moran, this is a lot to take in. Many people will be in disbelief when they meet you."

"But don't they have anything to talk about with their husbands?" I asked. "They have been gone for so long."

"Having their men leave for months at a time to bring their cows to graze in new areas or spend time with their other wives and children is the way of life, and there isn't much to talk about unless a cow or goat gives birth, the woman gives birth, or a lion eats a goat or a cow."

The only home that we wouldn't visit that day was Rokoine's, because his wives were already at the site where the major ceremony with thousands of Maasai would be taking place. Rokoine's wives were in the process of building their temporary home at the ceremonial site, which we would see tomorrow. Thankfully, except for Otumoi and Magilu, the trek between the houses ranged between one and three kilometers, so there was enough time and exercise between cups to allow my now-much-smaller stomach time to digest. Leken's wives fed us milk, beans, and rice. The expansion of the menu was a delight, but I paid for this sudden change in diet by running to the nearest tree every ten minutes.

The one real surprise was at Leken's enkang. After our meal, Leken took my hand and led me behind his home to a group of donkeys. Leken beelined to the smallest donkey in the pack: a baby female with a little tuft of white hair sticking straight up into the sky. He looked at me, looked at the donkey, and squeaked, "Mindy!" This was the first time Leken had ever said my name, so I hopped up and down and said, "Yes! Mindy!"

"He knows your name. He is introducing you to his donkey, Mindy," Lanet said, seemingly appearing out of thin air.

"Donkey? Mindy? . . . Huh?"

Lanet wrangled the baby donkey, wrapping his bicep around the donkey's neck and holding her front legs with his other arm. "Mindy, meet Mindy."

Slowly, I got it. "Leken has a donkey named Mindy?"

He laughed and translated my response to Leken.

"One day in orpul Leken was trying to figure out which animal best described you and finally he came up with a donkey, because your personality has a kick that can kill and you have a look that deceives your strength. I told Leken that your brother calls you donkey and that the Maasai from afar called you Tausi Punda, or peacock donkey. So now that you are part of his clan, he wanted to name a donkey after you. This way he can see his sister every day even when she is not in Loita."

Punda Mindy was super cute. If she hadn't been covered in fur and was minus the tail and pointy ears, I could have been looking at myself in the mirror. She brayed and kicked when Lanet held her down. Understanding her need to be free, I told Lanet to let her go, and with a final strong kick of her back legs, she trotted off.

We arrived at Lanet's home just as the sun was setting. He ushered us into the enkaji next to Noolamala's and showed us to our own separate rooms, complete with bed frame, mattress, and Superman sheets on my bed and space sheets on Becca's. In the corner of my room was the backpack I brought with me to Nairobi. Unzipping the front compartment, I found the treasures I had left behind: a ziplock bag with a new bar of Dove soap, avocado oil, nail polish remover, nail clippers, a new razor, Advil, and three sticks of spearmint gum. In the main compartment were three pairs of clean boy shorts, two sports bras, a pair of leggings, and a mock turtleneck.

I pushed a piece of gum in my mouth. The sweetness was so overpowering that my mouth watered, but with a few chews, I got used to the taste and my mouth instantly felt fresh and clean. Giddy about my newfound supplies, I asked Lanet if we could bathe. He returned with two plastic buckets filled with what I assumed was cow-saliva water. He placed the buckets in the hallway in between my room and Becca's, which was also used as a place to eat, as it was equipped with two wooden benches and a table.

"Where are we supposed to bathe?" I asked.

"Right here is fine."

"Are you sure that you want us to bathe in the same place you eat?"

"Don't worry, we will clean the floor before dinner."

As I untied my boots, clumps of dry mud dropped to the mud floor. Even though I had been in the forest for a couple of months and had learned to eat where I slept and slaughter where I ate, I still didn't feel comfortable bathing where I would eat. Then I reminded myself again that it wasn't bad, it was just different, and continued to remove chunks of mud from my boots. Becca and I sat on opposing benches and went to work. I unpacked the bar of soap and inhaled the freshness.

"Wow. I missed the smell of clean," I said.

Already shaving, Becca said, "I forgot what my legs and underarms looked like without hair on them."

I lathered the soap in my hands and inch-by-inch I washed the forest off me, happy that it would never completely wash out of me.

Before dinner, Lanet brought in a couple buckets of water and dumped it on the mud floor. As I watched the suds flow down the floor and out the door, Lanet said, "See, all clean. Now we eat."

For dinner we had more rice and beans. It felt foreign to be sitting at a proper table with a proper bowl and spoon, but what really felt wrong was that our unit wasn't complete: The rest of the Maasai were back with their own families. There would be no singing and dancing, no moran stories, and no snuggling in the cigar box. Feeling misty-eyed, I reminded myself that morans did not cry and turned my thoughts to what would be my final letter to Mr. Plank (see Appendix, Letter 8).

I CLIMBED INTO BED and stared at the mud ceiling. The mattress didn't feel nearly as good as I expected. Strangely enough, I missed the cold, hard earth. I drifted off to sleep, but when I awoke the next morning, I was not on the bed. I was curled up on the floor.

Over a breakfast of chai, Lanet told us that we would go to the ceremonial site (known as the *manyatta* in Maa) that day. The trek would be at least five kilometers, and once there, we would spend all day visiting with people. On the way, we discussed Lesikarr's and Turishoi's upcoming weddings. It would be a joint event to be held at Lesikarr's enkaji within the next few days.

"I understand that you don't send out invitations, but shouldn't you have a set date for the wedding? How will people know when to show up? What if they already have plans that day?"

"What plans? We are Maasai—we don't have plans. When the wedding is ready, we celebrate," Lanet said.

We approached the ceremonial site within a couple of hours. From the top of a hill, we had a perfect bird's-eye view. The site looked like a thousand-foot-wide pair of eyeglasses. At least two hundred small cow-dung huts spaced ten feet apart created each lens. Side by side, each brown circle formed the perfect OO. Each circle represented one side of the age group: the elders on the right side, the younger group on the left. This big ceremony would mark the end of moranship for one age group and would mark the coming together of the two sides to form one unit. As a unit they would move into the next stage of their lives, elderhood.

These ceremonies happen once every five to seven years and last approximately three months. The whole community comes to celebrate, and everyone is required to give gifts and spend the little money they have to help prepare and execute the celebration. It was still unknown when the ceremony would actually start and whether Becca and I would be part of the event. Everyone in our unit was hoping that the elders and the laibons would come together and agree to allow us to take part, but it was still a big hope.

As we arrived at the manyatta, Rokoine met us at the entrance, at the periphery. He explained there was a specific way that morans enter the manyatta—marching in a straight line, one foot in front of the other, with our spears angled at eighty degrees, almost straight to the sky. Following Rokoine, we proceeded through the gate, which was really an opening between the enkajis of two Chiefs. Women and children working on their temporary homes stopped and stared. Usually the women sang and danced when the morans made their entrance, but this time we were there, two white women with spears dressed in moran clothing. The sight of us struck them silent.

We kept walking until we entered the center of the manyatta. Lanet and Rokoine anxiously scanned the ceremonial site.

"What's wrong?" I asked.

"The women are supposed to sing when morans enter," Lanet explained. "No one is singing."

"They are probably not sure what to do because Becca and I are here."

"Yes, but news has spread that you and Becca are morans. They should respect you as morans."

I answered slowly, "As you said, this will be a process and we may find that not everyone will accept us."

Then I heard it, one female voice erupting into song. Another followed, and soon there was a crowd of fifty or so women singing and dancing around us. Their beautiful black heads bobbed back and forth while their deep, clear voices chanted. Beaded jewelry in every color of the rainbow covered their ears, necks, wrists, and ankles. One woman jumped to the middle of the circle to do a solo dance of leaps and stomps. On the way out, she gave another woman a high five, and she then took center stage.

AN HOUR OR TWO LATER the singing stopped, and the women went back to work hurriedly and diligently on their temporary homes. Construction requires a minimum of five hundred pounds of cow dung per hut. Doing the mental math, I figured that there was about one hundred thousand pounds of cow poop on this little hill. The architectural work that resulted was nothing short of phenomenal. Branches were woven and sticks were assembled one after another, a mixture of olive, acacia, and fig. Each branch had a strategic position in the dung. Entering one of these huts, I was struck by the remarkable utilitarian style in the compact six-by-eight-foot space.

Rokoine's wives fed us rice and beans and gave us cups of chai. Little kids came in and out of the home while we ate, always stopping in front of me or Becca to stare, then laugh and run away. As I shoveled the food in my mouth, the man in charge of the ceremony's operations entered and took a seat on a low footstool near the fire. Wearing a hunter-green fleece jacket on top of his olkarasha, his sleeves were rolled up and I noticed he was wearing an ornate bracelet of blue plastic beads.

"What's the meaning of the bracelet?" I asked Lanet.

"He is the Olotuno—a very senior and highly respected age group head. The community gave him the bracelet. If he decides that someone has done no good, he will take one of the beads off the bracelet and throw it to the ground in front of the person who has committed the unforgivable deed."

"Then what?"

"Then that person is kaput."

"Kaput?"

"Yes. The man is considered dead or goes crazy."

Giving him my best "please like me and don't drop a bead at my feet" smile, I greeted him with "Supa."

The man responded, "Hello. It is nice to finally meet the first two female morans."

"Wow! Your English is great!" I exclaimed.

"Thank you."

"You have a very impressive setup here," I said.

"Yes, we have been working for months, and the event will be here at the soonest. Thousands of Maasai will congregate. And then we burn everything to the ground right after the ceremony."

"Why?"

"It's part of the cleansing. There is a belief that any curses will be carried over to the next group if the same materials are used again. One never knows if someone has ill feelings for someone else and has cursed an age group or even one person in the age set. The burning makes sure that no trace of wrongdoing or malice remains."

"I have a lot of work to attend to," he continued, "but I wanted to tell you that I believe it is time for girls to have the choice to be morans. But you must know that many people in the tribe will not support this idea."

I responded quickly, "Our only goal was to prove that women are strong and brave enough to be morans. We accomplished that mission, but understand that whatever the tribe decides to do in terms of allowing Maasai girls to become morans or not is their decision." He nodded his head, shook our hands, and half hunched and half crawled out into the sunlight.

"That was intense," I said to Lanet.

"He is a very smart and good man, and it is important for you and Becca to realize that you are considered Maasai now. You are responsible for the tribe just like every other Maasai."

Becca and I had spoken about our commitment to the tribe, and we agreed that this was not an adventure we could ever just leave behind. The sooner we wrapped our heads around that, the sooner we would be of greater assistance.

Relaxing in Rokoine's home, we continued to discuss the ceremony.

"When will the ceremony begin?" Becca asked.

"There are some issues that need to be handled. Nothing can be left open before graduating to the next stage of life."

"Like what?" I asked.

Lanet translated for Rokoine, "The members of Lanet's age group, the one right below us, have been having sex with our wives."

I gasped. I knew that the rules of sex were lenient compared to Western standards, but no matter what culture, this wasn't cool.

Rokoine continued, "This typically wouldn't be a problem, but this time the women have fallen in love with many of the younger men. The other issue is that someone killed a man, so he has to pay a fine.'

"He won't go to jail?"

"There is no jail. He will pay forty-nine cows."

"That's it? He pays the cows and then he is a free man?" I asked.

"He will have nothing if he has no cows. His life is over. And when those two issues are resolved, the ceremony will begin."

"What does Lanet's age group have to do to make up for having sex with your wives?" Becca asked.

"Lanet's age group will pay a fine. When they give us gifts, we will forgive them."

"What about the women?" I asked.

"They have to give a cow or two, and if that is not enough, then they are whipped until they tell who they had sex with."

I felt sick, "Whipped?"

Lanet nodded and said, "It is custom. It will not be a surprise. They should not have engaged in love."

As the day came to a close, we left the ceremonial site and hiked back to Lanet's. I went to sleep thinking about the difference in treatment between the men and the women. I found myself judging their custom of whipping women versus making men give gifts for the act of falling in love. Even after all of the time I spent with the Maasai, I couldn't help but feel anguish about women being beaten. Why was it not a universal agreement that no one—man or woman—should hit or be hit based on behavior? Yes, there was injustice in every culture, but this struck a nerve and made me think I would pick and choose the values and principles I would retain from my Masaai culture and which ones I would reject. Even if I had been born and bred Maasai, I would most likely not react any differently, but then I wouldn't have the luxury to do so. Perhaps it was time for me to go back to California.

14

Passing the Torch

WITH NO BARK CALENDAR, I wasn't sure how many days had passed since arriving at the manyatta. Maybe two weeks? Maybe three? I had no idea, and it didn't matter. The only thing of importance was that it was the morning before the wedding and every living thing in Loita was aflutter. Flies did the tango on dung piles. Baby goats waltzed in the grass. The colobus monkeys cranked up their screeches as they swung from branch to branch. The Maasai were doing something alien to their usual modus operandi—rushing! They rushed to adorn themselves in beaded jewelry, they rushed to prepare gifts, and they rushed to slather their hair and bodies in a special burnt red soil (*ochre*) extracted only from specific areas overseen by a laibon.

"We're going to be late! We're going to be late!" Lanet hollered as he opened the front door of his enkaji, where Becca and I had been staying. "People have been at Lesikarr's enkaji since last night. The festivities should be in full swing. At least one thousand Maasai are coming to celebrate. We must leave at the soonest!"

"One thousand people?" I asked.

"At the least," Lanet said as he evaluated himself inch by inch with the tiny pink plastic mirror we had at orpul. Wearing a brand-new red tartan olkarasha, he was smothered under an eclectic combination of beaded necklaces, bracelets, leglets, and anklets. Spinning like a dreidel round and round, he showed off his Maasai finery.

"Now that I am a moran, I really have to redesign this uniform," Becca commented as she walked out of her bedroom, followed by Magilu in a sleepy haze. "This getup does not take boobs or hips into account. This outfit is sexist."

I looked at Becca, then at Magilu, then at Lanet. *Whatever happens in the bush, stays in the bush,* I thought.

Prior to leaving, Lanet's mama acted as my make-up artist and Noolamala acted as Becca's. As Noolamala mixed the red soil with cow fat, which would later paint our hair, I told Becca that I felt that my time in Loita was coming to an end. She agreed that we had accomplished what we set out to do.

"And who knows? Maybe the next time we come back, Maasai girls will be morans," I said.

"How cool would that be?" Becca said as Noolamala spread the thick red paint on her curly bob. With my hair already painted, Lanet's mama mixed red ochre and water, creating a thinner substance to draw a crisscross pattern, like fishnet stockings, from high on my thigh all the way down to my ankles. "I would totally hit the street in Los Angeles with my legs painted like this," I said.

"It is pretty sexy," Becca said as Noolamala painted squiggly lines and polka dots on her legs.

"All I need are a pair of black patent stilettos, and I would be good to go." And with sex on my mind, I asked Becca, "What's up with you and Magilu?"

A smile of pure infatuation swept across her face, and she said, "You know how we wondered if warriors kiss?"

Eagerly, I nodded and moved my hand forward in a "give me the details" gesture. "Well, they do kiss . . . and they are good!"

"For real?"

She nodded.

"So maybe you won't be leaving with me?" I asked.

"Don't be ridiculous. I have two boyfriends at home. But I can't deny that there is a serious connection with Magilu. He has this energy that I never want to be without."

Before leaving for the wedding, Becca and I found a signal and called our parents. We told them that we would be coming home soon and that we'd be in touch when we had final details. My parents still thought I was working for Under Armour, something I would have to deal with upon my return. But, surprisingly, I also sensed that they were proud of my having become a moran. My mother was so excited that I was coming home, "I'm doing a happy dance," she said and continued, "We will take you directly to Dr. Ransohoff when you get home. You might think you are fine, but who knows what illnesses you contracted that are lying dormant." On that high note, I also made a quick call to Queen Lee, who brought me back to earth with, "So you have finally decided to leave the cow poop palace?"

"Indeed," I responded.

"Good. It is time for you to come back and find a husband. After this experience a good Jewish man may not be so attracted to you, so maybe you shouldn't tell any prospects until someone actually proposes."

With a roll of my eyes, I said, "Good plan."

"Okay. See you soon and travel safe. I'll make a call to see if I can get you upgraded to first, but do shower so as not to offend others. Even thinking about what you smell like right now is revolting."

I said good-bye to Queen Lee and felt a little tingle of excitement when I thought about sipping champagne and being cozy in a soft blanket and cushy leather chair. I looked around my current environment, where women were sitting with legs crossed and babies on their laps, happily chatting while they painted ochre on each other. Children in tattered clothing chased each other with sticks while a couple of young girls hacked at a tree trunk with an ax. Luxury here didn't come in the form of champagne or cashmere, but rather in the form of family and community. I came to the bush thinking that the material items in my life were blocking me from being true to myself and what I needed to do was live without any attachments to get to know my truth, but with a shift of perspective I understood this: My identity wouldn't change if I was wrapped in cashmere or cotton, that what I needed to do was embrace my own eclectic personality.

THE TREK TO THE WEDDINGS was short. In less than three kilometers, the sound of deep chanting gently tickled the hills of Loita. As we came closer, the noise transformed from a gentle hum to a pounding in our hearts. From afar, all I could see was a sea of red, but the next thing I knew, I was engulfed and just as much a part of it as any other person there. Hundreds of morans ranging in age from early teens to late twenties congregated in circles, singing and jumping high into the crystal-blue sky. All were slathered in red ochre with various designs, from polka dots to wavy lines that started from the ankle and worked their way high up the thigh, with a break on the torso and beginning again on the face and head. Some had braided heads smeared in the earth's deep red substance, with thick, bold lines under their eyes and down their nose. Others had shaved heads smothered in red ochre, revealing only a glistening black face. Hundreds of ilkarash were from the same family of color, ranging from cotton candy pink to lusty red.

Feeling strangely at ease while surrounded by unknown faces and pulsating bodies, I instantly joined the chanting and jumping. With neck slinking back and forth like a boa, I fell into a hypnotic state. At least an hour had passed when Lanet grabbed my shoulder and guided me out of the Maasai mosh pit.

"The bride and groom are on their way! Come and greet them!"

We joined the grooms, Turishoi and Lesikarr. Turishoi was draped in a brown and white calfskin cape over his magenta olkarasha with layer upon layer of brilliant necklaces. The final accessory was a brand-new pair of white Converse sneakers. Lesikarr was covered with a silver-and-black-speckled calfskin, similar in looks to the cow we had slaughtered. His cape was slung over a bright red olkarasha with a happy white-flower pattern. He also wore many necklaces, bracelets, and anklets and had his legs painted with tic-tac-toe lines and tire sandals on his size thirteen feet.

The noise of a bumbling engine stopped the chanting, and all red heads turned to watch a rickety, rusted Land Cruiser jump along the parched grass like a cricket. Tied to the cracked bumper and headlights, where I would normally expect paper streamers, were olive tree branches. Squeezing through the throng of women, I got a closer look as the car jolted to a stop and at least ten people rolled out of the vehicle. The last person out was a stunning teenage girl dressed in a neon-blue-and-white-bejeweled olkarasha, wearing a white tiara with chains dripping down her face like angel wings. She was Turishoi's wife-to-be. Like a swarm of bees, the women buzzed around her, picking at her necklaces and poking at her olkarasha while singing and dancing. The group of at least a hundred women, the bride at their center, inched down the grassy path toward the entrance of the enkaji. The bride walked with what seemed to me leaden feet, all the while smiling proudly as she moved farther and farther away from her mother and sisters. Lanet explained that she was marrying for love, but terrified of the challenges of being responsible for a Maasai household.

Another car pulled up, this time a white four-door Mazda, but with just as many people rolling out in addition to two people riding along on the bumper. This time the bride was an even younger girl who looked around twelve years old, who was quickly absorbed by another group of women. This little girl's marriage was arranged and rather than a proud smile, tears gushed. Women tried to console the young girl as her emotions unraveled and, gasping for air between sobs, she made her way to the enkang to meet her betrothed, Lesikarr. She wept with such fury that I thought her legs would buckle beneath her. Maasai girls know from a very young age that this day will come, but it didn't stop my urge to scoop her up and take her home with me to a different way of life. But maybe she wouldn't want to flee, and maybe they would end up happy together. At the end of the day, it didn't matter what I thought. She was getting married; no other options existed.

Seeing this young girl made me think about whether her life would actually improve if she had the option to become a moran. Having that right wouldn't suddenly give her the opportunity to go to school or be able to choose her husband, but it might delay the age at which she got married because she would be a moran until she was in her twenties. Choosing to be a moran could give other girls some extra time. At the same time, I hoped that the introduction of women morans wouldn't completely change the Maasai culture, which in my opinion needed to be protected. It was a question—was I stirring up a controversy that would irrevocably alter their way of life that I mostly admired? Even though I was officially accepted as a moran, I was not Maasai and was never going to be. I understood and accepted that it was fully in the hands of the tribe members to make decisions on behalf of their culture.

Soon the women and men separated, which meant that the morans were not with the women. As morans, Becca and I joined the other warriors. The brides stood in the doorway of different enkajis while a hundred women decked out in brightly printed cotton ilkarash gathered in front, shouting out the gifts they were giving.

"Plates! Cups! Soap! Goat!! Olkarasha! Shoes! Goat!"

Becca and I had decided to give each bride a goat, and Lanet's mama shouted out our gifts for us, since the announcing of the gifts is never done by a moran.

When the gift giving was over, we were invited into the enkaji where the bride was to be blessed by an elder. Each home was packed with men and women drinking whiskey by the gallon. The brides sat on the cowhide beds while a new name was chosen for each woman. The tradition is that every new ceremony marks the beginning of a new life; therefore new names are given to the brides. Turishoi's wife was named Noonkishu, The One With Many Cattle, and Lesikarr's was named Noolepeta, The Mother of Morans.

With the naming ceremonies complete, everyone evacuated the enkajis to join the festivities. Out of the corner of my eye, I noticed a group of at least fifteen men directing a few goats to a semi-secluded area behind trees. I suspected they were going to slaughter the goats. I turned to Becca, "We should help out with the slaughter since we are morans." She nodded and we walked in their direction. Just as we arrived, two morans were suffocating one of the goats. Thirty eyeballs stared us down. I searched for a familiar face, but there wasn't one. I didn't know any of these men, and for the first time since arriving in Loita, I was scared. Feeling naked and weak, I hunched my shoulders like a defeated animal and took a few steps backward. Not knowing what was on their minds, I continued to walk one foot behind the other so as not to take my eyes off the men. Becca took my cue and walked away with me.

Back in the crowd, I searched desperately for Lanet through the hundreds of Maasai. Finally finding him, I yanked him away to a quiet spot.

With a look of concern, he said, "You look strange. What happened?"

My eyes searched out the group of men and I pointed, saying, "I was trying to help them slaughter the goats. I thought that is what morans are expected to do, and they looked at me like they wanted to kill me."

Placing his hand on my shoulder, he responded, "You heard yesterday that some men are angry that Topoika inducted you into the clan and honored you by accepting you as morans." Lanet scanned the property and the energy vaporized from his typical bouncy demeanor. "I was hoping that introducing you to the tribe on this day would not result in problems, but there may be physical beatings tonight."

"Beatings?"

"Yes. Topoika told the leaders of each age group that no one is to harm either one of you, but with alcohol, the senses dim and problems arise."

My neck stiffened, "Is it not safe for me and Becca to be here tonight?"

Expressionless, Lanet said, "I am not sure, but you cannot run and you cannot show them any sign of weakness. If there is any hope of the Maasai respecting you, you and Becca will need to remain at the weddings and conduct yourselves as morans."

Suddenly more afraid of what a human could do than an animal, I asked Lanet if one of the morans from orpul would stay near us tonight. Lanet nodded and said, "It looks like Magilu will not leave Becca's side, so remain nearby them, but again, you need to earn respect and the only way to earn respect is by conducting yourself as a moran." Lanet's eyes focused on an elderly man sitting on a grassy knoll. "That is my father. Let us go to him."

As we made our way, I couldn't help looking over my shoulder to see if someone was following me. I hadn't felt this level of fear even in the forest.

Lanet's father was sitting next to two other elders, who each looked to be at least eighty years old. With a salt-and-pepper five o'clock shadow, he sat with knees bent to his chest, wrapped in a wool blanket. The whites of his eyes had turned a mustard yellow. "Badass" should have been tattooed on his forehead. As we sat down, he immediately went into a tirade with spit spraying and his voice increasing by one octave after another. The other men around him grunted as he spoke. When there was a break in speech, I nudged Lanet and asked him what his dad was saying.

"My father is telling me that I need to give him some of my goats because one that I gave him last year is sick and will die soon."

"Is that all?"

"Not really. My father is a very good man, but he wonders why I brought girl mzungus to orpul." Lanet gazed off and said, "I hope my father does not suffer from problems because I committed to this mission."

I was quiet, thinking about the drama that his father was faced with because of Lanet's taking a chance on us. Lanet continued, "This reaction is to be expected by some, but we have to remember that there is another view—the one from the people who want to empower females. They believe that this will protect our culture from extinction."

WHEN THE MEAT WAS CUT, Becca, Magilu, and I sat with our age group of morans. This caused a bit of a stir, as it was tradition that women were not allowed to eat meat with men. We ignored the looks and waited for our cut. Finally one of the morans leaned over the fire and handed us each a piece of meat. After eating, we made our way back to the enkaji, I noticed three girls no older than ten trailing behind us, one of them being Kinyi, the little girl we saw herding cattle on the first day of orpul. I stopped, which made Becca stop as well.

"That is Kinyi. Remember her?"

"Yeah. She's the one who wakes up earlier than her brother so she can act like a moran." The young Maasai girls huddled together with all eyeballs on us.

"I guess that's her girl power crew," Becca laughed.

"Yeah. All of them have fire in their eyes. They could for sure protect the community from a lion attack. Just one look at their glares and you know they are serious."

"Totally," Becca said as we turned and walked away.

Back among the singing and dancing, I saw that two circles of more than a hundred morans each had formed in front of the goat corral. Deep, guttural *uh-uh-uh-uh-uh-uh* sounds projected from their throats as their heads swayed and their bodies shimmied to the rhythm. Becca and I joined the circle on the right, which was our side of the age group, the older side, noticing that the circle to the left watched the circle to the right sing and jump and then the roles reversed.

"They are competing," Becca said. "Each group is trying to sing louder and jump higher than the other." I nodded.

I surely wasn't going to win the jumping competition, but my loud voice seemed to spur some warriors to grunt and leap high into the sky. In this fashion we danced and sang for hours until our throats were too dry and scratchy to make another sound. Our competition continued until the first stars were seen in the sky. Then the groups united, and suddenly I was eyeball-to-eyeball with one of the very same morans who had looked like he wanted to kill me earlier.

I turned to Becca and she mouthed, "Oh shit!" Lanet's words rang in my head, "You need to earn respect." My lips tightened, and I stared back at him relentlessly. All of a sudden, he took his eyes off mine, whipped his head around, and smacked me clear across the face with his greasy ochred braids. My eyes bulged, not able to restrain my surprise. A crowd formed around us. Was I supposed to slap him with my hand? Punch him in the nose? As I hesitated, he whipped his head around once more and smacked me even harder with his braids.

"Hit him back!" I heard Lanet yell over the crowd, so I did. I flung my head and hair around with such force that I could hear the impact of my hair slap his face. The crowd grunted loud, and this time the moran opposing me hesitated. So I smacked him with my hair once more.

"He respects you!" Lanet called as he pushed to the middle of the circle.

Smack! His hair went across my jaw.

Smack! My hair went across his cheeks.

Smack! His hair brushed my forehead.

Smack! Smack! Smack! My hair went across his eyes, his forehead, his cheeks.

He stepped out of the circle and began jumping uncontrollably. A few morans ran after him to calm him down, and I was bombarded with morans poking and prodding me, as well as the three girls who had been following me all day. My face stung and my throat hurt like hell, but I couldn't help but feel proud.

A FEW HOURS LATER, the entire family from orpul and the three trailing little girls were gathered around a fire at Lanet's. We ate bowls of rice and beans together and, just as we were getting up to go to bed, Topoika spoke. Becca and I sat back down until he finished.

Lanet translated his words: "I know that your physical time in Loita is coming to an end, but your spirit will be here always and your work will be carried on through these three girls and others like them." He made room for the girls on the trunk and continued, "These girls will be the third, fourth, and fifth Maasai morans. They have already shown great courage by speaking to me and saying this will be so. I give you my word that I will stand with these girls and work with this community and others to get them and all other Maasai girls this right. And I will do this because women are strong enough and brave enough to be warriors."

Becca and I smiled, our joy reflected in the face of each member of our orpul family. I had never felt such a sense of accomplishment, nor such a sense of belonging. It seemed my work here was done.

15

A Double-Edged Sword

Becca and I left Loita a little over a week after the wedding. I wanted to stay for the big ceremony, but true to form, Maasai time was the polar opposite of on-point. Even after taking on many Maasai qualities such as a loving affection for cows, callused palms, and a stench of the savanna, I remained unable to sit still and could not fathom their lack of party planning. Even a ceremony of such grandiosity was going to start on Maasai time, which meant that only Ngai, the laibons, and the lions knew when it would begin. I was convinced that the expiration date for my time in Africa had come up.

Becca, on the other hand, did not feel a strong desire to go back to the United States. She was completely comfortable and very happy with life in Loita. At Lanet's enkaji she had a bed, a bush to pee on, rice and beans to eat, chai to drink, and Magilu to cuddle with. She was beyond thrilled with our accomplishment and was quite smitten with Magilu (and he was smitten with her).

When we agreed that it was time I went back to the United States, we decided to take Magilu to Nairobi for a safari into our lives. Decked in a canvas vest about five sizes too big, a Grateful Dead tie-dyed T-shirt, and khaki pants with a sword strapped to his beaded belt, Magilu was ready to head into the big city for the first time. Becca gave him loving eyes as she straightened his vest.

"What's he planning on doing with the sword?" I asked Lanet.

"You can take the moran out of the forest, but you can never take the forest out of the moran."

"Don't you think you should tell him that he can't carry a sword on him in broad daylight in Nairobi?"

"I will explain in the car. We have many hurdles to climb before we get him to remove his sword."

We trekked the five kilometers from Lanet's enkaji to the community center to meet a taxi that would take us to Nairobi. Lanet had ordered the taxi three days ago, but he still wasn't sure if the guy would show up. He explained that our backup plan was to stay at someone's home until the taxi or a bus arrived.

"But that could take days," I said.

With his lips in a hard line, Lanet replied, "Needing something from someone else is reason enough not to need."

Thankfully we only had to wait a couple of hours before the taxi rumbled up in a cloud of dust. I leaned my head against the window and watched gazelles gallop and zebras run in the opposite direction as our car hobbled up and down boulders and through elephant grass. As we left Loita, droplets of rain pelted the windshield.

Excited, Magilu spoke loudly and quickly in Maa while pointing to the windshield and then out the windows. Lanet grunted and said, "It hasn't rained in Loita for some time. Maybe close to a year. Magilu thinks that you and Becca are good luck. He thinks you brought the rain."

With a minor hiccup of getting stuck in mud and subsequently getting splattered with said mud as I pushed the car, we finally arrived at the main road. The evolution from life lived completely at one with nature to living in "civilization" was jarring. Elephant grass turned to a single-lane mud road, which then turned into a single lane of asphalt and then a four-lane highway. The cars traveling in every direction energized me, the street signs marking charted territory, the radio receiving a signal again. This existence was normal to Becca and me, but to Magilu it was a strange new world. Holding Becca's hand, his eyes grew wide as lights shone from every direction. Headlights flashed from the front, the side, and behind. Streetlights gleamed from above, and city lights spotted the sky in the distance. He pointed to the car in front of us and spoke in Maa. Lanet laughed and translated, "He wants to know why the car in front of us is pretending to look like a zebra." I looked ahead and saw the black-and-white-striped stickers signifying other drivers to take caution. The vehicle was a cement truck.

As we pulled into the driveway of a four-star hotel, I almost burst through the roof of the taxi thinking about a hot shower and the goodies in the mini bar. Bolting out of the bushmobile, I zipped through security and marched to reception, leaving bits of dried mud, twigs, and for all I knew lion excrement on the marble floor. A man and woman in their fifties dressed in coordinated outfits of fine linen were ahead of me in line. Standing behind them, all I could think about was what I would do first: clean myself or eat an ice cream sundae. The woman ahead of me gingerly turned to look at me and quickly turned back. She elbowed her husband, who didn't even need to make eye contact before nodding his head in agreement. The woman turned back again, this time pulling her orange Hermes scarf over her nose.

Suddenly I heard Becca call my name. I turned around and saw her, Lanet, and Magilu barred from entering by three security guards. I dropped my bags in line and went to see what the problem was.

"These security schmucks won't let us in!" Becca hollered.

I looked at the security guards, who looked at me deadpan. "What's going on here?"

A porter spoke up, "The man refuses to remove his machete."

I glanced at the sword, then at Magilu's bewildered face. I turned to Lanet, "You need to do something about this. I told you that he wasn't going to be able to bring his sword in here."

Lanet shrugged his shoulders. For the first time I witnessed him uncomfortable, seemingly not knowing how to navigate in this version of the world.

"Lanet! You are going to need to figure out how to make Magilu understand that it is safe in the hotel. There aren't any animals here, and the people will not hurt him." Lanet nodded and I continued, "Go take him on a walk while I get us checked in. Once I put money down for a couple of rooms, I will have more leverage."

I looked at Becca, who was distraught, her eyes on Magilu. I grabbed her arm, "Go walk with them. Make sure they don't get into any trouble." She nodded and I breezed past security once more.

When I got back to the check-in line, the linen twins were speaking with the hotel representative and pointing at me. With a maxed-out capacity for additional bullshit, I belted out, "Is there a problem?"

The woman's mouth dropped and the hotel employee approached me. "Miss, I am the manager of this hotel. I have not seen you here before. What is your room number?"

"I don't have a room number . . . yet. I was trying to check in, but your hotel has been a pain in the ass since the second I walked in the door."

"Well, Miss, I am sorry about that, but are you aware of our rates?"

Just as a rant of "Who do you think you are and give me your name because I am going to write to your CEO and chief legal council" was about to flow out of my mouth, I glanced down at my crusty boots, then made my way up my leggings with their various holes, to my dirty hands with chipped red nail polish.

My ferociousness softened, "I'm sorry. Let me start over. I have been in the forest for a few months. I forgot how I looked because my appearance hasn't mattered. I'm on my way back to California in a few days. I have a credit card that works. Oh, and the two men with me are Maasai warriors."

The hotel manager unclenched his jaw and said, "Of course you are welcome to stay if you are a paying guest, but please tell the warrior that he can't wear his sword in public areas."

I smiled, "Sounds reasonable."

By the time I finished checking in, Lanet, Becca, and Magilu (sans sword) walked past security and into the lobby. I watched as Magilu took his first baby step onto the shiny white-marble floor. Wobbling and looking at his reflection in the marble, he stopped, leaned over, and put one hand on the floor. Becca watched, giving him a "proud mom" look. He turned back and spoke to Lanet.

Lanet laughed, "He wants to know if he is walking on the sky."

I pressed the button to the elevator, and Magilu and Lanet had another exchange of words.

"He wants to know what happens when you press the button. I told him to follow me and he will be okay." He smiled and continued, "But he thinks we are on another planet."

We entered the elevator and as it began to move, Magilu bent his knees and braced himself on the handrail. By habit, he reached for his sword, but it was stored in Lanet's backpack, so he grabbed for Lanet's bag. Lanet pushed him to the other side of the elevator and said something in Maa that calmed him down.

We stopped at my hotel room first, where Magilu touched everything he saw. He turned the light switches on and off, on and off. He bounced on the bed up and down, up and down. He peered out of the window looking over the city. Finally he turned around to tell us he now understood what it felt like to be a bird.

Lanet told us that he wanted to visit friends in Nairobi, which was A-okay with me because I desperately wanted the time alone. Becca pulled Magilu away from the window, and everyone left. I immediately called housekeeping to see how quickly they could turn around my laundry. "Within three hours," they said. Perfect. I undressed, put all of my dirty stinky garments in a plastic bag, and left it outside my door for pickup.

I turned the knob of the shower to the left to let the water heat up. In the meantime, I clipped all of my nails and evaluated myself naked in the mirror. I hardly recognized what I saw: My breasts were smaller, tummy flatter, and derriere perkier. I looked at my face and hair—I could have been mistaken for a cavewoman. I would need to scrub once, twice, three times and maybe more just to get the dirt and dead skin off. And that is what I did.

The next morning over pancakes and scrambled eggs, Becca told me about Magilu's first bath. "Oh, Mindy, he was so cute. He looked at the tub and said *enkiteng,* the Maa word for cow. He thought the bathtub was a water trough for the hotel cows! I added a couple bottles of bubble bath, and you should have seen his face light up. He eyes grew wider and wider as the bubbles overflowed out of the tub. He played in that tub for like two hours. And then I showed him the television . . ."

"But all of the stations are in English," I interrupted.

Becca took a sip of orange juice and said, "Didn't matter. He watched *Happy Gilmore* three times in a row, and then hopped back in the bathtub."

"Seems like he had no problem adjusting," I said.

"He slept like a rock and Lanet told me that Magilu said he felt like he was sleeping on a cloud. But I, on the other hand, woke up on the floor wrapped up in a sheet."

"That's funny because I also found the floor more comfortable than the bed and I woke up totally freaked out because I forgot where I was. For a second I wondered if becoming a moran was a dream."

Becca smiled, "Definitely not a dream."

I nudged her shoulder lightly and said, "And the good news is that we are going home morans as opposed to going home in a box."

BEFORE WE PARTED—I to California and Becca, Magilu and Lanet back to Loita—we sat down with Nic to discuss the future.

"Only the laibons and the lions know what is next," Lanet said. "We don't have expectations. We have hopes, but no expectations. It is our hope that you will return one day. You are part of the Maasai tribe, so you will know what to do when the time comes."

Lanet, Magilu and Becca dropped me off at the airport. There were no words, just as if we were still in the forest. All we had and all we needed was a common understanding that this wasn't even close to the end of our time together.

On my way home from Kenya, I thought about how my relationship with my family would be all roses and rainbows. My father would hug me and tell me that my becoming a moran was his proudest moment, and that all of his concerns about my ability to find a job had vanished. My mother and I would have close but independent lives, and I would be able to eat chocolate cake and croissants freely. My grandmother's accessory count and her feelings about me would be simple and unconditional, and my brother would introduce me to a guy who embraced my donkey-ish nature.

But that tape didn't roll . . . just yet.

BACK IN SANTA BARBARA, my mom and dad greeted me at the airport with hugs and questions. Once we were in the car, my dad asked what was most on his mind: "Did you finish your report for Under Armour?"

I looked at him in the rearview mirror and said, "Huh?"

His eyes narrowed. He could smell the buffalo shit. With steam about to come out of his ears, he said, "The report for Under Armour. Isn't that the company you were working for in Kenya? Did they like your work? Do you think they will hire you full-time?"

Slapping my palm to my forehead, I said, "Oh yes! Of course. Under Armour! You mean Mr. Plank." And just as I was about to continue the lie by telling them that all went brilliantly well, something stopped me. I didn't want or even feel the need to hide. "Funny you should bring that up. The Under Armour marketing plan hasn't happened yet."

My dad pulled the car over on the shoulder of the road and my mom sat still, staring out the windshield.

I continued, "I was in touch with the CEO while I was in Kenya, but I didn't work for them."

My mom snapped her head around and said, "Then what in the world were you doing in that place for so long?"

"Well, I actually became the first female Maasai warrior."

"For heaven's sake, Mindy! What does that mean?"

My dad huffed, put the car in drive and said, "It's Mindy-speak for her still being unemployed."

AT DINNER THAT NIGHT, Queen Lee arrived dressed in a simple pair of wool slacks and a royal blue cashmere sweater with minimal accessories. "Anytime you need another Maasai melt to shed pounds, you let me know. I will fund your trip!" she said, looking me up and down. "You look fantastic!"

I hadn't stepped on the scale, but I was probably about twenty-five pounds lighter. It was nice to hear the compliment, but I knew I had gained far more than I'd lost.

Over lemon-herb chicken and steamed broccoli, I told my family about my experiences with the Maasai. I explained that because of my actions there was now an initiative to change a law so that girls can become warriors. My dad asked, "So how have you changed?"

It took me a minute to respond. The only thing that came to mind was that I didn't try to be someone I was not—that I had remained true to myself. I put my fork on my plate, looked up at my dad and said, "I actually don't think I changed."

He looked at me "How is that possible?"

"I learned while I was away that my heart is in the right place and I have the smarts to bring my dreams to life. And now I know how to throw a spear, kill a goat, and make a fire. So while I've changed how I look at myself, I am fundamentally still me. To quote my favorite disco singer, Gloria Gaynor, 'I am what I am.'"

My dad put his fork down, took a sip of water, looked me straight in the eyes, and said, "I have never been more proud of you."

Queen Lee lifted her G&T with four squeezed limes and said, "Cheers!" and everyone clinked their glasses.

PRIOR TO THE TRIP, I felt like I was walking in other's shadows. Now the only shadow in my existence is the one following me—my own. It took me time to notice it, but I can now see that the roses were blooming and the rainbow was present all along. It took looking at life from a different perspective to see the growth and feel the heat from the shining sun. Keeping that perspective is a continuous duty.

"At the soonest," as Lanet would say, I will head back to Loita to spend time with the tribe. It is my hope that when I go back, Kinyi and the other young girls I met around the fire on my first trip will be carrying spears and swords and accepted as morans. I like to think that those girls and I have something in common now as a result of my trip—a larger world view, a bigger tribe, a hand in determining our own destiny.

Epilogue

WITHIN A FEW WEEKS of my return, I moved back to Chicago. I spent most of the next year working on the first version of this book. I then became a full-time student at the University of Chicago Booth School of Business and graduated in 2012. In the meantime, the first version turned into the second, third, fourth, all the way to what I think is the hundredth version, which you are reading now.

While I never did hear from Mr. Plank, I decided I would re-send him the letters once this book was complete. And then one day the stars aligned before I even sent him the letters! While I was hiking the hills of Malibu, California, I met a sandy-haired woman who said, "I see that you like Under Armour." That one comment got me going about my experience with the Maasai and my one-way correspondence with Mr. Plank. She asked to see some of the letters. She later told me that her soon-to-be husband was an investor in Under Armour and a very close friend of—you guessed it—Mr. Plank! I nearly passed out from the twist of fate. As I write this epilogue, I have a vision in my head: me and Mr. Plank walking side by side down the halls of Under Armour, creating something cool that will get female hearts, minds, and bodies in motion.

Becca is part of a band that is playing all around the United States. She is still sketching and working on a graphic novel that shows her perspective of our journey. She has a new boyfriend, but still keeps in touch with Magilu. Whenever Magilu has access to Lanet's cell phone, he sends Becca an SMS. His messages are typically something along the lines of "&★^NHGxcve$#" or "ccc8plZRET★&%." But the big news among my family in the forest is that Magilu got married during the summer of 2011! He is a happy man and expecting his first child.

Topoika and Lanet are leading an initiative called "Operation Moran," which is working toward allowing girls the right to become morans. Lanet believes that the "law" to give teenage girls this right will be passed by 2016. We decided that the best way to benefit the tribe as a whole was to document and promote our story. We are also giving a percentage of every book sold to The Stillman Family Foundation, which builds clinics and schools for the Maasai. While money does not play a major role in a traditional Maasai's life, it is important in assisting in the face of drought and in the introduction of Western education and medicine.

Lanet and I speak often. We "share news" just as we would around a fire in Loita. He tells me about the packs of arrogant elephants that try to eat his corn, how difficult it is to get any means of employment, and how he feels that his government neglects the Maasai. Our relationship has been tested when he forgets my reality and I forget his. I am back in a place and in a position where I have access to food and water, and I live in a politically stable environment that offers tremendous opportunities to its citizens (if one decides to take them), but having your basic needs met does not mean that life is always jolly. When I make a mistake at my job, I still question my abilities and worry about the consequences. When someone says something hurtful, I still feel the sting. We didn't experience these "lost in translation" moments, as we like to call them, in the forest because we lived the same reality. Now, out of the forest I am still able to connect as I live with the same spiritual reality.

Letter from Lanet

Dear Reader,
I hope this finds you well. I am well myself.

I hope you enjoyed this book. You need to know that it is very important in the hearts of the Maasai. This book is an extraordinary story of extra ordinary women, my fellow morans, Mindy Budgor and Becca Stillman. Through their persistence, courage, and unending strength they have opened the door to a change in Maasai tribal law: allowing women to participate in warrior training and becoming morans. This will be voted upon at Ilmeshuki council of elders and the emanyatta steering committee on our next transitional manyatta. It is now fact that a number of girls in Loita have voiced their interest in becoming morans!

DATE: 26TH NOVEMBER 2012
DANSON LANET OLE LEKURUON

Appendix: *The Plank Letters*

Letter 1

To: Mindy Budgor
Subject: Marketing Opportunity – First Female Warrior!!

Dear Mr. Plank,

I just boarded the plane from Los Angeles to Nairobi with the hope of becoming the world's first female Maasai warrior. I gave you a call a few days ago—unfortunately we were unable to connect. But do not fear! I will keep you updated on my warrioress status through weekly letters.

Here is a short background on me: I'm a 27-year-old from Potomac, Maryland, a former ice hockey player, and an MBA-bound entrepreneur who was challenged a couple of months ago by a Maasai Chief while building a clinic in Kenya. The Chief said, "Women are not strong or brave enough to become warriors." I immediately wanted to prove him wrong (pushing my mental and physical limits is nothing new for me, and it's a lifestyle that your brand embodies in every stitch of fabric), but the deal was sealed when a Maasai woman said that women in her tribe have been trying to become warriors for generations. She believed the time for change had come, and apparently I, a white, strong, but pleasantly plump girl who had never even backpacked before, was the perfect guinea pig.

I forgot to mention that I recruited another girl—a midwesterner named Becca Bergman who is so gung-ho over female empowerment that the fact that our chances of survival are slim to none seem to breeze right past her like your revenue will soon surpass Puma's. Please don't hesitate to contact me. If I don't respond immediately, I am probably deep in the bush with no cell reception, but hang tight because I will get back to you ASAP!

Always Armoured,
Mindy Budgor

P.S. If you saw me now, you would surely do a double take. I am decked out in UA: boy short active underwear (style # 1001959), cold gear frosty black tights (style # 1001525), fire engine red tank top (style # 1201269), which hangs a bit lower than my black t-shirt (style # 1201574)—all of which sit nicely under my black jacket (style # 1204027). Confidence exudes when I am in your clothing!

Letter 2

To: Mindy Budgor
Subject: Marketing Opportunity – First Female Warrior!

Dear Mr. Plank,
A few hiccups so far, but nothing I can't handle. I, and the UA products that I wore on the plane, have made it to Kenya, but after a seventeen-plus-hour plane ride and then a six-hour car ride to the Maasai Mara to find the Chief, it was time to wash my shorts. Truth be known, I started to worry that I would have to search for the Chief with no drawers. After a thorough washing in something similar to a bathroom, I hung my shorts on three-foot-high blades of grass near my tent. I grabbed lunch and came back with the intention of flipping my boy shorts over like a steak sizzling on the grill. But what did I find? My shorts were fresh, clean, and DRY!! I am just so grateful for your moisture-wicking fabric!

I hope you don't mind if I vent for a moment . . . As you know, I made a pretty bold move by committing to this journey and all I wanted was a little support from friends (there was no way my Jewish mother, straight-laced father, investment banking brother, or grandmother who refuses to respond to anything other than The Queen were going to support this cause), but what did I get? A bet that neither I, nor my Under Armour are going to make it more than one day in the bush. A "friend" wrote, "You and your Under Armour are going to be ripped to shreds by the end of day 1." To think that I, an American woman whose biggest outdoor adventure was on a cruise ship to Alaska, would not endure this grueling and dangerous safari is one thing, but to doubt your brilliantly made products drew an unmistakable "line in the sand." My impression was that the excellence in the engineering of your brand was unquestioned. How could I be wrong?

When I get back to the States, maybe we should discuss how to change this error in perception. Yes, my Under Armour and I might incur minor injuries, but we are going to survive!

Always Armoured,
Mindy Budgor

Letter 3

To: Mindy Budgor
Subject: Marketing Opportunity – First Female Warrior!

Dear Mr. Plank,
Plan B is now in motion. This is none of your concern, but the Chief rejected us, which caused a minor snafu, but when one is committed, one can always create a Plan B, C, D, or even Z! Warrioresses here we come!

I asked Lanet, our new guide, if he had any questions prior to hopping on a ten-hour bus ride to his home. After the obvious question, "Why do you want to become a warrior?" he asked, "What's that symbol on every piece of your clothing? Those two shields crossing each other?" WOO HOO! My brand awareness strategy is already in motion!

I explained the practicality and science behind your brand, and just as we jumped into a mutatu he said, "I would like to see how that clothing holds up in the forest." Yes, he was skeptical, but I sat with head held high and shields shining in the sun knowing that his current doubt in UA products would turn to confidence.

Always Armoured,
Mindy Budgor

Letter 4

To: Mindy Budgor
Subject: Marketing Opportunity – First Female Warrior!

Dear Mr. Plank,
Today marks Day 1 of warrior training. Lanet took Becca and me deep into the forest with six other warriors ranging in age from sixteen to seventy-five. I think the plan is to stay here for at least two months. We are a good 50 miles away from a toilet, sleeping under the stars on a pile of crumply leaves and the food situation looks pretty bleak . . . we just slaughtered a goat and drank blood directly from the goat's jugular. I threw up. Not a good start. I don't know what we will be doing here and to be honest, I am trying to go moment to moment. However, I do have a recommendation for you. Lanet has proved to be a wonderful fellow and I think you should consider hiring him as your official African advisor. He is quite knowledgeable about the entire continent—including Madagascar, the Seychelles and Mauritius. Can we say opportunity?

I am sitting by the fire and all I hear are hyenas. I am pretty sure that a lion is watching me, but I am Armoured, so all is well.

Always Armoured,
Mindy Budgor

Letter 5

To: Mindy Budgor
Subject: Marketing Opportunity – First Female Warrior!

Dear Mr. Plank,

I think it has been a couple of weeks since my last letter. The excruciating training has left me mentally and physically exhausted. Lifting a pen at the end of the day feels like doing a sixty-pound wrist curl, so sorry for the radio silence. The good news is that I am still fully dressed in Under Armour under my tribal uniform and my brand awareness strategy is going viral and let me tell you why . . .

A few days ago when I was trekking to spear practice, I stopped at a local mama's home for chai. I noticed that the mama's breasts were hanging quite low. I asked Lanet if she ever wears any support. He laughed. How uncomfortable she must be on her daily treks, given that she has one hundred pounds of firewood strapped on her head and thirty liters of water hanging from each hand. I looked down at my own breasts and felt secure, protected, and properly positioned all due to my UA sports bra (style #1001216). I wanted this woman to feel the same comfort I felt, so I untied my olkarasha, lifted my UA tank top (style #1206284) over my head, removed my sports bra, and gave it to the mama. Her chest was larger than mine, but she was able to shimmy it on. The contraption mystified her, but after twisting her torso from side to side, she seemed to get a jolt of energy. She walked outside and started jumping and singing, smiling from notched ear to notched ear. Her son told me he hadn't seen his mama that happy since a borehole was dug two km away from her home (the previous water hole was six km away). I explained that she probably needed a larger size bra, but if she was comfortable, she should keep it. I trekked home braless, but due to your thoughtful consideration during the design of my tank top (with embedded breast support), I was not in the least bit uncomfortable.

Three days later, a boy herding cattle told me that his mama would like a boob holder too! You should have seen the boy imitate his mama. Frowning, he cupped his hands like he was holding breasts and swung them from side to side. Then he (and this is the part that you will love) patted his chest, pointed to your fantastic logo of interlocking shields on the neck of my turtleneck (style #1207246), and gave me two thumbs up. He extended his hand palm up and waited. Maybe he thought I was going to hand him a bra from my magical Under Armour tree?

Mr. Plank, please know that I am very careful about explaining the benefits of UA products when introducing your brand to an interested party. People in Africa are now not only beginning to be interested in athletic apparel, but they are specifically asking to be Armoured!

Always Armoured,
Mindy

Letter 6

To: Mindy Budgor
Subject: Marketing Opportunity – First Female Warrior!

Dear Mr. Plank,
Confession: I did bring another brand's pair of pants with me. For the purpose of this letter, I will call it Brand X. I made this decision because in order to truly understand the benefit and competitive advantage of our products (I hope it is okay that I called them "our" products), I needed to "get" the competition.

I wore Brand X's pants when we trekked our typical 15 kilometers through swamps and over boulders. The day was not only exhausting, but also incredibly uncomfortable. Every leaf, thorn, and twig clung to Brand X's pants as if they were intimate lovers. Even after two days and countless attempts to wash the debris off, nothing worked—the fabric seems to now be blended with the bush. Plus the fit just didn't make sense. I bought the right size, but the waist was too short and while my thighs are surely a bit plumper than Heidi Klum's, I am closer to the average woman's size. I decided that I wouldn't even give Brand X's junk to a hungry hyena, so I burned it in our campfire. Afterward, I promptly clothed myself under your shields. I can now sleep comfortably . . . well, not exactly because if you recall, I am sleeping on a bunch of cold, damp leaves.

I hope that you understand why it was essential for me to run this experiment. As I am sure you are aware, one can't operate in a silo if one intends to remain competitive. And now we have even more proof of excellence.

I trust all is well at headquarters. It would be great to hear what is brewing on your end. Besides the daily elephant attacks and hours of training, I have a lot of peace and quiet—the perfect atmosphere for idea generation!

Always Armoured,
Mindy Budgor

Letter 7

To: Mindy Budgor
Subject: Marketing Opportunity – First Female Warrior!

Dear Mr. Plank,
Let's talk about marketing. The backdrop of the forest and the warriors provides a plethora of perfect places for an Under Armour ad campaign. But I just left an ideal location. Let me take you there . . .

After a long and treacherous trek through a hippo pool (where I almost got eaten) and then up and down a massive mountain, we reached a waterfall. Water seemed to be falling directly from the sky. With the warriors blessing the earth, I thought about a culture dying from the drought finding their lifeline. It was magical and then I thought ... this could be the perfect setting to showcase Under Armour! How about a variety of scenes varying from surviving in the savanna to living luxuriously with the waterfall? We could show the durability of the culture along with the durability of Under Armour.

I hope these letters are getting to you. It would just be nice to know that someone has heard me beyond the trees. I have been pushed past my physical and emotional limits on this journey and these constant changes have come with intense feelings of fear and pain. I wanted to quit over and over. I have been hesitant to share these feelings with you because I wanted to appear unflappable, but just like all of the athletes who wear Under Armour, I am human and if I weren't experiencing pain, then I wouldn't be growing.

Always Armoured,
Mindy Budgor

P.S. When I was chased by a hippo I climbed a tree and snagged my pants on a branch. I now have a hole on the back of my pant leg that is about one inch in diameter. I thought the hole would expand, but I'm happy to report that it has not increased in size and the pants are fully functional. Your team is brilliant!

Letter 8

To: Mindy Budgor
Subject: Marketing Opportunity – First Female Warrior!

Dear Mr. Plank,
This letter is going to sound a bit odd. Since the end of July, I have been writing to you from the Kenyan bush while training to become the world's first female Maasai warrior. (After rereading those first two sentences, I see that this is more than a bit odd—this is flat out strange, but do me a favor and hear me out.)

I am a twenty-seven-year-old from Potomac, Maryland. I'm a former ice hockey player and an MBA-bound entrepreneur who was challenged a couple of months ago by a Maasai Chief while as a volunteer building a clinic in Kenya. The Chief told me that women are not strong or brave enough to become warriors. I, of course, thought this was ridiculous, but what really sealed the deal for me was when a Maasai woman told me that women in her tribe have been trying to become warriors for generations. If for some reason I was given the opportunity to break this barrier for women, I should take it seriously. So I did.

Training has been intense and there were plenty of times when I wanted to toss in my spear and go home, but this tribe (now my tribe) has taken my understanding of what a team is all about to a new level. You probably remember many experiences while playing football when a teammate covered your back or took a hit for you without blinking an eye. Yesterday was only one of a great many times when my team reinforced our oneness. I was almost bulldozed by a buffalo and the only thing that I could think about was the safety of my tribe—apparently they were thinking the same way. As I charged forward, they did as well and together we conquered the buffalo before it conquered us.

To make a long journey short, Becca and I proved the Chief wrong because we were inducted into a clan and are now the first female warriors. Furthermore, it looks like within the next few years a law is going to be changed to allow girls to become warriors. All good news!

Mr. Plank, I know that you are a very busy man, but there is a campaign or a platform that should be developed. Your brand has the unique ability to build an environment that women want to be invited into and stay involved with because of its core beliefs in empowerment and the essence of team—those beliefs got me to the finish line, as I am now a warrior, and I know that if those beliefs are amplified then they will get other women to their individual finish lines (whatever they might be). I will be back in the US within the next month. I would love to get together to discuss my experience and ideas.

Always Armoured,
Mindy Budgor

Acknowledgments

WITHOUT THE SUPPORT of my entire family and friends this book would have roasted in a fire in Loita a long time ago. In particular, thank you Anne T., Nancy KWOMAN, Vicky R., MOM, Queen Lee, Nana, Kellie ("Fifi"), Hilary, Lisa, Debbie B., Karin, Terry, Morgan, Lezlie, Susan, Jane D., Mikki, Marilyn H., Rana, Noelle, Allegra, Christine G., Neha, Avi, Ayesha, Mary X., Nandini, Shruti G., Ronit, Kristen E., Claudia L., Joann, Mary B., Nikki, June, Jocelyn, Cass, Ellie, Bevy, and of course, Kari.

Thank you Chicago Booth Class of 2012 and those in the Class of 2013 whom I spent time drinking caipirinhas with in Brazil. In addition, Professor Ginzel, Professor Davis, Professor Darragh, Professor Epley, Professor Urminsky, Professor Middlebrooks, Rosemarie Martinelli, Stacy Kole, and Julie Morton.

I also want to thank my core team of men who amazingly enough have never ceased to give up on me and who still pick up the phone when I call (most of the time): Adam, Dad, Ed R., Jeff W., Jeff J., Jeff B., Phil B., Barry K., Rob, David C., Tobin, Leeor, Micah, Lady Ellis, Zoltan, Zach, Eyal, Michael B., Robert L., Sam, Bant, Michael L., Matt P., David S. and my amazing attorneys John and Jon.

About the Author

MINDY BUDGOR is a 2012 graduate of the University of Chicago Booth School of Business. She started her first company while an undergraduate at the University of Wisconsin, and is moving on to new challenges in New York City. Mindy hopes *Warrior Princess* will bring attention to her tribe and empower readers to slap complacency in the face and take the reins in their own lives.